In Pursuit of Prosperity

IN PURSUIT OF PROSPERITY

Industrial Policy and the Politics of Economic Upgrading

Charles R. Hankla

University of Michigan Press
Ann Arbor

Published in the United States of America by the
University of Michigan Press
First published July 2025

A CIP catalog record for this book is available from the British Library.

Library of Congress Cataloging-in-Publication data has been applied for.

ISBN 978-0-472-07746-5 (hardcover : alk. paper)
ISBN 978-0-472-05746-7 (paper : alk. paper)
ISBN 978-0-472-90505-8 (open access ebook)

DOI: https://doi.org/10.3998/mpub.12122865

The University of Michigan Press's open access publishing program is made possible thanks to additional funding from the University of Michigan Office of the Provost and the generous support of contributing libraries.

Authorized Representative: Easy Access System Europe, Mustamäe tee 50, 10621 Tallinn, Estonia, gpsr.requests@easproject.com

This book is dedicated to my wife Anne-Sophie, without whom my French journey—and so many other journeys—would never have begun.

Contents

Digital materials related to this title can be found on the Fulcrum platform via the following citable URL: https://doi.org/10.3998/mpub.12122865

Brief Abstract

I develop and test a new theory that seeks to explain both the form and success of national policies designed to promote economic upgrading. Governments around the world encourage domestic producers to move up the value-chain, some hoping to secure their dominance in innovation, others struggling to escape the "middle income trap." I argue that the relative cohesion—matched or unmatched—of the state and private actors will inform the structure of upgrading coalitions and, by extension, the upgrading institutions that these coalitions may create or oversee. These dynamics, in turn, will condition whether upgrading policy is characterized by state dominance, private capture, corporatism, or pluralism. Moreover, I contend that governments will be most successful in creating effective upgrading coalitions when their level of cohesion is aligned with that of private actors and interest groups. I find support for my arguments using both qualitative and quantitative evidence. My qualitative tests use archival research and interviews to explore the policy process in postwar France—a highly informative case that is rarely examined by scholars of development—and in post-independence India. My quantitative models look at outcomes in sixteen countries across six decades, and I also explore the applicability of the model with a plausibility probe of the United States. My results shed light on a wide variety of economic policies and outcomes, while suggesting that policy-making styles are not fixed characteristics of countries but can vary both across time and, critically, across sectors of the economy. These policy-making styles, and the upgrading institutions and coalitions which support them, reflect the changing power dynamics and organizational resources of state and private actors and can evolve across time and space through a number of mechanisms. I conclude the book with an exploration of the implications of the theory in the modern globalized context. Upgrading policy, far from being a relic of the past, remains very much a viable option for states today.

Acknowledgments

This book has been a long journey, pushed to the side repeatedly by more urgent obligations at work and at home. This approach has meant that I have delayed the sense of satisfaction and closure that comes with completing a large project, but it has been a blessing as well. First and foremost, much to my surprise, the topic of industrial policy—decidedly "out" in 2008 when I took the first steps in this journey—has in the interim become "cool" again. I hope that this book will therefore take on less of a character of shouting into the wilderness and may rather find readers newly engaged with its subject and newly open to its arguments.

More than that, however, the years spent working on this project have allowed my thinking to evolve and develop in ways that have, I hope, made the argument richer. This is due in large part to the wonderful discussions I have had with scholars in a variety of fields during the intervening years. My home department—political science at Georgia State University—has always been supportive of my work and my travels, and I am deeply grateful to all of my colleagues. In particular, I would like to thank Carrie Manning, Mike Herb, Bill Downs, and John Duffield for their unrelenting support and substantive feedback.

Georgia State University, through its Research Initiation Grant and Research Intensive Semester programs, helped to finance a portion of this project, and I am grateful. I also want to extend my deep appreciation to Jorge Martinez-Vazquez, who has been a constant mentor for me for many years and has brought me into the policy sphere. Though this project is a bit different from our joint work in fiscal decentralization, he has been an inspiration for it throughout.

The ideas in this book were refined during a 2023 conference on industrial policy hosted by the Niehaus Center for Globalization and Governance at Princeton University and organized by Stephanie Rickard and Helen Milner. I deeply appreciate their excellent feedback as well as the ideas and suggestions from all of the participants, which included many of the country's top experts on the subject. In particular, Shanta Devarajan, in his role as my discussant, brought to bear both his scholarly expertise and real-world experience to strengthen the project.

I would like to thank participants in the 2019 American Political Science Association Convention, 2018 Emory Colloquium in Political Economy, and 2013 ICPP Conference in Grenoble for their careful consideration of the project. More specifically, my thanks go to Robin Best, Jennifer Gandhi, Mark Zachary Taylor, Nick Ziegler, and Joachim Wehner for their excellent feedback.

This project would not have been possible without the welcome that I received during my research sabbatical in France from Sciences Po Lille and from the Centre d'études et de recherches administratives, politiques et sociales (CERAPS) of the Centre national de la recherche scientifique (CNRS), where I was a fellow. It was a fantastic experience getting to know the faculty and students at these institutions and learning from deeply engaged French scholars. In particular, my appreciation goes out to Patrick Mardellat, Guillaume Duseigneur, Jean-Gabriel Contamin, and Pierre Mathiot. My thanks are also due to the archives and libraries that I used in Lille, Paris, and their environs. Any country would be proud to have such professional institutions stewarding their history.

In addition to France, my professional passion has been India—its politics, history, and culture. I had my introduction to this bewildering and wonderful country when conducting the fieldwork for my PhD in 2003. While I continue to work in India on a variety of topics—and indeed I am writing these words on a flight to Delhi—much of the primary research I use for this book comes from that early visit, financed by Emory University's internationalization fund. At that time, I was based at the American Institute for Indian Studies in Delhi, which I want to thank personally for their support. I have also received significant assistance from the Centre for the Study of Developing Societies and, later, the Policy and Development Advisory Group in Delhi and Presidency University in Kolkata. In particular, Pronab Sen, Jairam Ramesh, and Montek Ahluwalia took their precious time to meet with a budding, but quite callow, student of their country. For this I am forever grateful.

And, last but not least, I would like to express my great appreciation to another of my mentors, Rick Doner, whose careful reading of an earlier draft helped lead the project toward a new and more profitable direction.

I also owe a great debt to Madison Allums, Elizabeth Demers, Delilah McCrea, Danielle Cotu-Fattal, Marcia LaBrenz, and the excellent editors at the University of Michigan Press for their patience and their diligent support. And I am grateful to the reviewers of the book manuscript for their outstanding feedback, and to Patrick Munger for excellent research assistance.

The journal *Comparative Politics* and its publisher the City University of New York, along with the journal *Business and Politics* and its publisher Cambridge University Press, have both graciously allowed me to use portions of two articles published with them some years ago.

Let me close with a word about my family. First, while they may not be blood relatives, John and Karen Walson have truly become family over the years. I am so grateful for their continued friendship and support. The same goes for all of my friends; I won't test the patience of my readers by listing them, but you know who you are.

My parents, Robert and Alice Hankla, both professors and teachers of physics, were something truly special. I sometimes cannot believe my luck in having had them as my mom and dad. They inspired me to pursue knowledge and learning and, though the science I chose to pursue may not be a "science," I know they are smiling down on me from above.

My stepdad Jerry Davis, who entered our lives after my dad's passing nearly 30 years ago, has been an incredible blessing. An historian by profession, he has been attuned to my research from the beginning, and I have bounced numerous ideas off of him. He has become my second dad in every way.

My brother Allen, sister-in-law Nina, and their family have always supported and loved me, and I look forward to spending more time with them as their schedule becomes more flexible.

My French in-laws have, since my first visit in 1996, become my French family. I want to thank Philippe and Dominique Decouvelaere for welcoming a young American into their home who didn't speak a word of French and for putting up with my mistakes as I slowly learned about the language and culture. The same sentiments go for my siblings-in-law Juliette and Jerome and their lovely families, who have become a central part of my life. Joining this family has so deeply enriched my life. They could never have guessed that I would someday be allowed to vote in French elections!

Words cannot describe how proud I am of my daughters Emilie and Elizabeth. They have grown into incredible young women, curious, compassionate, and strong. Where did the time go? While I miss being able to lift you onto my shoulders, it is a joy of another sort to be able to discuss ideas and events with you now. I cannot wait to see what journeys you take next.

Finally, to my wife Anne-Sophie, our love has been a constant in my life since we first met at Trinity College Dublin in 1995. I don't know what I did to deserve marrying you, or indeed to deserve the serendipity of even meeting, but I am deeply glad we did (and not just because there is no way in which this book would have been written otherwise!). I am so excited for the next stage of our lives together.

Author Biography

Charles R. Hankla is Professor of Political Science at Georgia State University in Atlanta. He is also Director of the International Center for Public Policy (ICePP), which engages globally in research, professional training, and technical assistance in the areas of public finance, fiscal decentralization, and economic development.

Dr. Hankla's scholarly work has been funded by the National Science Foundation and the International Growth Centre, and he is a regular consultant with the World Bank, the UNDP, USAID, and the G20. His research has appeared in such journals as the *American Political Science Review*, *American Journal of Political Science*, *Comparative Political Studies*, *Comparative Politics*, and *Publius*. He has also published a co-authored book from Edward Elgar entitled *Local Accountability and National Coordination in Fiscal Federalism: A Fine Balance*.

ONE

Transformative Relationships

Rethinking Economic Upgrading

Sustained upgrading is the new benchmark of national economic success. Growth can be produced through temporary monetary or fiscal stimulus, only to peter out with mounting debt and inflation. Even the benefits of industrialization can be fleeting, as countries become stuck producing low value-added goods. Only upgrading, and the constant effort to remain at the high end of the value chain, can place a country's economy on firmer ground.

Economic upgrading can be defined as the process of moving up the value-chain in production (Porter 2011). It generally involves building deeper domestic linkages among firms with the ultimate goal of achieving constant productivity growth (Doner and Schneider 2016). The value-chain in question is very often global, with different components of the production process taking place in different countries (Milberg, Jiang, and Gereffi 2014). The most valuable elements of this chain require skilled workers and are typically associated with higher productivity and innovation; they may include, for example, research and development, product design, and marketing. Lower-value-added activities may encompass simple mass production or the procurement of raw materials.

Because of the benefits that accrue to countries at the higher end of the value chain, governments around the world have long been engaged in promoting economic upgrading. Technology is always in flux, and a place at the upper end of the production process can never be guaranteed for long. This is why even governments in highly developed economies regularly pursue policies aimed at building their national systems of innovation (Taylor 2016). Upgrading interventions even occur in ostensibly liberal countries such as the

United States, where Mazzucato (2015) and Weiss (2014) have highlighted the government's complex (but largely under the radar) efforts to secure America's leadership in innovation.

If leaders in the developed world are diligently pursuing economic upgrading, the issue is considered even more urgent in the capitals of the developing world. For the poorest countries, extensive growth is likely to be the focus of attention, with its emphasis on mobilizing investment and building the necessary framework for economic activity. But for those countries enmeshed in the so-called "middle income trap," economic upgrading can take on a critical aspect (Chiang 2018).

As Doner and Schneider (2016) point out, the World Bank classified 101 of the world's countries as middle income in 1960, and in the sixty years since, only 13 of these have graduated to high income status. In 2019, the Bank adopted a new scheme that counts 107 of the world's 218 countries and territories as middle income, very nearly half.[1] These countries face the peculiar situation of having exhausted the growth potential of pure investment. If they are to achieve high income status, they must effect the fundamental transformations necessary to move up the value chain.

When, then, is economic upgrading successful and when is it a failure? And, with so many states committed to economic transformation and so many experts ready to provide technical advice on how to do it, why are outcomes so mixed? I develop a new theory that seeks to explain both the form and success of policy efforts to move up the value chain, one which considers the organization of states and interest groups in an interactive model. Its key insight is that effective upgrading coalitions, and by extension effective upgrading institutions, are most likely when the state and private actors are characterized by a similar degree of organizational cohesion. Such beneficial matching is to be found in dual-cohesive *corporatist* systems as well as in dual-fragmented *pluralist* systems. It is absent in *statist* economies, where the state is cohesive and private interests fragmented, and in *captured* economies, where the state is fragmented and private interests cohesive.

Dual-cohesive corporatist systems, I argue, will be characterized by a single (or a small number of) large upgrading coalitions involving peak representatives of the state and private actors. By contrast upgrading in dual-fragmented pluralist systems will be managed by a large number of sector specific micro-coalitions. In both cases, however, the matching level of state-private cohesion encourages the cooperation necessary for upgrading to take hold. Upgrading in the two types of systems, however, may take somewhat different forms. Dual-cohesive corporatist systems are ideal for broad structural change and may facilitate the economic transformation needed by middle income countries to move up the value chain. By contrast, dual-fragmented systems, which bring together private and public sector specialists in particular industries, allow for more detailed and gradual upgrading in specific industries. Such systems may be of particular merit in already developed countries looking to maintain their technological lead.

That said, since the optimal structure of upgrading coalitions varies with the organizational characteristics of both the state and interest groups, they can take different forms in different times and places. Indeed, an implication of my argument is that the nature of ideal upgrading coalitions can even vary across sectors of a single country's economy and across relatively short periods of time. As the power and organizational resources of state and private actors shift, the structure of policy-making shifts with them. This dynamic can mean that effective upgrading coalitions appear in some economic sectors and not in others, and that they evolve in some periods and disappear in others. In order to achieve the most effective upgrading, therefore, it is sometimes necessary for countries to adapt their institutions quickly and purposively (Salazar-Xirinachs, Nübler, and Kozul-Wright 2014, Streeck and Thelen 2005, Mahoney and Thelen 2010).

Ultimately, what matters most critically for economic upgrading, I argue, is the right process of policy development and implementation. The key challenge is for countries to get their coalitions and institutions (rather than their proverbial prices) right. Although there are some fundamentals to good economic policy (see Rodrik 2007), the most effective specific approaches are likely to vary across cases. Only through the formation of effective upgrading coalitions is a country likely to empower upgrading institutions to implement the policies that fit its circumstances and needs, policies that can meet the difference between growth and stagnation.

To test my arguments empirically, I begin by leveraging an important case—France just after the Second World War. Much can be learned from this case. France is an excellent laboratory for evaluating my framework because, by moving from the 4th to the 5th Republics and from agriculture to industry, I can examine, with extensive archival research, all possible combinations of my independent variables. Moreover, the conditions faced by postwar France in many ways straddle those of developed states—upgrading to maintain their lead—and of middle income countries—struggling to move up the value chain. Unfortunately, few studies of economic upgrading consider anything but the very recent past, thereby failing to exploit what can be learned from earlier efforts. The near-universal focus on the "developing world" as a distinct entity means that the experiences of industrialized states have rarely been brought to bear on the economic development issues of today (but see Gerschenkron 1962).

I turn next to a deep examination of a critical lower- and (now) middle income case—that of India. Drawing on primary as well as secondary sources, I argue that the theory helps explain the relative success of upgrading policy during the early years of India's independence and again after 1991, as well as its stagnation for much of the 1970s and 1980s. I suggest that recent trends in Indian political economy may make future upgrading successes more challenging, at least unless the union government makes mutual cooperation with the states and the private sector a high priority.

Finally, to test the generalizability of my argument, I conduct a quantitative examination of the industrial upgrading success in OECD countries. I also explore briefly the important case of the United States, a high income, pro-market state that might be expected to eschew upgrading policy. I demonstrate that this is not the case and, more significantly, show how the US has developed a pluralistic form of upgrading that has assisted its efforts to remain at the top of the value-chain in many competitive industries.

I conclude with a consideration of what the book reveals about how upgrading policy can best be organized in various political systems, looking especially at recent developments in the United States, India, China, France, and beyond. In this context, I explore how upgrading policy can be achieved in the complex and globalized environment of today, where institutions such as the World Trade Organization (WTO) limit what states can do. I also include a brief discussion of the development of welfare policy in France to suggest how the theory might be adapted to throw light on issues in political economy adjacent to upgrading. In the final analysis, I argue that targeted state intervention, far from a relic of the past, is critical for the future success of countries seeking to develop their economies.

Upgrading and Industrial Policy

To promote upgrading, states must engage in *industrial policy*, a form of state action grounded in the belief that targeted government intervention can stimulate economic growth. Industrial policy differs from macroeconomic policy in its focus on specific economic actors, seeing some as more critical for achieving growth than others. And it differs from redistributive or welfare policies in its productivist orientation. In other words, industrial policy is not about redistribution, but rather about accumulation.

Within these constraints, however, industrial policy can take a wide variety of forms. In the first case, it can focus on extensive growth or on intensive growth (discussed below), and it can target specific firms (i.e., Airbus), industries (i.e., steel), or whole sectors of the economy (i.e., the high technology industrial sector). Industrial policies which are deployed with very specific targeting are consider vertical, while those which cover a wider proportion of the economy are classified as horizontal (Paus 2004, Salazar-Xirinachs, Nübler, and Kozul-Wright 2014, Warwick 2013).

Moreover, industrial policy can make use of a wide variety of instruments, each of which is not, by itself, necessarily a form of industrial policy. For example, states can encourage targeted firms, industries, and sectors by: (1) extending low-cost loans to preferred industries, (2) guaranteeing returns on risky investments, (3) using tariffs or quotas to offer protection from imported goods, (4) providing tax breaks, or (5) directly subsidizing production, inputs, or exports. Industrial policies which use quantifiable economic incentives are often called *hard,* while those in which the state acts as a facilitator or broker are termed *soft* (Harrison and Rodríguez-Clare 2010, Wade 2012). In this latter constellation of policies, governments simply encourage and cajole targeted firms and help to bring them into contact with suppliers, investors, and potential clients.

There are other ways in which industrial policies can differ from one another. In some countries, industrial policy is driven by a national (or sometimes regional) plan, one which is often centralized and specific. In others, it happens industry-by-industry, with little central direction or organized coherence. Furthermore, some states enjoy policy instruments which others lack. Countries where states play a major ownership role in the economy, or where they own or heavily regulate financial institutions, can obviously take actions that would be unavailable to others (see Zysman 1977).

There is considerably more focus today on industrial policy as a means of promoting *upgrading*. What do we mean by this term? Upgrading refers to the process of continuously employing new techniques, new methods, and new technology to move up the value chain of production (see Doner and Schneider 2016, Salazar-Xirinachs, Nübler, and Kozul-Wright 2014).

To understand upgrading, it is critical to understand value chains. Value chains have become the focus of a great deal of research since Porter's (1990) landmark study of competitive advantage. A good definition of the concept comes from Mitchell, Coles, and Keane (2009), who see value chains as describing "the full range of activities required to bring a product or service from conception, through the different phases of production, . . . delivery to final consumers and final disposal after use" (see also Kaplinsky and Morris 2001). In other words, value chains encompass the wide variety of steps necessary to design a product, produce it, and bring it to market.

Any value chain will contain activities that add high levels of value per input and others that contribute much less. For example, designing luxury clothes adds considerably more value per worker than growing the cotton or operating the sewing machine necessary to produce them. The challenge for firms and governments, then, is to upgrade along this value chain, to move from lower- to higher-value-added activities. Pieter van Dijk and Trienekens (2012) identify four ways in which a firm might improve its position on the value chain: upgrading products, upgrading processes, upgrading functions, and product differentiation.

However it is achieved, upgrading along the value chain is a form of intensive growth and can be distinguished from the more familiar extensive growth by its emphasis on constant productivity improvements within particular industries. A state's commitment to upgrading may involve efforts to move economic production from low-value-added to high-value-added industries, or it may mean encouraging existing industries to improve their productivity by moving up the value chain. By contrast, extensive growth occurs when, for example, capital investment allows for the purchase of more machines, or the building of more factories or the training of more workers in existing skills. It does not require learning or change but emphasizes savings (or borrowing) and investment.

This extensive growth has generally been the focus of traditional theories of economic development. If a country, rather than consuming what it produces, can save and invest, it can expand its industrial (or agricultural) capacity and grow. This is true as far as it goes, but we know from Solow (1970) that such extensive growth will eventually give way before the reality of diminishing returns. The more machines or workers are deployed to a particular industry, the less additional value each will produce, until eventually additional investment makes little sense. Instead, to sustain growth, countries need to incorporate new technology and new approaches to production. Only by doing this can they expect to launch themselves on a permanent growth trajectory.

Solow's recognition of the critical role of technological change was later incorporated into endogenous growth theory (Romer 1986), which modeled technological innovation as a function of investment in research and training. In this model, countries are not forced to rely only on the external progress of science to grow, but rather can spark intensive growth by channeling their resources in particular ways. Of course, time would show that even endogenous growth theory, while illuminating the process of development, depicts the process of incorporating innovation into the production process in a very simplified way. Most importantly, though, it leaves aside the political question of how to organize support for innovation.

In this book, my goal is to contribute to our understanding of the process of upgrading and how states can best encourage it. In exploring this question, my focus will be on the political and economic institutions that exist within countries, and on how their structures mediate the interactions between state and private actors which are so central to upgrading.

The Evolution of Industrial Policy

This book comes in the context of reignited interest in upgrading policy around the world (see Rodrik and Aiginger 2020). This new openness to government acting as a growth catalyst is the latest development in a long process of changing attitudes and practices in development and growth policy. While conceiving of certain forms of state intervention as "upgrading policy" may be relatively new, the idea of government as economic catalyst dates back at least to Colbert in the 17th century and Alexander Hamilton in the 18th. Normally, this approach is termed "industrial policy," though a number of other names—R&D policy, productivity promotion—have been applied. Industrial policy, of course, is not always focused on promoting upgrading; it can also be used to encourage extensive economic development and the like. But any understanding of the state's role in upgrading must begin with a brief look at how industrial policy has been applied in the recent past.

At the end of the Second War World, during the massive wave of decolonization that brought most of the world's states into being, economic development was emerging as one of the core global challenges. There were few who doubted that the newly formed states would have a central role to play in promoting this development. These were the heady days of the "big push" (Rosenstein-Rodan 1943), when economists believed that large scale investment would be enough to bring prosperity to emerging economies, just as it seemed to do with the Marshall Plan and reconstruction in Europe. There were, of course, numerous specific ideas about how best to encourage development, ranging from encouraging workers to relocate to urban factories (Lewis 1950) to promoting technology transfer. But with a few exceptions (i.e., Hayek 2005 [1945]), there was little dispute in these years that states would be called up to act as catalysts for growth.

Such views by professional economists, of course, gelled with the instincts of most emerging nation leaders, who were loath to sit by and "let the market work." So, the period from 1945 until roughly the early 1970s was characterized by massive use of what has come to be known as "industrial policy." As a reminder, industrial policies differ from more traditional economic policies in their privileging of particular firms and sectors over others. Unlike, for example, monetary policy or a fiscal stimulus rooted in Keynesianism, industrial policies are rigorously microeconomic and specific. Moreover, they can make use of a variety of tools, including subsidies, bank loans, investment guarantees, and trade protection to accomplish their mission. This aspect of industrial policy can make it difficult to pin down at times, since unlike most other economic policies, it is defined not functionally but by intent. So trade policy can be industrial policy, or not, fiscal policy can be industrial policy, or not, and so on.

Of course, as I will discuss in more detail below, there are many different forms of industrial policy. Most focus on industry, but (somewhat strangely, perhaps) industrial policy can also be applied to agriculture and services. Some industrial policy is carried out in a largely state-owned economy, though this sort is mostly a thing of the past. Today, industrial policy tends to be more subtle, offering nudges to largely independent private actors.

The immediate postwar period saw many emerging countries experiment with larger scale applications of the approach, most particularly those associated with import substitution industrialization (ISI). This development approach makes broad use of state powers to "substitute" products that would normally be imported with domestically produced goods, thereby stimulating the national economy by forcing domestic consumers to buy locally made products. It uses the powers of the state in a comprehensive way, creating import, export, and industrial licensing, quotas, and high tariffs, and generally providing favored industries and firms with generous fiscal incentives (see Kohli 2004).

But the failure of ISI to move countries to high income status (despite some of the benefits that it did produce), began, by the 1960s, to lead some countries to question the approach. The 1970s brought the oil shocks and stagflation in the rich world, and eventually the ascendence of more pro-market approaches in the United States, the United Kingdom, and the international financial institutions (see Frieden 2020). For many years after that, there was a consensus among policy-makers in much of the global North that efforts to promote upgrading are counterproductive. The reigning approach to economic progress was rigorously neo-liberal, embodied in the so-called Washington Consensus: an unfettered market will produce the best outcomes (Rodrik 2007). While more sophisticated advocates of this approach acknowledged that market failures might sometimes justify state intervention in the economy, they argued that this should be kept to an absolute minimum. The state, like the proverbial bull in a china shop, is likely to do more harm than good by getting itself embroiled in the complex workings of a modern free market (Lal 2000).

Soon, however, a new appreciation of the role of industrial policy in contributing to the success of the East Asian Tigers (Johnson 1982, Amsden 1992, Wade 1990, Evans 1995) led many thinkers to reconsider the role that states could play in upgrading. Within the United States, these new understandings were complimented with increased fears of the rise of Japan as an economic rival. All of this led to a renewed interest in industrial policy during the mid to late 1980s and the early 1990s, ironically under the leadership of the pro-market Ronald Reagan and George H. W. Bush (Newfarmer 1984, Premus and Bradford 1984).

During these years, Congress commissioned a number of studies on industrial policy and the administration added some additional tools to its economic policy repertoire, but ultimately the effort to create a cohesive American industrial policy fizzled out. The stagnation of Japan as a serious economic rival, along with the triumphalism of the end of the Cold War and the technology boom gave Americans the sense that others should copy their model, rather than the reverse. Of course, as we shall see, the United States has had a robust industrial policy for decades, though one which is decentralized and, indeed, deniable (Mazzucato 2015).

Internationally, the collapse of the Soviet Union seemed to call more statist approaches to economic policy into question. Indeed, during the period of neo-liberal triumphalism, Japan's insistence that international donors take industrial policy more seriously resulted in an analysis by the World Bank (Birdsall et al. 1993) attributing the success of the Asian Tigers to their harnessing of market forces. For a time, then, the role of the state as a catalyst for economic development was distinctly out of fashion, though it was never truly abandoned.

More recently, however, the ideological winds have noticeably shifted direction. Many observers attributed the 2008 "Great Recession" to unregulated financial markets, leading to vocal calls for state action in the United States and around the world. A number of countries used public funds to rescue financial institutions and businesses that were in danger of failing. Others tightened regulation on financial and real estate markets to prevent episodes of contagion from reoccurring (Kahler and Lake 2013).

At the same time, the rise of China as an economic powerhouse has replaced the old anxieties about Japan. Indeed, given China's enormous size and its state capitalist, authoritarian political system, the challenge that the country poses to the United States and the existing global system is orders of magnitude greater than that of Japan in the 1980s. In particular, the admission of Beijing into the World Trade Organization (WTO), despite the tight links between the state and large enterprises in the country, contributed to growing economic anxiety around the world. Would China's powerhouse industrial economy drive the domestic industries of its trading partners out of business? And do Chinese businesses enjoy benefits from the Beijing government that allow them to compete globally on uneven ground?

On the intellectual front, strict neo-liberal approaches to economic policy have also come under fire in recent years. As we will see in the next chapter, the neo-institutional approach in political economy is now mainstream, with its recognition that well-functioning market economies must be rooted in well-designed institutions (North 1990). Behavioral economists have increasingly called into question the rationality of market mechanisms, challenging some of the most fundamental assumptions of neo-liberalism (Shiller 2006). And recognition of the role of the state in development success stories has become overwhelming in recent years and increasingly difficult to discount. The focus of many scholars and policymakers is shifting from how to limit the state's role in the economy to how to improve the quality and efficiency of its interventions.

All of these considerations have led to a renewed interested in industrial policy in today's world (see Aiginger and Rodrik 2020). Nothing highlights this shift better than the recent actions of the United States government. As we will discuss later, the 2008 financial crisis and the "Great Recession" that followed gave birth not only to an enormous Keynesian stimulus and increased financial regulations, but also to striking new forays into industrial policy. During the Obama years, this new willingness to promote specific industries was embodied especially in the adoption of billions of dollars of direct subsidies for green industry. It was also visible in the government's role as a rescuer of the automobile industry. After 2016, the Trump Administration continued the shift away from neo-liberalism in economic policy but focused more on mercantilist trade policies and the perceived threat of China.

The really striking change came in 2021, when Joe Biden moved into the White House. So far, Biden has devoted more attention to upgrading and industrial policy than any of his recent predecessors. In particular, his administration has issued a detailed analysis of America's "supply chains," focusing on measures that the government should take to promote US production in several critical areas, notably semiconductor chips, rare earth metals, and vaccines, pharmaceuticals, and medical equipment (White House 2021a, 2021b). In keeping with past American practice, the report does not bill the measures as "industrial policy," but to the extent that it takes a microeconomic approach to favoring certain industries over others, that is exactly what it is.

This openness to industrial policy was made manifest in Biden's signature legislative initiative: Build Back Better. Though the full $1.2 trillion package failed to pass Congress, significant portions of it were included in two industrial policy bills (neither of which mention industrial policy) that became law in 2022—the CHIPS Act and the Inflation Reduction Act. The first of these pours billions into encouraging the manufacturing of semiconductors and microchips in the United States, while the second directs significant resources to clean energy industries. Together, they represent the most striking US commitment to industrial policy in years. That this is exactly what Biden's economic policy represents is made clear in the numerous media analyses of the bills, which discuss openly, from both sides of the political aisle, the increased profile of industrial policy (e.g., Krugman 2021, Hawley 2021).

Outside the United States, the policy space around upgrading is also expanding at a clip unseen since at least the 1970s. The Chinese government, much to the chagrin of many of its trading partners, is pursuing a massive and centrally directed upgrading strategy known as "Made in China 2025." A 2019 study by the US Congressional Research Service describes the initiative's goals this way: ". . . to modernize the Chinese economy, boost productivity, and make innovation a driver of economic growth. One key Chinese motivation for MIC 2025 is to avoid hitting the so called 'middle income trap' . . ." (1). More specifically, the plan envisions the channeling of hundreds of billions of dollars into lagging portions of the Chinese economy as well as into potential industries of the future. It may represent the world's most ambitious program of industrial upgrading.

The European Union, for its part, adopted upgrading as a specific regional priority in the Lisbon Process, and incorporated specific upgrading goals in the "Europe 2020" initiative which superseded it. In the French case, Macron, known as one of France's more pro-market presidents, has embraced industrial policy with a vengeance, seeing it as a way to reignite the dynamism of his country's economy. And in Asia, India's Prime Minister Narendra Modi, after previously abolishing the Planning Commission which had managed India's industrial policy for decades, is taking a second look at state-driven upgrading. The Indian government is now deploying a number of industrial and upgrading policies, with its key initiative termed "Make in India." Even the World Bank, once famous for its adherence to the neo-liberal "Washington Consensus," has begun warming to industrial policy, as seen notably in the Bank's 2006 Commission on Growth and Development report (World Bank 2008). We will return to these examples in more detail in the conclusion.

Of course, government upgrading policies are in many ways more difficult to implement today than they were in the past. The dense network of rules which govern international economic relations make certain industrial policy tools essentially off limits. The WTO is the key international institution regulating trade, and it is joined by a complex of bilateral, multilateral, and regional trade and investment treaties, many of which pose even more constraints on national governments than the global trading system. In particular, governments face challenges using tariffs, quantitative restrictions, and government procurement policies to promote domestic upgrading, as they may run afoul of international law (see Rodrik 2007).

At the same time, the renewed global interest in industrial policy indicates clearly that states remain able to promote upgrading when they choose to do so. As I have discussed, industrial policies, including efforts to promote upgrading, are characterized not by the policy instruments used but rather by the goals pursued. If the traditional instruments of trade policy are more difficult to leverage, myriad other options remain. Countries can use "soft" industrial policy to encourage and cajole firms to cooperate, share technology, and even merge. They can use "hard" industrial policies, including subsidies and low interest loans, to promote green domestic industries while fighting climate change. Or governments can invest in more "horizontal" measures such as infrastructure and education, which are generally permitted under international agreements. These do not aim directly at firms, but they are nevertheless forms of industrial policy, at least to some degree, because they impact different industries differently. Promoting science education, for example, is likely to benefit high technology firms more than those lower down the value chain. I will return in the conclusion to the question of which instruments of industrial policy remain open to states in the modern era. For the time being, the critical point is that industrial and upgrading policies are options for states, even those which are, in the aggregate, committed to free markets and open trade. Instruments are available which are legal under international trade law, and governments can layer domestic upgrading policies on top of support for (mostly) open markets at home and abroad.

Upgrading Policy: Intellectual Justifications

What, then, are the theoretical justifications of upgrading policy in the scholarly literature? Does its use rest on a strong intellectual foundation? The short answer is yes, but of course a contested one. As is well known, classical economic theory, going back to Adam Smith (2013 [1776]) highlights the power of the market mechanism to allocate the means of production—land, labor, capital, and perhaps information—in an efficient manner. The "invisible hand" transforms the self-interested search for profit into the social good of ensuring that a nation achieves the maximum productive outputs for its given inputs. Smith's insights were formalized much later by Arrow and Debreu (1954).

Of course, it was understood well by early scholars that the benefits provided by a free market rest on certain assumptions, and that when these assumptions are violated, allocative efficiency can collapse. Critical *market failures* of this type include: (1) imperfect competition (monopolies, oligopolies, and the like), (2) imperfect information (for example hidden pricing), (3) externalities or spillovers (which would include pollution, though spillovers can be positive, as we will see in a moment), (4) collective action and coordination problems, for instance between financial institutions and firms, (5) economies of scale, where producers become more efficient as they grow in size, allowing them to push out up-and-coming competitors, and (6) the presence of public goods (Olson 1971) which are neither excludable nor rival (such as clean air). Correcting such market failures constitutes the most widely supported basis for state intervention in the neoclassical economic tradition.

Drawing from this tradition, many neoclassical economists support efforts by states to provide public goods, regulate pollution, require business transparency, and prevent anticompetitive activities. All of these can be justified on the basic of well-established ideas in neo-classical economics and all are seen as market supporting rather than market replacing.

The problem comes, of course, when it is time to parse out exactly what is a market failure and what actions a state should take to correct it. Neo-liberal scholars, who embrace the neoclassical tradition but with a strong anti-state element, see market failures as relatively rare and unimportant. Rather, they fear that the consequences of state action to correct them will end up making the situation worse. As a result, sophisticated neo-liberal economists, while not denying the existence of market failure, fear so-called "state failure" even more (Lal 2000, Krueger 1990).

On the other side of the debate, many economists who also work within the dominant neoclassical tradition are more open to state intervention. They often identify market failures as endemic, especially in emerging economies, and tend to believe that markets will only function when states take action to correct these failures. These scholars also recognize the risk of state failure and corruption, and therefore emphasize the critical role played by strong public institutions in the functioning of market systems (e.g., Stiglitz and Greenwald 2015, Lin 2017, Easterly 2002, Acemoglu and Robinson 2006).

Within the neoclassical tradition, at least, these debates are at the center of how the state's economic role is understood. The problem is that a focus on market failures, at least as they are usually understood, can only get us so far. Perhaps, as some scholars have long asserted, the forms of state action needed to catalyze economic growth—especially for the long-term—are quite different from those needed to make the market work more efficiently in the short term (Rodrik 2007). After all, traditional economics emphasizes that the benefit that well-functioning markets can provide is allocative efficiency—getting the most output for a nation's input of land, labor, and capital. But long-term growth is a fundamentally more dynamic process, one that requires constant innovation. It should not be surprising that simply eliminating short-term market failures is not enough to drive the kind of upgrading that is at the heart of the modern understanding of economic development (see Evans 1995).

In an effort to incorporate change and innovation into the neoclassical understanding of growth, scholars have introduced the concept of *dynamic comparative advantage*. The idea of standard, or static, comparative advantage is well known. The English economist David Ricardo (2004 [1817]) developed it in the early nineteenth century to explain why, when two countries specialize in what each is most efficient at making and then trade, both are better off. This insight—that trade is a positive-sum-game and that countries (or individuals for that matter) should concentrate on their strengths and purchase everything else from exchange—is at the heart of classical economics.

Ricardo's model, however, assumed that comparative advantage was endemic to a particular country, and he devoted little effort to explaining its origin. In Ricardo's classic example of trade between England and Portugal, the former possessed a comparative advantage in cloth and the latter in wine. These were assumed to be essentially immutable, based on weather and the possession of adequate capital (though of course capital stock is not as fundamental to a country as rainfall). Nearly one hundred years later, Heckscher and Ohlin (1933) developed an explanation for why certain countries might specialize in particular industries, based on their relative abundance of land, labor, or capital.

Classical trade theory thus provided a powerful explanation for the benefits of free exchange as well as a way to predict broadly whether a country will trade manufactured goods, natural resources, or agricultural commodities. But it remained largely blind to potential changes in comparative advantage that can occur over time. After all, how can we explain why the United States has a comparative advantage in exporting certain knowledge-intensive services such as higher education or accounting, while Thailand has a comparative advantage in semiconductors (Doner 2009, Evans 1995)? Surely these export strengths are not fundamental to the United States or Thailand in the way that possessing oil reserves is to Saudi Arabia or Venezuela. How can South Korea develop a globally competitive automobile industry and India a globally competitive software industry seemingly out of thin air? And, to complicate things further, how can multiple countries develop a comparative advantage in a single product such as automobiles or airplanes?

Clearly, comparative advantage is dynamically created and destroyed and, beyond some basic predictions that can be made from factor endowments, its origins remain a bit mysterious. This observation leads us to a critical question: how can countries create a comparative advantage where it does not yet exist? This is a vital issue because some industries are higher up the value chain than others and are therefore more likely to contribute to long-term economic growth. Such industries possess more positive knowledge spillovers that can seed other industries and promote innovation, as we will discuss in more detail in a few moments. For the time being, it is enough to note that developing countries, and indeed all countries, have reason to believe that a comparative advantage in a desirable industry can be created even in places where it has never existed (see Krugman 1986).

The need to create new industries further up the value chain has particular resonance for middle income countries. Countries in the early stages of development, as we have already noted, can find success with fairly straightforward, traditional economic policies. As Adam Smith once put it, "peace, easy taxes, and a tolerable administration of justice" have often proven quite effective (Smith 2013 [1776], Besley and Persson 2011). When combined with the mobilization of investment toward labor intensive production, as envisioned by "big push" theorists such as Rosenstein-Rodan (1943), significant growth is often possible.

The problem, again, is that pure investment mobilization strategies can only go so far. This fact was made clear by Solow's (1970) groundbreaking work on the diminishing growth return to investment and, later, by endogenous growth theory (Romer 1986). Ultimately, without innovation, investment in new machines and methods will exhaust its potential and leave a country well short of high income status. Empirically, Rodrik (2007) has shown clearly that initiating a growth spurt is much easier than sustaining one. Nearly all countries have periods of high growth in their histories; the question is how to keep growing over the long term.

Moving from middle to high income status requires countries to move up the value chain in their production processes. It is no longer enough, for instance, to introduce mechanization to agriculture or to specialize in low skilled industrial manufacturing. Countries must increase their productivity and the value that they add to the goods and services that they produce (Paus 2014). They must create new comparative advantages in higher-value-added goods and services.

Creating this new comparative advantage often happens within the context of newly emerging global value chains (Gereffi 2018). The traditional view of trade, more or less accurate in the past, was that products were produced (or grown or mined) in a single country and then exported. The foreign exchange gained from these exports would then be used to purchase goods and services produced by other countries in which they, presumably, have a comparative advantage. The problem today is that a single complex product is increasingly produced in a multitude of different countries: design and management may occur in one country, raw materials may be acquired in another, different components may be manufactured in a third, fourth, or fifth country, and assembly may take place in a sixth. This reality has produced a disconnect between where on the value chain a country's exports lie and how much value-added that country has actually generated. In other words, a country may import a nearly finished high-value-added good (say a computer), make a relatively simple addition, and then export the product. While that export is high on the value chain, the value-added produced by the country remains low.

As a number of scholars have pointed out, this complex reality is certain to impact the sorts of industrial policies that will be most effective in spurring upgrading (Doner, Noble, and Ravenhill 2021, Gereffi 2018, Noman and Stiglitz 2017). Countries must now work with specific firms in a very targeted fashion to improve their position in the global value chains. They must interact with foreign multinationals that lead the global production chain, jockeying for an improved place. The focus now for development has moved from the creation of whole industries to better specialization in complex global production networks.

Before we shift our attention to the political economy of industrial policy, it is important to discuss a relatively new school of thought that has rapidly become one of the most influential approaches to upgrading policy: the need to create "a learning society" (Stiglitz and Greenwald 2015). This approach provides perhaps the clearest explanation for why certain industries might contribute more to long-term growth than others and might therefore be an appropriate target for state support.

The idea behind this approach, championed by former World Bank chief economist Joseph Stiglitz, is that the fundamental difference between successful and unsuccessful economies resides in the extent to which they are "learning societies." Such a society is one which incentivizes and encourages the dissemination of new knowledge within and across industries and educational institutions. This idea, of course, draws its inspiration from endogenous growth theory and the notion that long-term growth requires constant innovation, which in turn demands investment. But it sees learning in a much more expansive way than do traditional approaches.

Instead of identifying the production and transmission of knowledge largely with research and development activities, the learning approach sees it occurring whenever better techniques or technologies are incorporated into production processes, even when these are not in any sense new. A learning society, then, is one where the transmission and incorporation of knowledge, whether newly produced or just newly acquired, is easy and smooth. When this characteristic is present, and only when this characteristic is present, will long-term growth flourish. Indeed, for scholars of the learning society, the ability for economic actors in a country to learn is more important even than capital investment or other more traditional pro-development policies.

Obviously, the learning society approach has important implications for policy. Stiglitz and Greenwald (2015) argue that states should provide support to those industries which produce more knowledge spillovers. As noted above, spillovers, or externalities, are a form of market failure since they generate value outside market exchange. But spillovers can be positive, and many scholars argue that nurturing these positive spillovers is critical to development. Indeed, the central role of knowledge spillovers is not new to the recent learning approaches but has long been incorporated into political economy approaches. For example, scholars of agglomeration emphasize that the geographical proximity of high technology firms, as in Silicon Valley, can generate beneficial knowledge spillovers that improve the productivity of all actors (Rosenthal and Strange 2004).

What sets learning approaches apart is the idea that governments, instead of targeting particular firms or even industries, should promote the growth of the entire industrial sector. The idea is that the industrial sector is much more likely to produce knowledge spillovers than the agricultural sector, and so promoting its growth is a way to generate more learning without having to "pick winners." As we shall see in the next section, concern over whether governments can effectively "pick winners" is widespread among opponents, and even advocates, of industrial policy.

So, to summarize, the neo-classical justification for state intervention in the economy—to correct market failures—is almost universally accepted in principle. Neo-liberal economists and those more friendly to government involvement, however, can differ dramatically in how seriously they take such market failures and in how much they fear that "state failure" will accompany any effort to intervene.

But, taking onboard the insights Solow (1970) and later scholars of endogenous growth theory, it is not enough for governments simply to use their powers to make the market function more efficiently. Instead, while market pressures push a country to specialize in its current comparative advantage, its leaders must consider how to build a future comparative advantage in higher value-added goods and services (here see the work of Krugman 1986). Static comparative advantage, maximized through free trade and the market mechanism, will ensure that a country's factors of production are efficiently used in the moment. But without an understanding that comparative advantage is dynamic and can be built, that country, if it is low or middle income, will have difficulty moving up the value chain. In particular, middle income countries are going to need to consider carefully how they can promote economic upgrading, since they have likely exhausted most of the growth benefits that pure investment can bring.

Upgrading for such a country will demand a policy that encourages the growth of firms, industries, or sectors of the economy that are higher up the value chain and that are likely to generate more knowledge spillovers. Scholarship on global value chains would point to the need to work with individual firms in niche industries which are struggling to produce more value within a complex, multi-country chain of production. By contrast, the learning society approach would emphasize the need to encourage the growth of the industrial sector in general to strengthen firms where learning is likely to be more emphasized. It would also point to the need to finance more research, training, and the like.

The through-line is that higher-value-added industries and those which produce knowledge spillovers are vital to long-term growth and that the market mechanism alone is not likely to generate the incentives necessary to create or grow such industries. Industrial and upgrading policies are therefore a vital part of the state's role in the economy, along with, of course, the more traditional roles of overcoming market failures and maintaining macroeconomic stability. In other words, good industrial policies can be thought of as necessary, but not sufficient, contributors to economic development.

Upgrading Policy: Political Economy Perspectives

But if it is up to the state to encourage upgrading, how specifically can this be done? And how do different countries attempt to achieve this goal given their differing institutions and structures? A large literature in political economy addresses these critical questions. Much of this literature explores economic development more broadly, of which upgrading is only a part, but nearly all of it can help shed light on upgrading policy more specifically.

At the root of much recent research in the political economy of development is the scholarly turn toward institutions. A focus on institutions for development arose initially as a reaction to more mainstream economic models that emphasized "getting the prices right" as the key driver of economic growth. If the basic rules of the free market are in place (the argument goes) and guaranteed by an effective but highly limited state, development will follow. Despite this emphasis on spontaneously generated markets, some heterodox economists have always emphasized the role of institutions, most notably Karl Polanyi (2001 [1944]) in his classic work *The Great Transformation*. It was Polanyi who asserted that markets do not exist in a vacuum, but rather are embedded in a social and political fabric. For Polanyi, capitalist systems do not arise spontaneously but are rather *created* through state-driven institutional transformation.

It was not until the 1980s, however, that institutions—defined by North (1990 1) as "humanly devised constraints that structure political, economic, and social interaction . . ." and comprising "both informal constraints (sanctions, taboos, customs, traditions, and codes of conduct), and formal rules (constitutions, laws, property rights)"—were mainstreamed into the economics discourse. However, only a decade after North, their central role in development had become so widely accepted that the World Bank came to see the strengthening of institutional capacity as a core element of its mission.[2]

Within political science, of course, the key role of institutions has historically been less controversial. Nevertheless, the behavioral revolution of the 1950s and 1960s moved the avant-garde of the discipline toward the systematic consideration of mass behavior (Easton 1993). Scholars began to deemphasize institutions in politics, even eschewing the term *state* for *political system*. Again, it was in the 1980s when scholars such as Evans, Rueschemeyer, and Skocpol (1985) began to "bring the state back in" and reignite interest in the study of institutions. Since that time, many new approaches to understanding the role of institutions in politics and political economy have developed (i.e., path dependence) and many older ones have deepened (i.e., public choice). But the study of institutions has always remained at the center of scholarly interest.

Developments in the real world also helped to drive the turn toward institutions. These included the stagnation of some highly deregulated countries, combined with the success of some more guided economies (notably China, see Aghion et al. 2015). In the real world, institutionalists emphasized, market failures are ubiquitous; these include spillover effects, public goods, information asymmetries and, of course, collective action and coordination problems. Without good institutions, states will be unable to unleash the power of markets, upgrade, and achieve growth. With them, states will be able to develop economic policies that are appropriate to local circumstances and that are effectively implemented (i.e., Root 1996, Rodrik 2007, Wade 1990).

Which sorts of institutions are important? That, of course, is the key question and one which does not yet have a satisfactory answer. North (1990) and North and Weingast (2000) tend to emphasize the role of institutions, both formal and informal, in overcoming transaction costs, enforcing contracts, and protecting private property. In this conception, institutions are the necessary backbone to free markets. Other scholars have focused instead on broader institutions as critical for growth. These have included liberal democracy (Acemoglu and Robinson 2012), a capacity for income redistribution (Flechtner and Panther 2016), and state capacity (Huntington 1968, Osafo-Kwaako and Robinson 2013).

A growing research tradition—fitting within the institutional literature—eschews the more traditional focus on large scale tasks (i.e., industrialization) and macro-institutions (i.e., democracy) for a decidedly micro orientation (see Hsueh 2023). It begins with the observation that moving up the value chain requires confronting a daunting series of collective action problems, coordination problems, and intertemporal bargains (Paus 2014, Bardhan 2016, Waldner 1999). Overcoming these problems is unavoidably political and demands what Doner and Schneider (2016) call *upgrading coalitions* of state and economic actors committed to a common national strategy.

In other words, while endogenous growth theorists tend to focus on technological innovation as the driver of long-term development, these scholars emphasize that institutional innovation may be even more critical. Without the institutions, formal and informal, required to overcome the collective action and coordination problems inherent in upgrading, states are likely to be stuck in the middle income trap indefinitely.

Fundamentally, economic upgrading is very difficult for individual private or state actors to achieve on their own. Business leaders and entrepreneurs may be unable to move into a higher value-added industry without investors willing and able to take the necessary risks. Investors and entrepreneurs may be skittish without workers trained in the new industry, as well as without upstream and downstream producers to serve the industry and buy its products. Of course, workers are unlikely to receive training for an industry that does not yet exist, nor are related business likely to arise out of nowhere. And if state officials wish to encourage the creation of such a high-value-added industry, unless they are willing to adopt the largely discredited command economy approach, they will need to cooperate with business, finance, education, and perhaps labor. None of these actors can safely move forward without guarantees and cooperation from the others.

So what specific form do upgrading challenges take? Waldner (1999) points to the first mover challenges inherent in creating new industries and in upgrading old ones. In both cases, he argues, disparate actors need to coordinate their behavior to achieve an economic goal, but those who move first are taking an especially great risk. Moreover, upgrading represents a particularly severe challenge, since states normally avoid simply directing resources to generate a new factory. It falls to the state to encourage moving up the value chain with concrete policy tools such as investment guarantees, cheap financing, subsidies, and the like. Bardhan (2016) and Doner and Schneider (2016) point to additional roles that states may take to encourage upgrading. These include investing in vocational and higher education and coordinating its structure with the needs of business, improving infrastructure and R&D related to emerging industries, and facilitating relationships up and down the value chain.

Ultimately, the critical issue is to understand how these upgrading coalitions form, how they function, and when they are most effective. Here we can seek assistance from decades of insightful research on the developmental state. Beginning with Johnson's (1982) study of Japan, this scholarship developed as an effort to explain the extraordinary success of the Asian tigers (Haggard 2018). Developmental state theorists were unwilling to accept the standard story (enshrined in an official analysis by the World Bank [Birdsall et al. 1993]) that the economic rise of East Asia was due solely to pro-market policies. Instead, they pointed to the benefits of elite bureaucratic power (such as the Japanese MITI discussed in Johnson [1982]) which could assist the private sector in building a more dynamic form of comparative advantage (Hausman and Rodrik 2003, Harrison and Rodriguez-Clare 2010, Evans 1995). Such a form of comparative advantage was not a given characteristic of states, as assumed by David Ricardo (2004 [1817]), but rather something that could be built with systematic state and private action. In other words, middle income countries could develop consultative institutions that would facilitate upgrading and ultimately build a new comparative advantage in high-value-added productions.

As the developmental state literature evolved, it moved beyond its focus on elite state bureaucracies as the driver of upgrading and began to focus more on the dynamics of state-business consultation (Haggard 2018, Wade 1990, Amsden 1992). In other words, it explored upgrading coalitions. The most well-known result from this branch of the literature comes from a comparative study by Evans (1995); it identifies a relationship of *embedded autonomy* as the most effective consultative structure. Here elite civil servants are embedded enough with business to understand what it needs to upgrade, but autonomous enough to hold it to account.

Though the term "embedded autonomy" refers to a form of state-business consultation, it also reveals the developmental state literature's focus on elite bureaucracies. After all, it is about how state actors, not private actors, should behave. In other words, the developmental state literature remains quite focused on states as the drivers of consultation, seeing business interests as considerably more passive and virtually ignoring labor.

Interestingly, the reverse is true about a literature which is rarely in conversation with the developmental state because it was formed with Europe and Latin America in mind. This is the literature on *neo-corporatism*, considered by some to be antiquated as a field of inquiry but still very much worthy of our attention.

Scholars of neo-corporatism highlight the importance of interest group cohesion in the coordination of economic policy between the state and private actors (i.e., Schmitter 1974). In this literature, state-business consultation is as critical as it is for developmental state theorists, but here it is private interests which play the leading role.[3] For scholars of neo-corporatism, centrally organized business groups (and also labor unions, organizations that are largely ignored by the Asia-centric developmental state theorists) are in a better position to coordinate socially beneficial economic policies with the state. It is this peak-level cooperation that defines corporatism and distinguishes it from more pluralistic systems, where interest groups are fragmented and policy cannot take a coordinated form. In this conception, corporatism is not associated with a particular ideology or regime type but is rather a form of policy-making praxis.

Advocates of corporatism have touted its ability to generate macroeconomic stability (Garrett 1998), an equitable distribution of income (Freeman 1989), and, more broadly, mutually beneficial outcomes across all segments of an economy (Katzenstein 1985). Economic upgrading and growth are less central to scholars of corporatism, given their focus on the developed world, though Ornston (2012) has identified a new "creative" form of corporatism that leverages peak-level structures to promote economic transformation. Whatever the outcome studied, however, the implications for upgrading coalitions are clear: when private interests are better organized, consultation is more effective.

A third literature—*varieties of capitalism*—takes yet a different perspective on the question of state-business consultation. Again, this literature comes from the developed world and has rarely been applied to the questions of upgrading that concern us here. Nevertheless, it has clear implications for those issues.

This literature identifies the existence of distinct forms of capitalism in which institutional configurations in a variety of areas (education, industrial relations, finance, etc.) fit together to produce a cohesive political-economic system (Hall and Soskice 2001). Focusing primarily on the behavior of firms, scholars of the varieties of capitalism highlight the benefits of coordinated market economies (CMEs) in which multiple businesses, banks, unions, and often state actors coordinate their behavior outside typical market mechanisms. In such systems, they argue, the entirety of the political economy works together to create smooth, high-quality production of high-value-added goods. By contrast, in liberal market economies (LMEs), firms relate to their environment primarily through the market mechanism, drawing up contractual relationships with suppliers, buyers, and employees, and raising their capital primarily on private equity markets. The role of the state is limited in these systems, and they tend to excel at innovation and rapid adjustment to market conditions, but to be weaker in complex manufacturing.

Some recent scholarship has called into question the empirical predictions of this literature (i.e., Schmidt 2016, Streeck and Thelen 2005, Steinmo 2010). Skeptics contest the idea that particular political-economic systems are destined to be adept at predetermined forms of production. More fundamentally, some scholars even suggest that healthy state-private interactions may be critical for the long-term sustainability of market systems rather than just one of several ways to structure production systems (Iversen and Soskice 2019).

Whatever the case, the varieties of capitalism literature remains an innovative and sophisticated approach to understanding how the different pieces of an economy fit together. But it begs the question: how do these form-fitting pieces come together in the first place? In truth, varieties of capitalism has little to say about economic change and its causes. In it, we see the results of effective upgrading coalitions, but not their causes. More than that, the varieties of capitalism literature has a deterministic streak that likely overstates the structural constraints to economic policy making. Indeed, I argue here that institutions are not so mutually interdependent as to preclude different sorts of production arrangements existing at different times and in different industries within the same country.

Beyond these issues, scholars working within the varieties of capitalism tradition have expressed skepticism that liberal market economies such as the United States will be able to use industrial policy effectively (Hall and Soskice 2001). As we will see, there is reason to believe that this argument is incorrect. And, perhaps more significantly, the classification of all advanced political economies into these two abstract categories may be too ambitious; as some researchers have noted, France especially seems to be a poor fit for either economic type. Despite these critiques, however, the varieties of capitalism literature highlights well the benefits that can accrue with an efficient, interlocking national system of production.

A final scholarly approach to institutions and development focuses on the role of networks. This approach is similar to scholarship on upgrading tasks and coalitions, but it emphasizes the need for various economic actors to connect with one another in order to spur innovation (Cortell 2005, Taylor 2016, Schrank and Whitford 2009, Salazar-Xirinachs, Nübler, and Kozul-Wright 2014). For scholars in this tradition, it is not only adverse incentives and collective action problems that impede development, but it is the lack of interaction among the critical actors whose behavior must be coordinated for upgrading to occur. A core role of institutions, then, is simply to promote networks, whether between different private sector actors through business and professional associations, or between state and private actors through public-private partnerships, advisory committees, and the like. Such regulated forms of cooperation are critical to connecting key actors and to building trust among them to overcome the sorts of upgrading challenges that we have already discussed. As we will see, my theory is this book draws significantly on these insights.

Where does this leave us? Past research has dramatically advanced our understanding of the political causes of economic development. It has highlighted the particular challenges faced by middle income economies in their efforts to move up the value chain, especially as they relate to coordination and collective action problems. It has pointed to institutions as critical for overcoming these challenges, particularly upgrading coalitions of state bureaucrats, businesses, and (perhaps) labor. I turn in the next chapter to a discussion of how upgrading can best be accomplished, exploring at a more technical level insights from the literature about the sorts of institutions that are most likely to help economies move up the value chain. I then present my own theory in some detail and highlight how it fits into the ongoing conversation about upgrading.

TWO

How Can Upgrading Be Accomplished?

Building the Theory

What lessons can we draw from the political economy literature to inform how governments can best promote upgrading? I begin to answer this question with a discussion of the growing literature on "upgrading institutions," mining it for insights about how these institutions should be structured to maximize their performance. I then discuss the critical but amorphous role of the "upgrading coalitions" of state and private stakeholders that underpin any success that the institutions may enjoy. Finally, I turn to a detailed explication of my theory, which explores how the organizational cohesion of the state and private actors interacts to influence the form and success of upgrading policy.

Upgrading Institutions

Broadly speaking, upgrading institutions are state or quasi-state bodies that intervene in the economy to promote upgrading. Research and experience teach that there is no single way to structure an organization focused on upgrading. These institutions range from planning commissions that enjoy significant formal powers to loose forums for consultation among critical actors. They sometimes operate at the national level, coordinating economic policy across multiple sectors and regions of the economy. Other times, they may be regional or local institutions that encourage upgrading only within a circumscribed geographical area. Countries may possess a single powerful upgrading institution, such as Japan's famous Ministry of International Trade and Industry (Johnson 1982). Conversely, numerous different ministries, agencies, and sub-agencies may play the role of upgrading institutions within a single country, as is the case in the United States with disparate actors such as the Defense Advanced Research Projects Agency (DARPA), the Small Business Administration (SBA), the National Institutes of Health (NIH), and innumerable others.

More than that, some upgrading institutions may be insulated from political actors, and others may include them. Some may be centralized and deal with the economy (or the industrial sector) as a whole, while others may be laser-focused on particular firms or industries. Some such institutions may exclude labor, and others may incorporate it. Some may allow private businesses to play a significant role, while others may be very much state driven. Some upgrading institutions may be endowed with significant powers over policy—whether favorable loans, investment guarantees, tax breaks, or something else—while others may primarily serve as a forum for networking and collective planning.

Despite all of this variety, the literature points to a number of "good practices" in institutional construction that are likely to produce the best outcomes. One good practice for which there is near unanimity across different scholarly programs is the need for institutional strength and coherence. For developmental state theorists such as Evans (1995), this means above all that state institutions must be autonomous from the private sector. In other words, they must be able to discipline capital without themselves being "captured" by the private sector (Amsden 2001). This sort of institutional capture is destructive to upgrading because it means that private actors are able to coerce the state into providing them with rents rather than forcing them to become more competitive. After all, what private business would choose the hard road of upgrading when the easy path of government protected rents is available?

One critical question related to institutional autonomy is whether successful upgrading is limited only to countries with high levels of institutional coherence, most of which are found in the developed world. Of course, having strong political and administrative institutions is a very positive thing for development, as well as for other tasks of government. Fortunately, as Johnson (1982), Wade (1990), Amsden (1992) and others have shown, a number of countries that lack strong institutions overall have successfully promoted upgrading by creating a specialized, elite development body. Committed governments, then, are sometimes able to generate the coherent bureaucracy necessary for upgrading to work, even when other institutions of government do not function as effectively.

Connected to the need for coherence is the critical issue of accountability.

If the firms receiving state support for upgrading are unaccountable, they might see such support solely as a source of rents without doing the difficult work necessary to move up the value chain. So, government officials promoting upgrading must be able to remove state support when private actors are abusing it. At the same time, these state actors must be accountable, since there is always a risk that they will seek kickbacks from unproductive firms. How to balance this accountability with the need for autonomy is one of the major challenges of upgrading.

A third characteristic of institutions that is critical for upgrading is the capacity for policy flexibility. The traditional approach of neo-liberal economists to development is to recommend specific policies, perhaps including trade liberalization, privatization, or even the channeling of investment. By contrast, most scholars of institutions focus much more on process, emphasizing that the "correct" policy is likely to vary significantly in different circumstances. Given this fact, the key goal is to create institutional structures that can draw relevant information from all sources (firms, government agencies, experts, etc.) and rapidly adapt to changing circumstances (Salazar-Xirinachs, Nübler, and Kozul-Wright 2014). Such institutions must allow consultation, to be sure, and they must also be cohesive and autonomous. But these characteristics alone are not enough. Effective development institutions must be able to adjust to market conditions and to the changing needs of various state and private actors, something that can be challenging when making decisions that have important distributional effects.

Even institutions that can adapt rapidly will likely be more effective if they control certain levers of policy that can incentivize upgrading. Simply building networks between firms, banks, researchers, unions, and other actors is useful, but upgrading institutions can do much more if they can offer more material incentives to move up the value chain. And the state institutions responsible for upgrading are also those in the best position to determine what sorts of support will be most effective at promoting upgrading. Of course, the more powers that these institutions have, the more accountability will be required.

The Techniques of Upgrading Policy

Beyond the good practices of institutional design, the literature also provides lessons about what precisely the state should be doing to promote upgrading. As noted above, there is near consensus around the importance of policy flexibility, but a number of general guidelines can still be gleaned from prior work. These are in general compatible with one another, though they tend to lay their emphasis on different points.

One common refrain, articulated most clearly by Mazzucato (2015), is that the state should not replace or "crowd out" the private sector, but should rather "do what no one else is doing." This perspective provides a needed corrective to the idea that industrial policy is fundamentally anti-market, a more polite cousin of Soviet-style central planning. Rather, there are certain tasks which, due to coordination problems, market failures, and risk, private firms will refuse to undertake. If upgrading is to occur, at least at a higher rate, state authorities will have to take their place.

What are these specific tasks that only the state is able and willing to do? They can vary widely depending on context, but they often include some of the following:

(1) Financing or insuring risky, but potentially transformative, business activities that private financial institutions are unwilling to underwrite. As Mazzucato (2015) and Noman and Stiglitz (2017) point out, even venture capitalists tend to be more risk adverse and more oriented toward short-term rewards than is commonly understood. The state is generally the only entity willing to take a risk on basic and applied research that might take years to bear fruit economically. But it is precisely this sort of research that is most critical for upgrading.

(2) Acting as a networking service for firms, universities, financial institutions, unions, up- and down-stream producers, and other actors whose behavior must be coordinated in order to move up the value chain (e.g., Cortell 2005, Taylor 2016). Often, without state assistance, these actors face coordination or first-mover problems that undermine any incentive for a single actor to begin the process of upgrading. State actors can also go beyond mere matchmaking by providing material incentives or guarantees for these actors to cooperate (Waldner 1999).

(3) Providing policy support in the form of subsidies, trade protection, tax breaks, low-interest loans, investment guarantees, and the like to keep firms in business as they restructure to produce new goods and services for which they have not yet developed a comparative advantage or scale economies. One critical market failure that can impede upgrading is the presence of economies of scale. Many high-value-added industries are characterized by these scale economies, meaning that products become cheaper to produce—

and more profitable—as firm size increases. A critical result, well understood by advocates of import substitution development policies in the mid-twentieth century (i.e., Prebisch 1959), is that established firms can undercut the competitiveness of up-and-coming competitors, driving them out of business before they are able even to get started. This dynamic, not surprisingly, results not only in monopolies and oligopolies, but can also present roadblocks to building new areas of comparative advantage. One solution to this challenge is erecting trade barriers so that domestic producers have protected access to domestic markets. Another is to subsidize exports so that domestic firms are able to charge competitive prices on international markets, even as they seek to develop scale economies. In the conclusion, I discuss what sorts of policy approaches are available in today's globalized world.

(4) Disciplining firms to upgrade rather than to seek rents. This task, of course, is complementary with the one above. Supporting firms as they move into higher-value-added areas risks creating dependence on state assistance, something that has plagued previous development efforts. Upgrading institutions, as I discussed in the previous section, must be able to hold private firms to account, demanding that they take active steps toward upgrading or risk losing public support (Evans 1995).

Another way to put all of this is that upgrading institutions should dedicate themselves to performing the tasks necessary to promote development. These include overcoming market failures (especially scale economies, coordination problems, information asymmetries, and the like), building networks, and providing material incentives for moving up the value chain. Through their networking activities, such institutions should also build upgrading coalitions in the various industries where they work.

It is worth discussing a final, but critical, topic on the question of what upgrading institutions should do. The state's role in development often brings to mind images of central planning, with government bureaucrats scribbling on input-output tables in their efforts to direct the economy. As we have already discussed, except for a very few cases, this understanding of state-directed development is antiquated and simplistic. The question remains, however, whether some form of central planning, at least "indicative" rather than coercive, is a useful exercise. I argue here, as we will see, that both centralized and decentralized approaches to development can be effective when the state-society relationship is properly aligned.

Our last topic here concerns the very practical question of which firms and industries the state should support as it endeavors to move up the value chain. There are, not surprisingly, several different takes on this question in the literature. Some scholars (i.e., Stiglitz and Greenwald 2015) emphasize the role of positive externalities, arguing that the state should prioritize supporting economic actors that generate large knowledge spillovers. Such firms and industries are generally those which are already higher on the value chain relative to others in the domestic economy. The idea is that, if these firms and industries grow, the knowledge they generate will spill over into adjacent industries, either through the sharing of employees or through mutual cooperation or co-location.

But should states begin with an existing firm and assist it to move up the value chain in its existing business, or should they bring relevant actors together to move into an entirely new industry? The literature does not offer a clear and consistent answer to this question. Choosing an existing firm would be a less complicated and easier way to promote upgrading for those concerned about state failure. But it may well be that, in many countries, the high-value-added firms to support simply do not exist. Moreover, some scholars would maintain that the state needs to step in where the private sector cannot, and that this means in catalyzing new industries (though these could well be operating by existing firms moving into new areas).

One major critique of industrial—and by extension upgrading—policy is that the state is lousy at picking winners. This is no doubt true. But, as Mazzucato (2015) points out, the costs of investing in a multitude of failed industries are often offset many times over by a single success. So, even if the state fails in its choices most of the time, the relevant question is one of cost-benefit, and this generally falls in favor of intervention, at least when it is done well.

With all of this in mind, two scholars have pointed to ways in which the question of "picking winners" can be better systematized or even avoided altogether. Justin Lin (2017), like Stiglitz a former chief economist of the World Bank, has proposed a potential solution. In essence, he argues that states should identify an industry to support that represents as short a leap from the country's existing capacity as possible. This can be done by beginning with the country's existing comparative advantage and then selecting higher-value-added industries that are as close to what the country can already do effectively as possible. This risk adverse strategy seems to minimize the dangers of failure, but some have also criticized it for being too timid.

A second, more aggressive way to solve the "picking winners" problem is associated with the "learning society" model of Stiglitz and Greenwald (2015). They argue that, since the industrial sector in general is likely to produce more positive spillovers then the agricultural or service sector, it is enough for states to promote further industrialization more broadly. This is welcome news for those worried that the entire enterprise of industrial policy rests on the alchemy of choosing the right recipient of state largess, but it is also likely to run into resource constraints. Such a broad strategy may also make little since outside the context of low-income countries.

In thinking about how to choose where state support should be channeled, it is worth thinking about two final points. First, promoting knowledge spillovers and a knowledge-based economy more broadly is not just a question of creating new technologies and processes. It may be, especially for developing countries, more a question of effectively incorporating existing knowledge into the production process. As scholars have long understood, the spread of new knowledge is not smooth, and even when it is freely available it may still be a challenge to apply. Significant upgrading can occur with any original research and development.

Finally, given the proliferation of global value chains (Gereffi 2018), upgrading often involves competing with other firms in other countries for a higher position in a single product's chain of production, one that is often run by a multinational corporation. This fact complicates traditional approaches to upgrading, since it introduces a global component not just in marketing and competition, but also in production.

Upgrading Coalitions

Well-functioning institutions, however, are not enough; rather, boosting national productivity will remain elusive without the active engagement of *upgrading coalitions* (see Doner et al. 2021; Doner and Schneider 2016). These coalitions, which can take a variety of forms, comprise critical state and private stakeholders who share a common commitment to achieving higher-value-added production. Without the explicit or at least tacit support and cooperation of these actors, upgrading is not likely to achieve success. In other words, successful upgrading requires both empowered institutions to carry out industrial policy and the social and political backing that only coalitions of critical stakeholders can provide.

Despite the importance of these upgrading coalitions, however, they can be tricky to define and theorize. Who are the key actors and organizations that must come to agreement for upgrading to take hold in an economy? And, since upgrading coalitions are often informal, how can we know whether such a coalition exists in any given country or economic sector? These questions have no easy answers and form part of the reason, as we shall see, that I devote much of the empirical part of the book to qualitative case studies.

We can say, however, that upgrading coalitions manifest in a number of predictable ways. In many countries, for example, the critical actors required for upgrading policy to work, whether at the national, sectoral, or regional level, are incorporated into the upgrading institution itself. Examples of this phenomenon include (with some caveats) the National Development Council which for years oversaw the broad actions of the Planning Commission in India.

Indeed, scholars have long emphasized the benefits of such an approach. Researchers from a wide variety of traditions—the developmental state, corporatism, networks, upgrading coalitions, and beyond—are nearly unanimous about the key role played by consultation mechanisms that bring together private and public actors. Though there may be some differences in emphasis around how such institutions should be structured and around what their principal goal is (building connections, overcoming collective action problems, promoting accountability, etc.), there can be little doubt of their importance to successful upgrading. A corollary of this need for consultation is the critical role of embeddedness, a term coined for this context by Evans (1995) to indicate when state officials are close enough to the private sector to understand development needs. Root (1996) is even more emphatic in his analysis of the role of formal consultation mechanisms in upgrading, seeing them as critical to success.

At their best, then, upgrading institutions can provide a space for networking and consultation among relevant public and private actors in a particular industry targeted for upgrading. Elite government administrators may be directing the institution, and they may consult with executives from firms in the industry as well as those up- and down-stream, business associations, labor unions, bankers and leaders of financial institutions, experts and researchers, educational organizations and universities, and more. In such cases, the distinction between upgrading coalitions and upgrading institutions nearly dissolves.

At other times, however, upgrading coalitions may be amorphous and difficult to identify. In some countries, the United States is an example, there are numerous state institutions that encourage upgrading at different tiers and in different sectors, often without a clearly stated mandate that this is their task. In these cases, upgrading coalitions essentially stand behind the more formal institutions taking specific actions to promote upgrading. Even when upgrading institutions do not formally incorporate consultation mechanisms for key members of these coalitions, real consultation can, in some instances, be quite robust behind the scenes. There is also a considerable amount of diversity in the relative power of the state versus private interests in these upgrading coalitions; in some cases, for example in many Southeast Asian countries, the state is so overweening that consultation happens only intermittently (Haggard 2015). This variation will become a critical element of the theory I will develop in a moment.

Upgrading coalitions, in my conception, can refer either to (1) the political coalition of higher-level actors who come together to promote upgrading, or (2) the coalition of lower-tier actors who promote upgrading in specific industries. In many centralized systems, as we will see, an informal, high-level upgrading coalition creates and empowers formalized state upgrading institutions. In decentralized systems, upgrading coalitions may exist only at the lower-tier, in specific industries or regions. They may then stand behind decentralized upgrading institutions such as specific departments or agencies within a national or a sub-national ministry.

Upgrading coalitions can include a variety of different actors. Peak-level coalitions, for example, will generally include the leaders of governing political parties, business associations, financial institutions, and the like. Those at lower tier may comprise the leaders of individual firms or industrial groups as well as government administrators, technical experts, and so on. To complicate matters, it is not always immediately apparent which actors and organizations constitute upgrading coalitions.

Whether unions are involved varies quite a lot from country to country, as other scholars have highlighted. The developmental state, as it generally manifests in East Asia, has tended to exclude and even to repress labor (Kohli 2004). In Europe and parts of Latin America, by contrast, labor has been more fully represented in the councils of government (Schmitter 1974). In France, as we shall see, unions have experienced an on-again, off-again relationship with upgrading consonant with the traditionally conflictual relationship between labor and capital in that country. While the role of labor is not the focus on the argument here, it is worth noting that the inclusion of unions generally contributes to a more peaceful factory floor and a more redistributive form of growth. On the other hand, it can potentially slow aggregate growth by allocating more capital toward wages and less toward investment. I theorize below the specific ways that state and business leaders may interact in upgrading coalitions.

Institutions, Coalitions, and Upgrading: A New Theory

It is apparent, then, that we know a great deal more about the politics of economic upgrading than we did just a few decades ago. In particular, we are now able to appreciate the role of strong coalitions and good institutions as a necessary, if not sufficient, component of successful upgrading and long-term economic development. Nevertheless, though we understand much more about the central role of coalitions and institutions and the functions they must serve in upgrading, there remains work to be done in explaining when these institutions are more likely to form, what structures they take, and when they are most effective. These are the questions that I seek to answer in the book.

Of course, what constitutes a "strong" coalition and a "good" institution varies dramatically depending on context. Consequently, I begin this section—where I lay out my theory on the politics of economic upgrading—with a few key definitions. For my purposes, upgrading coalitions are groups of key public and private actors who join together to promote moving an economy up the value chain. Institutions, for their part, are structures, formal or informal, developed by and through the members of these coalitions to carry out specific upgrading policies. Finally, industrial, or more specifically upgrading, policies are the specific actions carried out by these institutions and other parts of the state to advance economic development and productivity.

It is worth remembering that many countries never develop fully functioning upgrading coalitions, or they develop these coalitions in some industries and not in others. Likewise, some countries do not possess upgrading institutions, while others have such institutions organized in a top-down fashion and with little stakeholder buy-in. My starting point is that, although upgrading institutions can take many forms, they are unlikely to be effective in the absence of working coalitions of key actors, both public and private. As such, what matters most is not the specific policies that upgrading institutions carry out, as these will vary by circumstance, but the more basic social coalitions that undergird them.

Upgrading institutions may include political institutions at the national or sub-national level, autonomous bureaucratic institutions devoted specifically to promoting upgrading, private business and labor organizations, quasi-public consultation committees, and even informal networks that exist between actors in government, business, and finance. A country may have any number of these institutions, ranging from none to a single strong bureaucracy at the national level, to hundreds of informal organizations spread out across different industries. It is these institutions, when they exist, which carry out industrial or upgrading policies.

For such institutions and such policies to work, however, they need to be supported by upgrading coalitions of critical actors who are committed to coordinating their actions to promote development. This fact has sometimes been ignored in the developmental state literature, which tends to focus on bureaucratic strength rather than the fundamental social and political foundations of upgrading (see Bardhan 2016; Doner and Schneider 2016). Upgrading is not simply a technical challenge, but more basically a political challenge. Upgrading coalitions may include senior national politicians to provide political cover, as well as business and labor leaders, bureaucrats, bankers, and others. They may also comprise complex lower-tier groupings of relevant government officials and private actors.

As we will see, my focus in this book is primarily on the upgrading coalitions and whether they are formed in a cohesive fashion, a fragmented fashion, or a mismatched fashion. I will argue that, where state and private actors possess similar levels of organizational cohesiveness—whether high or low—effective upgrading coalitions can form. However, when there is a mismatch in organizational cohesiveness between state and private actors, these upgrading coalitions will be unlikely to take shape. As a result, efforts at economic development will be characterized by the dominance either of the government or of private interest groups, an arrangement which is unlikely to lead to positive outcomes.

The structure of upgrading institutions, for their part, will follow more or less from the structure of the coalitions. In other words, countries defined by organizationally cohesive state and private actors will generally create a single (or a small number) of national upgrading bureaucracies, while those where both actors are more decentralized will possess numerous, often informal and industry specific, institutions. Both of these arrangements are capable of generating effective industrial policy, though they do so in contrasting ways and with contrasting strengths. On the flip side, when there is a mismatch in the organization of state and private actors, upgrading institutions will be absent or ineffective, existing without the support of strong state-society foundations. Countries in this position are unlikely to produce and implement effective industrial policies and will have a harder time moving up the value chain.

The Argument

With all of this in mind, I begin the development of my theory with the proposition that upgrading coalitions will be most effective when a balance of power exists between state and private actors. Such a situation will reduce the twin risks that the state either dominates economic actors, ignoring their needs and the realities of the market, or that the state is captured by these actors, providing publicly funded rents that allow them to turn a profit without making efforts to move up the value chain.

At the same time, my theory recognizes that there is no single structure that upgrading coalitions must take to be effective. For such coalitions to work, of course, it is necessary that both state and private actors be committed to upgrading. But this commitment is not sufficient. If the relative power of state and private actors is not balanced, it can lead either to state or private dominance rather than productive cooperation. At the same time, a corporatist structure, where upgrading bargains are made at the national level by cohesive and centralized state and private actors, is only one pathway to success. Indeed, a more decentralized structure, where multiple state-society coalitions exist to promote upgrading in different industries, tiers, and geographical locations, can be equally efficacious, as long as powerful political actors back the approach. And it is entirely possible for the same country to have both sorts of coalitions functioning in different sectors of the economy or at different time periods.

What, then, of upgrading institutions themselves? These too can efficiently take a number of forms. In some countries, especially those where strong state actors interact with cohesive business interests in the creation of upgrading policy, such institutions may comprise national political and business leaders themselves. In others, characterized by a more decentralized state and less cohesive private interests, such institutions may take the form of numerous, lower-level consultation committees organized by industry, or they may be characterized by informal networks. But, as we will see, I argue that countries where the relative influence of state and private actors is mismatched, due especially to their organizational cohesion, will be less successful at upgrading. Such countries may possess institutions with similar formal structures to the ones described above, but true policy will be one-sided, dominated by the stronger actor.

In building my theory, then, I am concerned with the internal cohesion and centralization of the state and of key private interests. These private interests generally include business associations and their member firms as well as agricultural groups and farmers. They can also include, in certain circumstances, labor unions and members of civil society more broadly, including for example research organizations and universities. It is these groups which will form the core of any upgrading coalition. By extension, how the organizational structure of these groups interacts will play a critical role in shaping the effectiveness of the institutions responsible for upgrading.

For my purposes, the cohesion of private interests means, for the critical cases of business and agriculture, that (1) representation of the sector is dominated by a single group, (2) this single group organizes a significant portion of participants in the sector, and (3) this single group is, at least to some degree, organizationally cohesive. An interest group can be considered cohesive when its executive is able to determine its bargaining position and impose that position on the membership, or when its rank-and-file are so united on an issue that they act as one. This same principle applies, with some alteration, to universities and civil society groups which may play a role in upgrading. Here, to take the education sector as an example, if professional and higher education are dominated by a small number of organizations, there is more cohesion than if the education sector is large and diverse. I do not consider state dominated interest groups, which are especially common in autocratic systems, to be cohesive because they do not represent the independent preferences of private actors.

For the state, cohesion means that it can speak and act with a unified voice on most economic policy matters, and that it is insulated enough that private interests can find few openings to exploit. Cohesion can take many forms in a democracy. For example, a state is cohesive when a powerful executive controls most of the levers of policy or when a single disciplined party dominates the legislature. States may also be cohesive when decision-making is in the hands of a powerful bureaucracy, but this argument can be taken too far, as I emphasize below in the French case. Often, at least in well-functioning polities, even strong bureaucracies are powerless to take any sweeping initiative unless their political masters are on board.

In other words, a state is more cohesive when there are fewer veto players that must agree to policy changes (Immergut 1990). For this reason, authoritarian states, by my definition, are generally considered cohesive, since power in such systems tends to be concentrated. That said, some authoritarian states are more cohesive than others, depending on the degree to which power is centralized in an individual, a party, a wealthy class, or an institution such as the military.

By contrast, a state is fragmented when there are multiple "access points" through which private interests can influence policy; these access points can result from party system fractionalization, weak governing party organization, or strong legislative power (Ehrlich 2011). Fragmentation can also include the existence of empowered sub-national governments, though, for my definition, this is not a requirement. It is worth emphasizing, however, that cohesive states, by my definition, are not necessarily "stronger" than fragmented states. In other words, the concept as I am using it concerns the centralization of policy-making authority rather than the capacity of state institutions. Of course, a minimum of state capacity is necessary for any effective upgrading strategy, but exploring variation on this variable is outside the scope of this book. Rather, I am assuming here a minimum level of state capacity and looking rather at the cohesiveness or fragmentation of decision-making authority.

How do these institutional structures interact to produce different types of upgrading coalitions? First, I contend that, when a country's political institutions are cohesive and its business, labor, and farm interests are fragmented, the economic preferences of the government will largely determine state policy. As discussed below, prior research has found that political cohesion tends to insulate policymakers from interest group power. This is because more cohesive political institutions provide fewer access points through which interest groups can influence policy (Ehrlich 2011). When policy is controlled by a small number of individuals at the center of power, changing that policy will be more challenging for private sector interests than when decisions result from a more fragmented process. The greater insulation of a cohesive state, combined with a fragmented and unorganized structure of interest group power, will provide governments with maximum freedom to carry out their economic policies. Under such conditions, state authorities are unlikely to face coordinated opposition to their decisions and will be in a better position to play one private sector group against another. A *statist* economic policy will be the outcome.

In addition to a mismatched pairing of state cohesion and private fragmentation, I also classify a system as statist when the state directly owns or otherwise controls the bulk of firms. In such countries, it is the state calling the shots in upgrading even more than in places where the private sector is real but fragmented. It should be noted, however, that parastatal firms which enjoy significant autonomy can be considered, for the purposes of the theory, as private entities which potentially act to counterbalance state power.

Turning to the second of my four categories, when a country's political institutions are cohesive and its business, farm, and/or labor representation is as well, state officials will have to consider the preferences of organized interests. The cohesive political institutions will, however, provide political leaders with a modicum of insulation, allowing them some room to pursue their preferred policies. Put differently, interest groups will have difficulty influencing the cohesive policy process on the front end, but, by the same token, political leaders will need to consider the possible response of private interests to their enunciated policies. Under these conditions, upgrading coalitions will be *corporatist* in nature, with outcomes determined by bargaining among representatives of the state and the peak-level interest groups. Both state and interest group leaders will begin the bargaining process with internally formulated preferences, but also with an understanding that coordination will be required for effective upgrading. And, in keeping with the corporatist mold of policy formation, only a small number of influential actors will be given a seat at the table when that coordination takes place.

Business associations will almost always be among these actors, but the status of labor unions will depend upon their organizational resources. As we shall see in the French case, the role of workers' representatives in upgrading coalitions was marginal at best. For their part, banks and financial institutions are often among the most important players in the implementation of upgrading policies. In some contexts, representatives of these institutions may participate in corporatist coordinating bodies, but more often they will be made to carry out the resulting policies through a variety of nationally distinct mechanisms (see Zysman 1977).

In a third case, where a country's political institutions are fragmented but its interest representation is cohesive, government officials will have little opportunity to resist the power of organized business, labor, or agriculture. These interest groups will have the ability to inject themselves into the upgrading policy formation process itself by lobbying legislators, ministers, bureaucrats, and other influential state actors. And, once the policy is made, they will have the power to threaten coordinated non-cooperation if the government's decision does not accord with their desires. Consequently, economic policy outcomes will reflect the preferences of these cohesive interest groups, and the state's preferences will be effectively *captured* by organized social interests. As a result, efforts at upgrading in these cases are likely to devolve into exercises in rent seeking.

In the final case, when both political institutions and interest organizations are fragmented and decentralized, policymaking will embody the *pluralist* model most closely, with smaller interest groups lobbying multiple different state actors to affect policy. State leaders will be heavily constrained by these interest groups but will have some ability to build different winning coalitions to maintain office. Policy will reflect the interests of these state-society coalition members. For example, business associations may fracture by sector of the economy and, likewise, different state agencies may be responsible for economic policymaking in different industries. In this scenario, the ultimate result will be state-private sector coordination at the sectoral or issue level rather than the national level, with different actors involved in coordinating different elements of economic policy. Such a process would be open and fragmented, with important roles to be played by different components of government and the private sector.

What might we expect upgrading institutions to look like under each of the four models of potential upgrading coalitions? Because these institutions derive their effectiveness from the relative organizational resources of states and interest groups—as embodied in the coalitions discussed above—they may be present in one sector of the economy and absent in another. They may evolve across time within a single country, and they may also disappear from one decade to the next. These dynamics can follow any of the four logics of institutional change identified by Streeck and Thelen (2005). Old institutions may be "displaced" by new, or their purpose may change through "drift." New institutions may also be "layered" on top of old ones, or existing institutions may be "converted" to a new purpose. Whatever the case, they will eventually come to reflect the changing power relations within the upgrading coalition. In order to maintain effective upgrading institutions, therefore, countries will need to carefully adapt them to the changing structure of public-private coalitions in their societies.

Bearing this in mind, we can expect upgrading institutions to mirror, at least to some extent, the structure of the underlying coalitions. (As noted above, though, institutional structures may be out-of-sync for a time with coalitional dynamics). For example, when both the state and private interests are cohesive, and upgrading policy therefore follows the corporatist model, we can expect upgrading institutions, or indeed a single upgrading institution, to exist at the central level. There may exist, for example, a national development council that generates a national plan to direct upgrading and development activity for a specified number of years. Another model consistent with corporatism is to create upgrading institutions made of elite and autonomous bureaucrats. This approach is most associated with Japan and the so-called Asian Tigers—South Korea, Taiwan, and Singapore—where powerful central authorities coordinated the development process to great success (e.g., Amsden 1992, Wade 1990). Such a structure, to be effective, must itself rest on a broad public-private coalition like the one described above, though one that delegates policy implementation powers to experts. In South Korea, for example, leader Park Chung-Hee himself chaired the council which oversaw upgrading (Haggard 2015).

In an alternative framework, where both state and private interests take on a decentralized character and policymaking is pluralist, upgrading institutions are likely to be decentralized as well. They might take the form of consultation councils made up in much the same way as the peak-level councils found in corporatism, but at a lower tier and repeated across a multitude of industries and issue areas. Or they may be more informal, comprising networks of government officials, business leaders, bankers, universities, and the like who work toward a common goal.

Finally, when the cohesion of state and private interests is mismatched, there may be no upgrading institutions at all, with policymaking dominated by a powerful state or by overweening business groups. On the other hand, there may exist such institutions but, not resting on a firm coalition foundation, these are likely to be ineffectual.

In which of these four cases are we most likely to see effective upgrading coalitions that will result in improved economic outcomes? My theory suggests that the state will be most successful in promoting economic upgrading when its level of cohesion is aligned with that of interest groups. I argue, then, that cohesive governments cooperating with cohesive business, labor, and agricultural interests in a corporatist framework, along with fragmented governments cooperating with fragmented business, labor, and agriculture interests in a pluralist framework, will be in a good position to shepherd the economy. By contrast, government-dominated and interest group-dominated economic systems will be less successful in promoting upgrading.

The logic is that cooperation between the state and interest groups is critical for economic management. Only countries with effective upgrading coalitions are likely to develop and implement policies that will help them move up the value chain. The creation of these upgrading coalitions is largely a function of the structural characteristics of the state and interest groups, and whether these characteristics force actors to consider one another's preferences. In this sense, my argument is compatible with most scholars in historical institutionalism (see Mahoney and Thelen 2010), who focus on the role of shifting power to understand institutional structure and institutional change. When state actors or interest groups are able to use their organizational advantages to dominate the other, I assume that they will. Only when they share similar organizational resources will these actors be forced into the types of upgrading coalitions that are likely to produce the best outcomes. When both the state and private interests are cohesive, these upgrading coalitions tend to be centralized and expansive, and when both are fragmented, micro-coalitions tend to manage upgrading in individual sectors of the economy.

While previous research has tended to emphasize either the benefits of a cohesive state or of cohesive interest groups, rather than the benefits of combining the two, the corporatist logic of coordination is fairly straightforward. Cohesive state authorities enjoy centralized access to the key policy tools necessary for overcoming the collective action problems inherent in upgrading. These include subsidies, guaranteed credit, tax benefits, investment insurance, and the like. Cortell (2005), for example, in his innovative study of the US and Britain, argues that centralized government tends to lend itself to industrial policy better than decentralized government, at least when networks are dense. Similarly, Zalk (2014) and Ferraz, Kupfer, and Marques (2014) point to the benefits of centralized industrial policymaking in South Africa and Brazil, respectively. As we will see, I agree that centralized government can create effective industrial policy, but I also emphasize that industrial policy is equally viable in decentralized systems, though through a different mechanism.

Cohesive private actors, for their part, are well placed to communicate to government authorities what they need to accomplish upgrading, and they are in a unique position to implement the resulting policies effectively. When a cohesive state coexists with cohesive private interests, both sides will be forced to cooperate in the making and implementation of upgrading policy, and the results are likely to be effective.

The logic behind the benefits of a fragmented state meeting fragmented interest groups may seem less apparent. Past research on the salutary effects of a strong state, not least in the developmental state literature itself, might make this portion of my argument surprising. But my contention is not that weak states are inherently positive for upgrading, but rather that states with a multitude of power centers can coordinate well with interest groups possessing the same characteristics. These states are not weak in the sense of having low capacity, but rather pluralist and decentralized. When states organized in this manner coordinate with interest groups that are also fragmented and decentralized, the result should be a series of sector specific upgrading policies. These policies will be developed by those state and private actors with a deep understanding of the needs of the specific sector along with an ability to implement their decisions effectively.[1]

On the other hand, when institutions are such that either side can effectively ignore the preferences of the other, the quality of policymaking and implementation will suffer. In state-dominated systems, for example, we would expect the linkages between government agencies and interest groups to be weaker, something that is likely to impair the development of realistic policies (see Evans 1995). Even when these links are well developed, the absence of a coordinated interest group preference may also intrude on the development of an effective policy. A dominant state must still understand the needs of the private sector to construct effective upgrading policy, and when these private actors are not able to speak with a single voice, this task is complicated considerably. Furthermore, problems are likely to spill over into the implementation process, since the state cannot count on coordinated interest groups to assist in carrying out a jointly determined policy.

In the reverse case, where interest groups are dominant, their overwhelming power can lead to redistributional policies that impair competitiveness. It is always easier for private actors to engage in rent-seeking than to compete on world markets. When these actors dominate the policymaking process at the expense of the state, they are more likely to demand subsidies, trade protection, and other benefits than the more challenging policies that can contribute to long-run growth. As theorists of the developmental state have pointed out, strong states with an interest in the aggregate welfare of the country are more likely to develop and implement such policies (see Johnson 1982, Wade 1990). Corporatist and pluralist systems will make economic policy in very different ways, I argue, but the outcomes will reflect a broader level of social and political buy-in than policies produced in state or interest dominated countries.[2]

In addition to its implications for which sorts of upgrading coalitions and institutions will be most effective, the theory also speaks to the different strengths and weakness that dual-cohesive and dual-fragmented structures might possess. We can anticipate that dual-cohesive upgrading coalitions, and the institutions through which they operate, will often produce a coordinated national plan. This plan could be more or less authoritative or more or less indicative depending on the ideology of the regime, but it is likely to be created and implemented nationally. Such an approach means that coalitions comprising cohesive state and private actors are in an especially good position to create new industries or to significantly expand existing ones, in short to create "national champions" that require a tremendous rerouting of resources. Ziegler (1997) in his study of French and German industrial policy makes a similar point. Both the state and business are represented by peak-level organizations that can think big and make major changes in the national economy. For these reasons, dual-cohesive systems may work especially well in middle income countries looking to transform into the "learning societies" at the top of the value chain.

The strength of dual-fragmented coalitions lies elsewhere. These micro-coalitional structures allow for more detailed, smaller scale, upgrading of disparate existing industries. Each upgrading coalition and institution is less nationally coordinated than in dual-cohesive systems, operating instead at the industry or local level. But each involves considerably more detailed expertise on the specific needs and challenges of a specific industry. For this reason, upgrading in dual-fragmented systems is more grassroots, less centralized and dramatic, but at least as transformative as in dual-cohesive systems. It may be particularly suited for already developed economies seeking to continue the upgrading process.

Another way to think about the effectiveness of matched coalitions—paired cohesive or paired fragmented—considers their ability, and that of the institutions through which they work, to carry out the key tasks of upgrading highlighted earlier in the chapter. To what extent can matched coalitions and institutions overcome collective action problems, promote networks, promote learning, and support industries with positive spillovers? Are they in a better position to perform these tasks than countries with unmatched coalitions or with none at all?

In the final analysis, all of these tasks require coordinated action between the state and private actors. Overcoming the collective action and coordination problems inherent in upgrading, such as the need to coordinate research, training, and investment in the creation of new capabilities, requires that state institutions reduce the risks faced by private actors taking a step into the unknown. Otherwise, the risks of being a first-mover may deter any advances in productivity. It also demands a private sector willing to take these risks, which are after all never entirely mitigated by public guarantees. This means that the state and private actors must cooperate toward the common goal of upgrading. The same is true for promoting learning and encouraging productive networks.

If the state possesses more organizational resources and is therefore dominant, this cooperation will be difficult to achieve. State officials will be able to ignore the needs of the private sector in their policymaking while the private sector will be unlikely to share private market information with state actors they cannot control. This arrangement leads more to top-down policy than to the level of cooperation needed for upgrading. Similar problems arise when the private sector is dominant, only in this case the risk is that dominant firms will be able to use upgrading policy as a cover for rent seeking.

Do matched coalitions and institutions embody the institutional features identified earlier as "best practices": (1) flexibility, (2) accountability, (3) autonomy, and (4) consultation and embeddedness? Consultation and embeddedness follows from the arguments above. When the state and private interests have matching organizational resources, there will be a higher level of consultation among the actors. After all, each will be unable to take significant action without the other. The constant interaction between the key actors, required by their similar organizational resources, increases the likelihood that policy will respond in a flexible way to changing market conditions. As for autonomy, state dominance will of course maximize state autonomy, while private sector dominance will maximize the autonomy of firms. But their joint autonomy is best maximized when they share similar levels of cohesion. In this case, state and private actors are able to make decisions which consider the preferences of the other but which are independent.

What, then, does accountability mean in this context? It is true that state accountability to the broader citizenry for positive economic outcomes will be maximized in a democratic setting, something which is outside the scope of this book. And it is also true that firm accountability to shareholders and stakeholders is in part a function of corporate governing institutions, also outside the scope of this book. But within the context of upgrading coalitions and institutions, mutual accountability is also critical. For upgrading coordination to work, private actors must be able to trust state upgrading officials, and state officials must be able to rely upon the private sector. This two-way accountability functions best in balanced upgrading coalitions. I present a summary of my theory in Table 2.1, along with corresponding portions of my case study below.

In this book, I take my inspiration from the prior literature, but introduce several key innovations. First, I combine political institutions and interest groups into a single interactive framework. In this sense, my argument is similar to Hall's (1986) comparison of French and British industrial policy, but in that classic book no specific framework for understanding outcomes is developed and the focus is entirely on planning. I also draw on the work of Haggard (1990), who sees development policy outcomes as resulting from the interaction of actor preferences and institutional constraints, and Levy (1999), who points to the benefits of strong social capital in informing the decisions of interventionist states. I attempt, however, to flesh out in more detail the expected outcomes from different combinations of institutional constraints and preferences. In addition, I develop predictions both for the nature of the policy process and for the effectiveness of policy in promoting economic upgrading.

Moreover, I argue that a complete explanation of economic policymaking requires an understanding of how state cohesion and interest group cohesion interact. To be sure, scholars of corporatism and the developmental state are both interested in the relationship between government and interest groups. Neither approach, however, fully theorizes the organizational structure of both state and private institutions. Theorists of the varieties of capitalism (i.e., Hall and Soskice 2001), for their part, emphasize the interlocking structures of institutions, which they argue tend to fall into distinct coordinated and uncoordinated categories. This characterization, while it yields powerful insights, understates the significance of "mismatched" state and private institutions, which can produce quite distinct outcomes.

I also emphasize, unlike most prior research, that corporatism and pluralism, statism and capture, are not fixed characteristics of countries. Rather, I argue that they can vary both across time and, critically, across sectors of the economy. My approach is in contrast to most theories of corporatism,

TABLE 2.1: Theory

	State Cohesion	State Fragmentation
Interest Group Cohesion	**Corporatism** **(Dual Cohesive)** **Upgrading Coalition(s):** At central level **Upgrading Institution(s):** At central level. Likely either a National Development or Agricultural Council or an autonomous bureaucracy backed by the coalition. **Upgrading Outcomes:** More effective. Special strength in national planning, creating large new industries, and basic structural transformation. **Case Example:** French Fifth Republic Agricultural Policy	**Capture** **(Mismatched)** **Upgrading Coalition(s):** Non-existent or unbalanced **Upgrading Institution(s):** May or may not exist. Will be ineffective. **Upgrading Outcomes:** Less effective. Greater focus on private rent-seeking than on upgrading. **Case Example:** French Fourth Republic Agricultural Policy
Interest Group Fragmentation	**Statism** **(Mismatched)** **Upgrading Coalition(s):** Non-existent or unbalanced **Upgrading Institution(s):** May or may not exist. Will be ineffective. **Upgrading Outcomes:** Less effective. Greater focus on clientelism or visible government schemes than on upgrading. **Case Examples:** French Fifth Republic Industrial Policy India (1969–89, 2014–Present?)	**Pluralism** **(Dual Fragmented)** **Upgrading Coalition(s):** Decentralized to industry or local level **Upgrading Institution(s):** Numerous formal or informal upgrading institutions at industry or local level **Upgrading Outcomes:** More effective. Special strength in detail-based upgrading of existing industries. **Case Examples:** French Fourth Republic Industrial Policy United States India (1947–69, 1989–2014)

varieties of capitalism, and the developmental state, which imply that these characteristics are relatively fixed elements of individual countries (see Gilpin 2001, Lijphart and Crepaz 1991, Schmitter 1974). It is true that some scholars have pointed to the ways in which structure of policymaking can vary within countries. Keeler's (1987) focus on the corporatism of agricultural policy, in contrast to industrial policy, in France is an example of this recognition, as are Pinglé's (1999) work on "developmental ensembles" in India and Hsueh's (2023) sectoral studies in Russia, China, and India. That said, the assumption that the basic structures of economic policy making are fixed national characteristics remains pervasive in the literature.

Another contribution of the theory is to develop a unique classification of upgrading systems, one which begins with coalitions, continues with the institutions they undergird, and concludes with the sorts of policies they can pursue. As part of the theory, I emphasize that effective upgrading coalitions, and as a consequence effective upgrading institutions, can take different forms. I argue that these forms, while almost infinitely complex, can be classified into two broad categories—dual-cohesive (corporatist) and dual-fragmented (pluralist)—and that each of these has specific characteristics and strengths.

Finally, in emphasizing the key role played by upgrading coalitions, I emphasize the alignment of powerful state and private interests in individual countries. This approach, taken by some more recent studies of industrial policy and upgrading (Doner et al. 2021) is in contrast with the traditional focus on bureaucratic autonomy and strength associated with developmental states. Like Kohli (2004), I argue that upgrading cannot take place in a power vacuum, at least not for long. Good upgrading institutions will not long persist in the absence of effective upgrading coalitions to stand behind them.

Economic Upgrading in Postwar France, Independent India, and Beyond

I test my arguments empirically using a mixed methods approach, one that combines two field-work-based case studies with a large-N model and a short, qualitative plausibility probe. Such an approach allows me, first, to explore the disparate upgrading coalitions and institutions in two key countries, while evaluating the theory's ability to explain the causal processes behind them. It also makes it possible to test the generalizability of the theory, and especially of its implications for upgrading success, in a broader quantitative model and to establish, as a first cut, the theory's ability to make sense of the critical US case.

In Chapters 3 and 4, then, I present my first empirical test of the theory using a case—postwar France—that is normally not considered in scholarship on economic development, both because it is somewhat remote in time and because it is considered a "high income" case. But France just after the Second World War faced many of the same challenges that confront modern middle income countries. It had an industrial base, one severely damaged during the war, but its productive efficiency had fallen behind that of Germany, Britain, and especially the United States. Consequently, there was a sense of urgency among French policymakers that the country needed to retool and upgrade or be left behind. As a result, the experiences of France during this period are particularly relevant to the many industrialized modernizers of today, namely those middle income countries that have achieved a certain level of economic development but that are seeking to upgrade further their productive capacity (Doner and Schneider 2016).

At the beginning of the period that I examine, 1944 to 1968, France experienced a sharp break with its past as it emerged from the trauma of occupation and war. This makes the case interesting not because the pursuit of economic upgrading requires such a break, but because many countries that have dedicated themselves fully to economic change have done so following some internal or external political shock. Scholars of qualitative methodology have long argued that such crises can form "critical junctures" where institutional transformation is possible (see Capoccia and Kelemen 2007). Under such circumstances, old institutions can be "displaced" by new (Mahoney and Thelen 2010). It thus makes sense to examine a country seeking to transform its economy after some watershed event because the hypothesized relationships will be in clearer relief.

Moreover, studying postwar France allows me to vary each of my key independent variables and therefore permits a comprehensive examination of the theory. France under the Fourth Republic (1946–58) was characterized by relatively fragmented political institutions paired with fragmented interest representation in the industrial sector and cohesive interest representation in the agricultural sector. The country's political institutions were then transformed in 1958 with the establishment of the Gaullist Fifth Republic and its strong president. This new cohesive state in turn faced, for the most part, the same structure of interest representation that had confronted its predecessor. By examining how French economic policy varied from the Fourth to the Fifth Republics and from the industrial to the agriculture sector, I am thus able to examine all of the variation present in my model.

In effect, therefore, I am adopting a most-similar-systems research design (see, for example, Meckstroth 1975), where I seek maximum variation on the independent variables of interest and minimum variation elsewhere. By examining a specific country in detail, I am better able to hold potentially confounding cultural, social, and economic factors constant while I investigate the effects of changes in my independent variables. To complete my qualitative analysis of postwar France, I draw on the secondary literature in both English and French, as well as on an extensive examination of primary sources. These sources include memoirs of the key actors during the period, government and interest group documents maintained in various French archives, and contemporary journalistic accounts.

I adopt a similar methodological approach in Chapters 5, 6, and 7 as part of my second major case study—that of independent India. This analysis extends the theory to a critical developing state and demonstrates its relevance for understanding upgrading in lower- and middle income countries. I show how varying levels of state cohesion—driven largely by changes in the structure of national contestation—interacted with relatively weak private actors to influence the effectiveness of upgrading policy in that country. More specifically, I argue that India, with its fragmented and decentralized interest groups, has vacillated between pluralist and statist forms of upgrading. The pluralist periods, which include the early years of Nehru's premiership as well as the decades between the collapse of the Congress Party's dominance in 1989 and the advent of the supremacy of the Bharatiya Janata Party, or BJP, in 2014, saw more effective economic outcomes than the statist periods of centralized party control.

This sort of detailed historical analysis is appropriate to test my theory's implications for the formation of upgrading policy (though somewhat less its implications for policy success, which is why I supplement the analysis of this point with quantitative models). My theory specifies not just a hypothesized relationship between independent and dependent variables, but a full causal process. In this context, process tracing allows me to test whether the causal mechanisms highlighted by my framework actually produce the economic policy process predicted (Mahoney 2003). Identifying upgrading coalitions can also be quite challenging in a quantitative context but is more tractable within a case study.

As I have already noted, measuring the process of policymaking is best done using the qualitative examination of the French and Indian cases, but exploring economic outcomes can also be accomplished in a large-N setting. Indeed, a quantitative study provides the best laboratory for exploring the effects of different institutional arrangements on economic outcomes across countries and years. And, as Lieberman (2015) has argued, combining quantitative tests with comparative historical analysis is an effective way of fully testing probabilistic theories like mine.

With that in mind, for the large-N portion of the analysis, found in Chapter 8, I explore how different configurations of state and interest group cohesion influence four economic outcomes associated with upgrading success. To make this assessment, I estimate a series of models using data from sixteen developed countries across six decades. My focus remains on the developed world because good data on interest group structures is limited to these cases, and also because even developed states are in a constant process of upgrading and modernizing. The results from the quantitative models provide strong evidence for my hypothesized relationships. Also in this chapter, I briefly extend the argument to the postwar United States through the Biden Administration, with the goal of exploring whether the theory can plausibly be applied to this critical case. Relying on the secondary literature, I show how the combination of America's fragmented state and fragmented interest groups have made for effective upgrading across a number of prioritized sectors.

I conclude the book in Chapter 9 with some reflections on the implications of my theory for understanding upgrading policy, both on a scholarly and a practical level. I discuss France, India, and the United States going forward, and I also bring China briefly into the discussion. Furthermore, looking beyond upgrading, I also suggest—using welfare policy in France—that the theory could be useful in illuminating a variety of policy areas. Finally, I draw on my theory and my empirical analyses to make some predictions about the future of upgrading policy and where it might be most successful.

In the end, I emphasize that what matters most critically for upgrading is not fundamental characteristics of states such as geography or deep history, though these do set the circumstances under which they must operate. Nor is it transient factors such as choosing the "right policies," which in any case can vary depending on national and international circumstances. Indeed, it is certain that today, given the constraints placed upon economic policies by a growing number of cross-border agreements and by the tremendous pressures of mobile capital, different sorts of policy tools are required to modernize than were used in the past.

Rather, what matters most is the right process of policy development and implementation. There remains much that states can undertake, and in fact do undertake, to encourage economic transformation. In other words, while industrial and upgrading policy may take different forms today, they are no less relevant than they were fifty or seventy-five years in the past. Getting the process right when developing and implementing these policies helps countries take the actions that fit their circumstances and needs, actions that can transform the material future for their citizens.

THREE

Postwar France

Fragmentation and Cohesion

In this chapter and the one that follows, I present my first test of the theory outlined in Chapter 2—a temporally and sectorally comparative study of postwar France.[1] Diving deeply into this historical case allows me to explore the causal relationship between the structure of the state and private actors on the one hand and the organization of economic upgrading on the other. As noted in the previous chapter, I argue here French industrial policy during the Fourth Republic saw a fragmented state interacting with fragmented interest groups, producing a largely effective pluralist upgrading policy that helped propel France in the 1950s to record levels of growth. By contrast, agricultural policy during the same period was stagnant and ineffective, due mainly to the ability of cohesive interest groups to capture the fragmented state. Things changed after the transition to the Fifth Republic in 1958, when the state became significantly more centralized and cohesive. During this period, which we trace here through 1968, it was agricultural policy which was effective, leading to a rapid growth of productivity in the countryside. This success was the result, I argue, of the corporatist structure that was possible in agriculture as a consequence of the dual-cohesion of the state and private interests. Moreover, the corporatist agricultural policymaking of the Fifth Republic was especially effective in producing a comprehensive transformation of the sector, whereas the Fourth Republic's industrial policy was more suited to gradual, sector-by-sector upgrading. Unfortunately, industrial policy became less efficient in the Fifth Republic, taking on a statist structure with government institutions so dominant that they were able to ignore the critical input of private actors and force their preferences on business. All of this accords well with the expectations of the theory.

France emerged from the Second World War with its economy and infrastructure devastated. Nearly two million buildings had been damaged, extensive areas of farmland had been rendered unusable, and both train and ship transport were at a virtual standstill (Eichengreen 2007). But the country's technocratic elite also saw in the destruction an opportunity to set France on a path toward economic upgrading that had eluded it for decades. As a consequence, the first twenty-five years after the war gave birth to French economic policy as we know it today. Those years began with a turn to large-scale indicative planning and dirigisme in an effort to reconstruct the French economy. The postwar period also saw a dramatic expansion of the French welfare state and an unprecedented growth in the public sector's social role (Nord 2010). French leaders adopted these policies as part of a broad economic upgrading strategy, pursued at a time when the dangers of permanent stagnation loomed in the aftermath of occupation and war. These policies continue to structure the economic debate in France today, whether over welfare benefit cuts, government support for national champions, or the expansion versus deepening of the European Union. And their importance does not end with France. Dirigisme and indicative planning have been emulated in a number of countries around the world, and French policy continues to leave its mark on the structure of European integration (Balassa 1978, Loriaux 1999).

France is generally considered to be a statist country, one where the government and, especially, the powerful civil service call the shots in economic policy (Schmidt 1996). It is often thought of as an outlier in studies of European political economy, neither liberal nor corporatist nor pluralist (Hancké 2002, Esping-Andersen 1990). I argue, by contrast, that France was sometimes statist, but also sometimes corporatist and pluralist, and even sometimes dominated by private sector interests. My model helps explain why the French case has historically been so vexing for scholars and teases out the various ways that economic policy has been made in the country.

Testing my argument in the postwar French case requires, as a critical first step, evaluating the relative cohesion and fragmentation of state and private interests during the two periods I consider. Only once we can identify when and where these institutions were matched or mismatched can we develop consistent expectations as to the nature and effectiveness of industrial policy. I use this chapter, then, to detail the institutional structures of the Fourth and Fifth Republics, with an emphasis on how France transitioned from a fragmented polity to a cohesive one. After I complete this analysis, I devote the remainder of the chapter to examining the relative cohesion of business associations, labor unions, and agricultural interests in France. The analysis shows clearly that business and labor remained highly fragmented during both periods, with some internal variation. By contrast, French agricultural interests were significantly more cohesive. After taking up the question of institutional structure in this chapter, I devote the next chapter to exploring how industrial and agricultural policy was made during the two periods, and when each was most successful at promoting upgrading in the country.

A Tale of Two Republics: Fragmentation and Cohesion

When France emerged from German occupation in 1944, a provisional government took power under the leadership of General Charles de Gaulle, head of the Free French during the war. In the following year, the French people elected a constituent assembly to draft a new constitution, ultimately ratifying the result by referendum in October 1946. This new constitution, which gave birth to the Fourth Republic, retained most of the key institutions of the defeated Third Republic, including a weak presidency and a strong parliament (MacRae 1967, Vinen 1996). But after four years of occupation, many of the institutions from the pre-war period, including those dealing with economic policy, had been lost or altered. New institutions formed under the wartime Vichy regime were largely rejected by the new leaders of the Fourth Republic, though some continued in altered form (Nord 2010). For these reasons, we can observe a process of institutional displacement, but also to some extent institutional conversion, in the immediate postwar period (Streeck and Thelen 2005).

Just after the Liberation, the provisional government was centered on the person of Charles de Gaulle and the inclusive institution of the Conseil national de la Résistance or CNR (Hitchcock 1998, Nord 2010). Ever since it had become clear that Nazi Germany was losing the war, the CNR, representing many different shades of the French Resistance, had been developing plans for the postwar order. In the economic sphere, these plans were broadly social democratic but vague, envisioning not a command economy, but one where the "commanding heights" would be largely in public hands (Nord 2010). There was also great hope for a modernization of the French economy and for greater opportunity for members of the working class and peasantry. And, as in other European countries, the Beveridge Report in the United Kingdom inspired great hope for the creation of a just welfare state.

Of course, the task of governing a country just emerging from the trauma of war and occupation is quite a bit more complicated than planning for a bright future. After the Liberation, de Gaulle's provisional government rejected much of the CNR's plan and focused instead on reestablishing the necessities of life: repairing infrastructure, dealing with the complexities of postwar justice, repatriating prisoners of war, and helping prosecute the war as it moved into Germany itself (Hitchcock 1998). Indeed, the greatest economic debate of the early postwar years was between René Pleven and Pierre Mendès-France and concerned the trade-offs between inflation and austerity (Kuisel 1981, Rioux 1987). Mendès-France believed that the French needed to weather a period of low consumption in order to emerge into brighter economic times, while Pleven advocated looser fiscal and monetary policy to get the economy started. De Gaulle, sensing the desperate mood of the French people, sided with Pleven and reflated the economy. The focus, at least in the short-term, was to be on easing economic woes rather than on fundamental, but painful, transformation.

As the Constituent Assembly debated what form the new French constitution would take, de Gaulle hoped to correct what he saw as the weak institutions of the Third Republic, institutions he blamed for the collapse of 1940 (Baum 1958). De Gaulle was especially averse to recreating a "republic of parties," one dominated by bickering factional interests that neglected the composite will of the French people (see de Gaulle 1971). Unfortunately for the general, however, the old parties had reformed, along with some new ones, and were pushing for the reestablishment of a parliamentary system. After suffering under the Vichy dictatorship, many French politicians were not in the mood to create a strong president and simply wanted to return to the old system. When he saw the way the wind was blowing, a disgusted Charles de Gaulle resigned his position as chair of the provisional government in January 1946. The constituent assembly duly drafted a constitution putting power back in the hands of a dominant National Assembly, and it was put up for a national referendum in May. The French people, however, rejected the new constitution, forcing the assembly to add a second parliamentary chamber. This time, in October 1946, a narrow plurality of the French people approved the draft and brought the new republic into being (see Baum 1958, Hitchcock 1998).

The authority structures that evolved from this constitution were fundamentally fragmented. First and foremost, the position of the president remained essentially powerless under the Fourth Republic. The Third Republic, which lasted from the end of the disastrous Franco-Prussian War to the German invasion of 1940, had also possessed a weak presidency. But the office of president under the Fourth Republic was if anything even weaker, perhaps from the understandable fear of dictatorship that haunted the aftermath of Vichy. According to Chapter 4 of the constitution, the president was to be elected by both chambers of the parliament for a seven-year term.[2] On a day-to-day basis, he was primarily a figurehead, called upon primarily to nominate formally the council of ministers, the prefects, and other top positions. Indeed, Article 38 made clear that "every act of the president of the republic must be countersigned by the president of the council of ministers [prime minister] and a minister."[3]

Real power rested with the lower house of parliament, the National Assembly, which selected the government and the prime minister, termed in France the president of the council of ministers. As in most parliamentary systems, deputies in the National Assembly were empowered to form and to remove the government, and the prime minister and members of the cabinet were drawn from among them. The upper chamber, the Council of the Republic, was indirectly elected and possessed primarily consultative powers (see MacRae 1967, Rioux 1987). As Article 48 of the constitution stated, "the ministers are collectively responsible before the National Assembly for the general policy of the cabinet and individually for their personal acts. They are not responsible before the Council of the Republic."[4]

Scholars of parliamentary democracy have long understood that such systems can paradoxically empower the executive, in the person of the prime minister (Huber 1996). When a single party controls the majority of seats in parliament, and when authority in that party is centralized in the national leadership, the prime minister can use the threat of dissolving the government to force recalcitrant co-partisans to toe the line. She can also use the power of candidate selection, by threatening not to renominate disloyal members, to enforce adherence to the government's program.

While such prime ministerial dominance may describe the United Kingdom (at least until recently), it was quite foreign to the French Fourth Republic. Though its prime ministers could hold significant powers with the backing of a majority in the National Assembly, the Fourth Republic was characterized by a fragmented party system which put severe limitations on their actual authority (Vinen 1996).

This fragmentation had several sources. First among these was the electoral system. The Fourth Republic replaced the two-round majority electoral system of the Third Republic with proportional representation (PR), a system that gave impetus to multiparty politics (Judt 2011). Indeed, the first political scientist to draw the link between proportionality and multiparty politics, Maurice Duverger, was living in the French Fourth Republic and trying to understand its unstable dynamics (Duverger 1964). As scholars have come to understand well, the ability to win seats with only a small percentage of the vote, a core characteristic of most PR systems, makes it possible for finer shades of ideological and social differences to form their own parties and be successful. And sometimes even small parties can serve as "king-makers," without whose support governments will fall.

The second key cause of fragmentation during the Fourth Republic, therefore, can be found in the party system. In the years immediately following the ratification of the constitution, a quasi-stable system of tripartism developed, whereby power was shared between the Christian Democratic MRP, the revitalized Social Democratic SFIO, and the Communist PCF (Blum 1958, Suleiman 1974). The Mouvement républicain populaire (MRP) was the only one of the three to emerge during the tumultuous years following liberation; the SFIO and PCF had both been major political players in the prewar years.

That the French right would coalesce during these years under a centrist and Christian Democratic banner is not surprising (see Vinen 1995, Vinen 1996, Nord 2010). Many significant figures on the right had held positions in the discredited Vichy regime and were temporarily barred from politics. Others who had been less closely connected with Pétain's government were nevertheless compromised in the eyes of many French for their collaborationist past. Furthermore, many French business leaders and local notables were either active supporters of Vichy or at the very least had made accommodations with it.

For all of these reasons, a new and untainted right was needed, and Christian Democracy, which had never won a significant following in France before, was the order of the day. The MRP was centrist and new, and it was therefore capable of representing the right under its chastened postwar circumstances. For its part, the resurgent left in both its communist and non-communist forms, which had dominated the resistance movement and continued to distrust the right, joked that MRP stood for "machine à ramasser les Pétainistes" (a machine for gathering Petainists) (Vinen 1996). But, in the interests of national unity, they found points for cooperation.

The Section française de l'Internationale ouvrière (French Section of the International Workers Movement or SFIO) was an important party from the days of the Third Republic. It was founded in the early twentieth century from a merger of France's earlier socialist parties, and under its iconic (and martyred) leader Jean Jaurès moved in a social democratic direction and away from a focus on revolution. It was also the party of Léon Blum, the prime minister during the Left Front government of the 1930s who took the first steps toward creating the French welfare state. The Parti communiste français (French Communist Party or PCF), for its part, had split from the SFIO in 1920 over opposition to its increasingly moderate direction and lack of loyalty to the Comintern (Berman 2006, Nord 2010, Judt 2011). The PCF remained in thrall to its Soviet mentors, and its leader Maurice Thorez had passed the war holed up in Moscow. But the French communists had also been the most resolute anti-fascists during the dark days of the occupation and had emerged from the war with a great deal of credibility and good will. In short, now that de Gaulle had retreated from politics, it seemed to everyone that the resurgent left would dominate the postwar years.

These predictions, however, turned out to be mistaken. The nationalizations of the postwar period (discussed below) exhausted themselves very quickly, and the French state turned away from hard left policies. Cold war pressures led to the successful banishment of the PCF from power in 1947, when Prime Minister Ramadier made clear that his government would no longer include communists. From this point on, power in the Fourth Republic was shared among the MRP, the SPIO, the centrist Radicals and UDSR, and the rightist-liberal UNIP. With a few exceptions (the Radical Pierre Mendès-France and the Socialist Guy Mollet are the most notable), no Fourth Republic prime minister was able to stay in power for more than a few months at a time. While some politicians held the prime minister's office multiple times, and also circulated among the key ministries of state, shifting party coalitions meant that stable government was next to impossible (Vinen 1996, Rioux 1987, MacRae 1967).

Perhaps it was inevitable, with the introduction of proportional representation, that there would be many different parties holding seats in the National Assembly. Of course, simply having a multiparty system does not automatically lead to unstable coalitions in parliament. Some countries are able to manage large coalitions in a lasting fashion through carefully constructed power-sharing agreements developed either before elections or after. For example, before the BJP's commanding victory of 2014 made coalitions unnecessary, Indian politics was dominated by two enormous party alliances, each formed before elections and centered on one of the two dominant parties (see Chapter 8). In the Netherlands today, coalitions are generally formed after elections but, with carefully constructed common platforms, manage to hold power for years rather than months. Indeed, Mark Rutte held the prime minister's chair for more than thirteen years, despite the fact that his party, the largest in parliament, generally holds only around 20% of seats.[5]

By contrast, the degree of coalition instability in Fourth Republic France was much greater. Indeed, in the twelve years from 1946 to 1958, twenty-two different prime ministers from six different political parties held power across twenty-six terms. This means, of course, that the average length that a Fourth Republic prime minister spent in office was less than six months (see MacRae 1967). Indeed, the constant changes in government had become so endemic that Georges Bidault (1967) notes in his memoirs that, during a particularly contentious session of the National Assembly, "the no confidence motion tied, and the government was thus barely allowed to continue. Querelle believed it had fallen and made the customary speech." Of course, many of the same party leaders served from government to government, and so a coterie of experienced ministers did form even in the midst of constant coalitional changes. But since these politicians rarely stayed for long at the same ministry, they were unable to exercise consistent control.

Some have argued that the fragmentation and instability of the Fourth Republic has been overstated, and that, in the absence of consistent political leadership, the elite civil service served as the nation's glue. For these observers, the Fourth Republic was effectively cohesive due to the power of its bureaucrats (see Debré 1981). It is certainly true that the authority of the administration meant that day-to-day governance functioned in France, despite the fragmentation of the National Assembly.

The elite Corps de l'État, associations of state administrators who often colonized power in key ministries, provided a structure to government decision-making that was sometimes lacking among the elected leadership (Suleiman 1974, Hayward 1986). The French administration has long been organized hierarchically along the lines of these corps, the most important of which are the Inspecteurs des Finances, Conseillers d'État, and members of the Cours des Comptes. These administrators must pass rigorous examinations, and they are generally trained at the École nationale d'administration (now the INSP) and given plum positions across the organs of state. This system creates a powerful esprit de corps across the top levels of the French bureaucracy and also connects senior state and private sector positions through the system of pantouflage, which we will discuss in more detail in a later chapter.

In economic policy, the Commissariat général du Plan (CGP), headed initially by the energetic Jean Monnet, provided a central coordinating point for industrial policy and upgrading (Monnet 1978, Nord 2010). The CGP, however, was organized quite differently from other state institutions; Monnet had secured the freedom early on to select administrators without regard to their corps and even those (academics, for instance) without a corps altogether. In fact, the CGP operated outside the usual lines of authority in the government, a fact established by Monnet when he insisted to de Gaulle at the moment of the organization's founding that he report directly to the prime minister (Monnet 1978). This special status gave the CGP, at least in its early years, an unusual amount of power over economic policy in France, but it also created enemies in the Finance and Industry Ministries who contributed to the downgrading of the CGP in its later years.

Despite the strength of the public administration during the Fourth Republic, many scholars (i.e., Chagnollaud 1996) have argued that its ability to act independently has been greatly exaggerated. Indeed, the evidence indicates that the power of the civil service to effect policy change was severely limited without the direction of the fragmented political authorities. As a senior civil servant during the Fourth Republic, François Bloch-Lainé, put it:

> It is certain that the [senior administrators], especially those in the Finance Ministry, had more freedom of action and more personal influence when the ministers passed quickly, when the governments changed often. People say that things worked during the Fourth Republic thanks to them, despite the political instability. . . . [But the senior administrator], whatever his liberty, is limited in his efficiency. There were a thousand essential things that he could not do nor obtain. Deprived of solid and constant governmental support, he was an infirm person who leaped around without constraint. He limps, he hops, and he doesn't go far, even if he walks a long time.[6]

So the large number of parties holding seats in the National Assembly contributed significantly to fragmentation in the Fourth Republic, as did its endemic cabinet instability. But does this party system fragmentation and cabinet instability signal the sort of fragmentation identified by my theory? For my purposes, government fragmentation means that power is not concentrated in the hands of a few but is dispersed widely. This fragmentation means that decision-makers in the state can more easily be influenced by private interests, due especially to the higher number of access points. By the same token, it means that government does not speak with a single voice and that its initiatives can be harder to pin down and more complex to implement.

All of this was certainly the case for the Fourth Republic, and the constantly shifting cabinets contributed significantly to the state of affairs. The complex coalitions that formed and reformed during the period made it impossible for any prime minister to impose discipline on the other ministers. Often, ministers holding key portfolios came from different parties with different constituencies and agendas, and so they often acted quite independently of other members of the government. As de Gaulle's advisor Peyrefitte (2012) noted, Fourth Republic ministers regularly talked separately to the press, giving mixed signals, a practice that de Gaulle rapidly ended during the Fifth Republic. But if a Fourth Republic prime minister had tried to impose a single platform, other parties would surely have threatened to withdraw from the coalition and topple the government, and indeed they often did. This ensured that fragmentation of power was the order of the day.

Compounding the fragmentation of authority within the party system was the uneven internal structure of the parties themselves. While some of the parties, such as the SFIO and the PCF, were quite organizationally cohesive, with national party leaders firmly in control, others, such as the Gaullist RPF and the Radicals, were highly fragmented and internally split (MacRae 1967).

Like most communist parties, the PCF was strongly centralized and institutionalized, possessing clear lines of authority. The SFIO was similar, while the new center-right MRP was organized a bit differently, cohesive but not to the degree of the left parties. The most fragmented parties in the Fourth Republic tended to be on the traditional right. Conservative politics in France, going back decades and even centuries, has been dominated by powerful "local notables" (Hoffmann 1974). These individuals, landowners, professionals, and business leaders from the provinces, continued during the Fourth Republic to hold outsized power on the right, especially outside the MRP.

The Radical Party emerged from a bourgeois movement dating to the early nineteenth century and coalescing into a party at the very beginning of the twentieth (MacRae 1967, Vinen 1995). It was initially quite radical in its opposition to clerical and aristocratic power, but in the context of the postwar world was considered centrist. That said, it could be quite difficult to pin the Radicals down to a cohesive ideology given their fragmented and weak organizational structure. Indeed, the Radical Party was divided among a left, center, and right wing, each with its own leadership. Corralling the local notables and the national politicians toward a single platform proved impossible. The UDSR and the classically liberal UNIP were no different. These parties were also based on local notables and took quite disparate positions depending on which of their internal leaders was ascendant.

Perhaps the strangest party of the postwar period was the RPF, which was organized around the leadership of a figure who had essentially disowned it (Vinen 1996, Peyrefitte 2012, Ehrmann 1957). Charles de Gaulle, disgusted by the return of party-based parliamentary government, had withdrawn to his estate in Colombey-les-Deux-Èglises. His conservative nationalist politics of French *grandeur*, however, did not quite retreat with him. Instead, de Gaulle's intellectual followers created a new party, the RPF, and attempted to organize a new French right. The heroic legacy of the general meant that this movement could not be attacked for a history of collaboration, as could some of the other right parties. And its brand of conservative politics was distinctly nationalist and centralized, modern if you will. It was based on an image of a strong France acting on the world stage, rather than on preserving traditional society. But Gaullism's time had not yet come; without the support of the general, the party declined and gave way to its competitors.

During its brief period of influence during the Fourth Republic, the RPF was generally more top-down than other right parties, though its reliance on notables and its rejection by de Gaulle kept it from coalescing firmly.

How did the decentralized and weak organizational structure of most French parties during this period contribute to the overall fragmentation of the Fourth Republic? Because these parties lacked a clear leader and an agreed platform, power was highly dispersed within them. This meant that fragmentation in postwar France was not limited to cross-party differences within constantly shifting coalitions but was also present within the parties themselves. Different actors controlled different intraparty factions and often called for different sorts of policies. To take an example, Pierre Mendès-France led the left wing within the centrist Radical Party, often competing with the right-wing Radicals led by Edgar Faure (Hayward 1966).

In summary, then, the state during the Fourth Republic was highly fragmented. The multitude of parties in the National Assembly, driven by a highly proportional electoral system and deep ideological and social divisions, kept power from coalescing. This effect was exacerbated by the instability of cabinets and the fact that many of the Republic's political parties were themselves internally fragmented, especially those on the right which relied on local notables. A strong bureaucracy helped to avert a crisis of governability, at least until the pressures of the Algerian War unleashed forces that the Republic was unable to control. But even the bureaucracy was split among different corps and ministries, and, more importantly, was unable to take coordinated and centralized action in the absence of centralized leadership. As we will see in the next section, however, things were to change when de Gaulle returned to power in the wake of the Algerian crisis.

The Fifth Republic

The structure of French government underwent a dramatic change in 1958 with the advent of the Fifth Republic. The crisis that led to this institutional shift was precipitated by the Fourth Republic's inability to deal with decolonization in Algeria (de Gaulle 1971, Peyrefitte 2012, Nord 2010). The French public was split over whether to continue fighting the Algerian independence movement, the FLN, despite the increasing costs. Some French, including many on the right and in the military, saw keeping the French Empire intact as critical for the country's pride, especially in the wake of the German occupation. The situation was complicated by the fact that, unlike in Indochina, which France had lost shortly before things in Algeria came to a head, there were more than a million European French, termed pieds-noirs, living there. Most of these settlers, some of whom had lived in North Africa for several generations, were vehemently opposed to Algerian independence and stood in the way of any reasonable settlement.

As the situation descended into crisis, intimations by the French government that it would consider leaving Algeria led to the beginnings of a coup by a clique of hardline French generals (Kedward 2005, Maier and White 1968). The resulting fear of military dictatorship and even civil war led to the recall of de Gaulle, who was waiting for his moment in his small town retreat. Many French had concluded that de Gaulle, with his unique stature, was the only person who could hold the country together. His return to government quelled the coup attempt, as supporters of empire concluded that a man so focused on French greatness could not fail to rescue the situation across the Mediterranean. And those concerned for the future of French democracy put their hopes in de Gaulle's commitment to free government as their hope for a better future.

But de Gaulle, for his part, was not ready to return as just another Fourth Republic prime minister. Rather, as a condition of his return, the general demanded a new constitution that would correct all of the problems that he had been criticizing for years (Peyrefitte 2012, de Gaulle 1971, Maier and White 1968). This new constitution, which inaugurated the Fifth French Republic, introduced a number of significant changes to the French polity.[7] First, it created a dramatically stronger president of the republic. As we have already discussed, the presidency under the Fourth Republic was largely symbolic; heads of state played a role in calling for the formation of government but had few other real powers. Actual authority rested with the head of government, known as the president of the council or, more commonly, the prime minister.

Under the new constitution, authority was moved from the prime minister to the president, who could now appoint the prime minister, with parliament's approval. Moreover, the president was empowered to dissolve parliament and call for new elections (Article 12) and also given significant decree powers that permitted many executive actions to be taken without the consent of parliament (Article 13). De Gaulle quickly concluded that these new powers were incompatible with the selection process for the president that had been used under the Fourth Republic. Under the previous constitution, the president was chosen by an electoral college made up of the two houses of parliament. De Gaulle believed that democratic principle, as well as practical politics, required that a more powerful president be chosen by the people (Peyrefitte 2012, de Gaulle 1971, Maier and White 1968). In 1962, therefore, he held a successful referendum creating a directly elected president, and the first direct presidential elections in more than one hundred years were duly held three years later. France's transition from a parliamentary system to one with a strong president was complete.

Unlike in the United States, however, the Fifth Republic maintained the position of prime minister, perhaps from a desire to maintain continuity. Under France's new system, as noted above, the president would appoint the prime minister and the government, subject to the approval of the National Assembly.[8] The prime minister would take responsibility for the day-to-day running of the government, and especially for domestic issues, while the president would set the broad direction of the country while presiding majestically over foreign affairs. Such a division of power in the executive made sense in the context of the 1950s and 1960s, though after de Gaulle's death it would lead periodically to contested authority under "co-habitation," when different parties controlled the presidency and parliament (Hall 2008).

Many of the president's new powers came at the expense of the National Assembly, which had enjoyed a position of dominance during the Fourth Republic (Debré 1981).[9] Perhaps the clearest sign of the Assembly's diminished role was the fact that ministers in the Fifth Republic, unlike those in the Fourth, were most often technocrats and rarely from a parliamentarian background (Suleiman 1974, Bloch-Lainé 1976). Indeed, ministers were prevented by the Fifth Republic constitution from holding any concurrent national-level offices, including seats in parliament (Article 23). As a result, deputies, especially those from outside the ruling party, were looked down upon by senior civil servants and government officials, and they were considered almost powerless by lobbyists (Suleiman 1974).

One important reason for the impotence of the parliament under the new constitution lay in the government's ability to leverage the vote of no confidence as a cudgel for driving through legislation that might not have been popular with ruling party deputies. Following a pattern identified by Huber (1996), when faced with a choice between having their way on a particular issue and risking the collapse of the government, most deputies went along with the executive. Of particular importance is the constitution's famous (some would say notorious) Article 49, Paragraph 3:

> The Prime Minister may, after deliberation by the Council of Ministers, make the passing of a Finance Bill or Social Security Financing Bill an issue of a vote of confidence before the National Assembly. In that event, the Bill shall be considered passed unless a resolution of no-confidence, tabled within the subsequent twenty-four hours, is carried as provided for in the foregoing paragraph. In addition, the Prime Minister may use the said procedure for one other Government or Private Members' Bill per session.[10]

This section allowed the government to pass particular bills unless legislators forced a vote of no confidence, thus pushing the burden of initiation on the Assembly. More than that, the executive under the Fifth Republic could package bills together so as to force legislators to vote against measures they supported if they wanted to bring down a single measure they opposed. This sort of strategic packaging made it increasingly difficult for the parliament to oppose the initiatives of the government.

The Fifth Republic dispensed with the proportional electoral system of its predecessor, replacing it with a two-round majoritarian system like the one mostly used under the Third Republic (Judt 2011). For National Assembly elections, this system required 50% of votes cast and 25% of votes registered to win in the first round. If no candidates achieved this, a second round would be held pitting only the top two (and sometimes three) candidates against one another. While the proportional system of the Fourth Republic made it possible for small parties to win seats in the National Assembly, this new system rewarded the larger parties, those who could survive into the second round. As a result of these changes, party fragmentation was reduced dramatically and government became much more stable (Suleiman 1974, Judt 2011). The Gaullist UNR and its successors essentially dominated the National Assembly and the Presidency until the 1970s, and only two presidents and four prime ministers held office during this period.

Two more factors contributed to the cohesion of authority during the Fifth Republic. First was the dominant personality of Charles de Gaulle himself, whose role in government was hardly questioned, at least until 1968 (Pinay 1984). De Gaulle's special status, of course, originated from his position as the leader of the Free French during the Second World War. When many other French leaders were accommodating themselves to the new Vichy regime, de Gaulle fled to London to begin working against the Germans and their supporters in France. Four years later, he returned triumphantly at the front of an exile army that participated in liberating France and that, for many, helped to restore the country's honor after the humiliations of collaboration.

De Gaulle's willingness to step away from politics in 1946 when it became clear that the "government of parties" that he so detested would return only increased his reputation as someone "above it all."

So, when de Gaulle returned to power in 1958, preventing the collapse of the French government and forestalling a coup, he was hailed by many as a hero. Moreover, his rhetoric of restored French greatness ("grandeur") allowed him to place his institutional changes within a broader context of postwar restauration (Peyrefitte 2012, de Gaulle 1971, Maier and White 1968). In other words, a strong government is required for a strong country, and only a new constitution, presided over initially by a leader of true greatness, can deliver what France needs. Compounding the individual power of de Gaulle, as emphasized by Suleiman (1974), was the dominance of a single party (sometimes with different names) from 1958 through the election of Giscard in 1974.

A final source of the Fifth Republic's cohesion was the resurgent power of France's elite administrators, who were frequently able to take charge of key ministries during the period (Bloch-Lainé 1976). There is some disagreement in the secondary literature over the changed role of France's powerful bureaucrats in the Fifth Republic. On the one hand, some scholars assert that the weakness of the political leadership under the Fourth Republic made civil servants all the stronger. In this story, the administration was able to act however it wanted in the absence of guidance from elected leaders.[11] On the other hand, scholars such as Crozier (1970) represent the Fifth Republic as particularly bureaucratic, seeing France in this period as a "blocked society," over-governed by hierarchical, closed, and technocratic elites.

I argue here that, as the earlier quote by Bloch-Lainé makes clear, there is only so much that civil servants could do without direction and support from government. So, while civil servants may have acted with some autonomy in day-to-day affairs under the Fourth Republic, their ability to wield the powers of the state was limited. In the Fifth Republic, by contrast, senior civil servants increasingly brought their technocratic skills to bear as full government ministers. Unlike in the Fourth Republic, in the Fifth Republic civil servants often filled the highest positions of the state, relegated no more to the service of elected ministers (see Suleiman 1974). Of course, with the firm and technocratic leadership that these civil servants brought to the ministries of state, junior civil servants may have been more constrained than before. But overall, the Gaullist state allowed the elite administration finally to come into its own.

In the final analysis, therefore, the increasing cohesion of the French state produced by the new Fifth Republic had a number of disparate sources. Among other things, the party system was less fragmented, the ruling party remained constant, the presidency was greatly strengthened at the expense of the legislature, and the civil service took over political roles that had previously been denied them. In later chapters, we will explore how this new cohesion played out in industrial and agricultural policy.

Business and Union Fragmentation

In making industrial policy, the French state of both periods partnered with businesses that were organized in a decidedly fragmented fashion. On the face of it, this fragmented structure might not be obvious. Immediately following the end of the occupation, the French state, at that point under the sway of a resurgent left, nationalized a number of the country's largest firms, particularly those controlling transport and key utilities (Sheahan 1963, Nord 2010). Not only that, but many private French corporations were members of the CNPF, the peak level French business association (Ehrmann 1957, Wilson 1987).

But industry representation was in reality not at all cohesive. First, as noted in the section above, only a relatively small percentage of industry was ultimately nationalized. Nationalization in France began in 1944, soon after the Liberation and before the war had even ended. It was driven in part by anger at the *patronat*, the class of business owners, for the willingness of many to collaborate with the Germans and the Vichy regime. It was also to some extent a natural consequence of the left-leaning ideology of many resistance leaders, strongly represented on the CNR, which envisioned a mostly socialist economic structure after the war (Nord 2010, Kuisel 1981, Vinen 1996). A similar left wave swept through other European countries, notably the United Kingdom, as citizens sought to give meaning to their suffering and to rethink long-held social structures.

In France, the first nationalizations happened soon after the Liberation and focused on businesses, such as Renault, whose owners had collaborated with Vichy and the Germans. They also included many of the coal mines in northern France, where workers had taken over production more or less spontaneously after the war. The final wave of nationalizations brought much of the transport sector, including rail, ports, and air, into state hands. Also nationalized was deposit banking, insurance, telecommunications and, of course, electricity (Baum 1958, Vinen 1996). When the nationalizations were finished, the state had taken control of significant economic resources in the country.

That said, the government nationalized a smaller portion of the economy than many on the left would have preferred. Indeed, the vast majority of French businesses, including large ones, remained in private hands; only about 15% of

French value-added (Cohen 2010) and 25% of capital formation (Vinen 1996) was controlled by state-owned enterprises. Moreover, apart from the communists, there was little appetite among even left-leaning French elites to create a truly state-run economy. Indeed, the nationalizing fervor had exhausted itself by 1947, the same year that the PCF was excluded from government and its influence well and truly contained (Nord 2010).

As important as the limited extent of nationalization was the fact that even state-owned industries were given a significant amount of autonomy (Baum 1958). A common phrase of the time was that "nationaliser ce n'est pas étatiser," that nationalization is not the same as state-dominance (Baum 1958). This reality was reflected in the management structure of the newly state-owned industries, which were rarely placed under the control of ministries but rather given significant discretion to act according to market conditions. Indeed, the most constraining new rules placed on these industries dealt with the requirement to include stakeholders in their leadership bodies, including labor (Keeler 1987). As we shall see, however, these rules did not play out in France as they did in neighboring Germany, in part because the largest union soon refused to participate.

Fragmentation in the business sector also reflected the structure of business associations, notably the largest of the time, the Conseil national du patronat français (CNPF). In the early years after liberation, the influence of the patronat was at a low point. Many business owners, worried about their assets and often sympathetic with its brand of conservatism, had supported the Vichy government that was created after the fall of France in 1940. Vichy was indeed quite pro-business, though it also had a strongly corporatist bent as evidenced by its system of Comités d'organisation (Nord 2010).

As the controlling presence of Nazi Germany over Pétain and his ministers became increasingly difficult to ignore, especially after the occupation of the south in 1942, some members of the business elite moved into the resistance camp. But others remained neutral or indeed supportive of the regime. This blemished the reputation of the patronat after the war, even among conservatives such as de Gaulle. More than that, traditional conservative parties based on local notables and backed by business were completely discredited, and for a number of years the political right in France was dominated by Gaullist nationalism and Christian democracy with limited business influence (Balassa 1978, Peyrefitte 2012, Vinen 1996, Kedward 2005).

It was in this environment that the structures of business representation were reconstructed in the early years after liberation. Assisting in the steady strengthening of business influence was, of course, the ability of the patronat to mobilize financial resources for candidates and parties. Also important was the leadership of Georges Villiers, whose strong resistant credentials helped give the organization he represented more credibility in postwar France (Vinen 1995, Ehrmann 1957).

The most important factor ensuring the fragmentation of business was the structure of the CNPF itself. The organization's members were not individual businesses but rather smaller business associations divided by region, economic sector, and firm size, and these had quite fractious interests that made it difficult for the CNPF to agree on anything (Wilson 1987). An excellent example of the organization's structure is provided in Ehrmann (1957). He describes how a company producing metal boxes in Bordeaux might join a metal box syndicate in the same city and then a larger one in the Gironde department. This organization might in turn become a part of the French metallurgy organization, which, for its part, might then be a member of the CNPF. So, an individual firm would be a member of at least three smaller organizations prior to its involvement with peak-level business association.

These divisions inevitably led to irreconcilable disagreements among the CNPF's component members. For example, the CNPF remained agnostic in a critical parliamentary debate about the location of infrastructure investment in France, largely because its members were unable to agree on a common program (Wilson 1987). The differences were not just geographic. The size of firms was of equal importance, as was the industry represented. Indeed, the wealthiest business associations often disposed of budgets in excess of that enjoyed by the CNPF, and they were not afraid to use their resources for their individual benefit. These dynamics were confirmed by CNPF chief Pierre Ricard in a 1947 letter to Monnet lamenting that it would take considerable effort and internal debate for the patronat to come to any single position about planning.[12]

So, the CNPF was itself quite a fragmented organization. More than that, while it remained the dominant representative of the patronat during the period under study, the organization was not the sole business association that mattered. The CNPF also had an important rival in the CGPME, which represented small and medium sized industries and often vocally took positions in conflict with those of the CNPF.[13] Because small- and medium-sized businesses were less tainted by the occupation, the CGPME and its leader, Léon Gingembre, took a more aggressive political stance in the early postwar years. Ultimately, due surely to its weaker financial resources, the CGPME was integrated into the CNPF structure, but it was able to retain a veto on the broader organization's decision-making (Wilson 1987, Ehrmann 1957, Vinen 1995).

Another rival for influence were the independent Chambers of Commerce, created in the immediate postwar era as a quasi-corporatist regional grouping to represent business (Wilson 1987, Ehrmann 1957, Keeler 1981a). These never became tremendously powerful, but they did serve as an alternative area of business representation. A rival from a different direction was the Centre des jeunes patrons (CJP), a grouping of progressive younger business leaders who understood their role as encouraging business leaders to take up a socially responsible role. Their vision of the patronat served as yet another alternative to the dominant narrative (Vinen 1995, Ehrmann 1957). All of this fragmentation led de Gaulle's advisor, Alain Peyrefitte (2012, loc 10633) to note that "the CNPF is incapable of imposing a discipline on its troops. . . . The delinquency of the business association struck me strongly. . . . The patronat is lamentable!"

If business representation was fragmented, labor interests were even more so. While some variation in union structure and in the organization of unions occurred between the immediate postwar period and the late 1960s, the overall fragmentation remained. Unions in France were highly divided along ideological lines, with the largest syndicate in France, the Confédération générale du travail or CGT, under the sway of the communists (Howell 1992, Rioux 1987, Ross 1981, Wilson 1987). This ideology, not surprisingly, made the CGT reluctant to work with the state and business leaders and inclined it rather to advocate for broad social transformation. Other major unions took a more social democratic or Catholic orientation and were more willing to participate in upgrading policy, but these tended to be smaller.

In addition to the ideological divides, some unions focused their representation on the traditional working class, while others were made up of public sector or highly skilled workers. Such divisions obviously made it more difficult for organized labor to speak with one voice in interacting with the state. But perhaps the most important factor ensuring the fragmentation of labor representation was France's very low union density, the percentage of workers who are members of labor union (Howell 1992, Wilson 1987, Kuisel 1981, Schmidt 1996). This stood at around 15%, meaning that French labor unions were not in a position to claim representation over anywhere near a majority of French workers (Hayward 1986).

The overall structure of syndicalism in France is often held out in the literature as exceptional in Europe (Howell 1992, Hayward 1986). First, and perhaps more notably, is the fragmentation of labor representation discussed above. While most comparable countries were characterized by a single dominant union, such was not the case in France. Moreover, French unions were (and are) quite weak compared to their counterparts in much of western Europe, not only because they organized a smaller proportion of the working population, but also because they operated in a strongly market-based labor system. Unlike in the evolving neo-corporatist systems of countries like Austria and Sweden, French unions, as we shall see, played little role in policymaking (Howell 1992). Their relationship with government and business was simply too toxic to sustain this form of corporatism, and the relative weakness and fragmentation of French unions removed any incentive for policymakers to take them seriously as equal partners. Even unions in pluralist Britain tended to be more influential than those in France. This fact is due in part to their greater union density, but also to the tight association of British syndicalism with the Labour Party. This link ensured that union leaders in the UK had a place at the policymaking table and influence in parliament (Hayward 1986).

To understand why cooperation between business, the state, and unions in France was complicated, we must return to the origins of syndicalism in the late nineteenth century. The repression of the communards in 1871, a socialist uprising that occurred in the wake of the Franco-Prussian War, undermined early efforts to organize labor (Judt 2011, Howell 1992). Rather than associate with a political party, as occurred in the United Kingdom, unions in France took a more anarcho-syndicalist tenor, suspicious of state power and reluctant to cooperate too closely with electoral politics (Hayward 1986).

As noted above, the predominant union in France has long been the CGT. This union, which grew dramatically during the leftist United Front government of the 1930s, was closely associated with the French communist party, which itself broke from the Socialists when Jean Jaurès moved the party away from advocating violent revolution. The head of the CGT was, in fact, a member of the Politburo of the PCF, though the union did enjoy a fair amount of autonomy from the party (Wilson 1987).

Nevertheless, this communist, anarcho-syndicalist heritage complicated any effort at cooperation between the state, business, and France's largest union during the postwar period. Rather, the predominant sense on both sides was one of mistrust. Union organizers were suspicious of the motives of businesses and saw the state, in Marxist terms, as in the pocket of capital. State and business leaders, for their part, were reluctant to cooperate with an organization that called, officially at least, for violent revolution. While it is true that the CGT agreed to participate in the planning process during its first years, taking part in the modernization commissions, the union soon concluded that this form of cooperation was useless and indeed counterproductive (Mioche 1987). As we shall see, it therefore withdrew from formal cooperation with the state (Howell 1992).

Of course, the CGT was not the only French union of importance. The CFDT (Confédération française démocratique du travail) was another early union. Unlike the CGT, the CFDT was associated with social Catholicism and loosely linked to the Socialist Party, and for this reason tended to be more focused than its communist counterpart on the immediate material conditions of workers rather than on broader political change. This orientation meant that the CFDT was more inclined to cooperate with planning in France and more willing to discuss productivity increases with the state and business (Hayward 1987, Wilson 1987, Hall 2008). But, as it represented a relatively small percentage of workers, the CFDT's participation, while meaningful, represented only a limited advancement in the incorporation of labor into upgrading plans.

Another significant union was the Force ouvrière (FO), which broke from the CGT in 1947 over its communist ideology (Nord 2010). The FO, like the CFDT, saw itself as focused primarily on the specific working conditions of its members rather than on broader political issues. It became the primary union representing the most organized section of the working population in France—the public sector. As a result, its involvement with the specifics of upgrading was limited. Beyond these three unions, there were a number of other smaller ones that played relatively minor roles, but nevertheless contributed to fragmentation.

To summarize, then, the key private interests in industrial policy—business associations and labor unions—were highly fragmented. Both were characterized by a number of important interest organizations rather than a peak-level group. The patronat, for its part, did coalesce to some extent within the CNPF, but that organization was deeply decentralized and often unable to act as a result of its internal divisions. It was more a collection of interest groups than an interest group itself. In labor, the primary source of fragmentation was, first, the low percentage of the working class that was organized and, second, the existence of a number of ideologically antagonistic syndicates. As we will see in the next section, the situation in agriculture was quite different.

The Cohesion of Agriculture Interests

The peak level association in agriculture, the FNSEA (Fédération nationale des syndicats d'exploitants agricoles), was France's most powerful and cohesive interest group. As in industry, there were divisions among French farmers, especially between the large agriculturalists of the North and West and the small growers of the South and East. Still, most of the FNSEA's individual members were farmers themselves rather than trade groups, making it easier for the leadership to coordinate policy across the divisions. And, even more importantly, the FNSEA, at least before the 1960s, was able to unite its constituents over a policy on which they could all agree—high prices (Keeler 1981a, Wilson 1987, Moravcsik 1998).

The history of the FNSEA, like that of the more fragmented CNPF, dates to the immediate years after the Liberation. In 1944, the provisional government appointed the leftist resistant François Tanguy-Prigent to oversee the reconstruction of agricultural representation into a sort of democratic version of Vichy's corporatist "Corporation paysanne" (Cleary 1989). Tanguy-Prigent created the Confédération générale d'agriculture (CGA) to take the place of the Vichy system, placing it in charge of the newly created FNSEA, which was itself tasked with organizing the regional syndicates (Rioux 1987, Keeler 1987).

Part of Tanguy-Prigent's motivation for empowering the CGA was a fear that, should the local syndicates dominate agricultural representation, the traditional conservatism of farmers might manifest itself and make the sector (in his lights) a regressive force (Keeler 1987). Despite Tanguy-Prigent's best efforts, however, the state-sanctioned and progressive CGA was soon eclipsed by the FNSEA. More than that, the 1947 agricultural elections put conservatives firmly in power in the FNSEA, which in short order was able to sidestep the influence of the somewhat artificial CGA as the primary voice of agriculture in France (Knudsen 2009).

Of course, agricultural interests were not perfectly unified under the FNSEA's leadership. The organization represented a number of departmental FDSEAs, some of which were significantly wealthier and more organized than others. Moreover, differences existed between the wealthy *gros* or large farmers of the North and the Paris region and the mostly smaller farmers in the Center and South, and differences also persisted across commodities (Keeler 1987). That said, the organization, and farmer interests in France more generally, remained stunningly cohesive. As one FNSEA leader, Michel Debatisse, put it, agriculture has "what most industrial unions dream of—a united and unitary syndical movement."[14]

To conclude, then, the move from the Fourth to the Fifth Republic represented a significant shift from a fragmented to a cohesive polity. The Fifth Republic centralized executive power in the president, weakened the National Assembly, led to nearly two decades of single party dominant government, and empowered the elite bureaucracy. Among private interests, business leaders were represented primarily by the highly fragmented CNPF, an organization of organizations, while labor was weakly mobilized and split among ideological syndicates. Only agricultural interests, through the powerful FNSEA, were able to interact with the state as a cohesive, peak-level group. In the next chapter, we will explore the implications of these structures of upgrading in France.

FOUR

Postwar France

Upgrading in Industry and Agriculture

If my theory is correct, we would expect industrial upgrading policy during the Fourth Republic—consonant with the dual fragmentation of the state and interest groups—to be characterized by a *pluralist* pattern of decision-making, one where numerous micro-coalitions oversee upgrading in specific sectors of the economy. By contrast, we would expect industrial upgrading policy to be *statist* under the more cohesive institutions of the Fifth Republic, with the state able to impose its will on the private sector. Moreover, we would anticipate industrial policy during the early period to be reasonably successful, especially at gradual, sector specific change, while during the later period overweening state power would lead to much less efficient outcomes.

In this chapter, I begin by evaluating the evidence for these expectations and find broad support for the theory. I then turn my attention to upgrading in the agricultural sector, drawing on the analysis of state and agricultural institutions from Chapter 3 to explore whether my theoretical expectations about agricultural policy are borne out by the historical evidence. In this domain, I anticipate that agricultural policy under the Fourth Republic will be *captured* by the preferences of the organized farmers' lobby, which was much more organizationally cohesive than the state. During the Fifth Republic, however, I expect that agricultural will embody a negotiated settlement between cohesive state and agricultural interests in the *corporatist* fashion.

After comparing the making of industrial and agricultural policy across the two republics, I then turn to a discussion of the theory's implications for the success of upgrading policy, both in industry and agriculture. Up to this point, I have focused primarily on the theory's predictions for the process of industrial and agricultural policymaking in France and have only touched on its implications for upgrading success. In this portion of the chapter, I turn my attention to that critical issue. I ultimately conclude that, as expected, the dual-fragmented, pluralist industrial policy of the Fourth Republic, along with the dual-cohesive, corporatist agricultural policy for the Fifth, were more successful than upgrading efforts undertaken with mismatched levels of fragmentation. I then finish the chapter with a brief examination of upgrading in France since the 1960s.

Industrial Policy and Planning in the Fourth Republic

Under the Fourth Republic, the predicted pluralism of industrial policy accords well with the structure of economic planning that was introduced during the period. At the behest of Jean Monnet, de Gaulle authorized the creation of the leading state planning institution, the CGP, just before he left office in December 1944. Monnet's vision was to develop a form of indicative planning, distinct from the command-oriented Soviet version, which could coordinate public and private sector efforts at reconstruction and upgrading (Monnet 1978, Mioche 1987). This vision was not Monnet's alone but was very much part of the zeitgeist in postwar France, and indeed in postwar Europe more broadly. In a few years, it was also to become central to economic thinking in the postcolonial world as well, as we will see in future chapters. In the French case, planning had actually been tried to some extent during the Vichy period and was theorized by a group of young economists known as the X-Crise (Nord 2010).

Unlike Vichy planning, and of course the Soviet variety that preceded it, French planning would be more democratic and considerably less corporatist. Robert Marjolin, in a 1947 description of the state of the economy and the goals of planning, stated that "What is required, in other words, is the modernization of the French economy. This is the raison d'être of the plan. To increase not only production but also the productivity of labor, this is its fundamental theme."[1] But in order for these ideas to reach fruition, Monnet understood early that his commission would need to be attached directly to the executive. Only in this way would its bureaucratic position be robust enough to weather the power struggles that were sure to come. Fortunately for Monnet and for French planning more broadly, de Gaulle agreed to his proposal. More than that, Monnet was able to convince the general's successor, Prime Minister Félix Gouin, to follow the same practice (Monnet 1978, Kuisel 1981). This move signaled the new Fourth Republic's commitment to planning and gave the CGT, which would remain quite a small institution with little political power in its own right, a surprising degree of leverage during its early years.

The First Plan, named for Monnet, would run from 1947 to 1950 and be extended later to 1952 (Monnet 1978, Mioche 1987, Adams 1989, Balassa 1981).[2] As I discuss in more detail in the next chapter, many historians and economists credit the plan, and those that followed in its wake, for much of the rapid recovery, growth, and indeed transformation of the French economy during the postwar period. It not only provided direction, coordination, and motivation for French industry, but it was also critical for obtaining funding from the United States under the Blum-Byrnes Agreement and the Marshall Plan (Nord 2010).

During this early period, there was broad agreement that planning was necessary to secure France's future. Even the communist labor union, the CGT, was on board with the principle of planning. Pierre Le Brun, the secretary-general of the syndicate, in a statement to the first Conseil du Plan (which oversaw the broad strokes of upgrading policy) on November 26, 1946, gave the organization's "considered agreement" to the process.[3] The CGA, speaking through its secretary-general of agriculture Philippe Lamour on November 27, 1946, also expressed support for the planning process, stating that his organization "closely participated in the elaboration of the plan."[4]

French business, characteristically, was represented at the Conseil du Plan by two leaders—Gingembre from the CGPME and Ricard from the larger CNPF—and had difficulty coming to a single position on planning. Ricard, highlighting the newness and decentralization of his organization, stated "I am not qualified today—and I deeply regret it—to give the official point of view of the French patronat."[5] Gingembre, for his part, felt that he was not being adequately consulted by the state planning apparatus. Interestingly, in 1952, he composed a letter to Lamour, his colleague on the Conseil du Plan, complaining that the CGP had not convened the group frequently enough and suggesting they draft a complaint letter together.[6] The CGP attributed this lack of meeting to "the current government crisis."[7]

The first plan was economically and statistically quite simple, at least compared to what would come next. It involved little formal economic modeling and focused its attention on only five industries. French planners considered these five industries—coal, electricity, steel, agricultural equipment, cement, and transport—as especially critical for economic recovery (Monnet 1978, Adams 1989). The plan used carrots and moral suasion rather than legal obligations to ensure its targets were achieved. Even its earliest proponents understood well the critical "spiritual effect" that creating an "économie concertée" (a term coined by the second CGP chief, Étienne Hirsch) could create (Nord 2010). And, indeed, the plan would prove spectacularly successful in motivating participation from key economic actors and in achieving its goals.

One significant form of leverage possessed by the planners, and by the state more generally, was money (Loriaux 1999, Cohen and Bauer 1985, Bloch-Lané 1976, Eichengreen 2007, Rioux 1987, Kuisel 1981). The First Plan was financed largely by American money from the Blum-Byrnes Agreement and, later, the Marshall Plan. This was channeled primarily through the Fonds de modernisation et d'equipement (FME), created in 1948 under the auspices of the CGP and focused on extending long-term loans for upgrading. This fund was supplemented by other government accounts with different purposes and also by money from the newly nationalized banks, which extended credit at discount rates to firms prioritized by the state (Pinay 1984, Eichengreen 2007). Later, after the departure of Monnet, the Ministry of Finance reasserted itself and brought all of the funds under its control, merging them into what would become, after 1954, the key source of plan finance—the Fonds de développement économique et social (FDES) (Rioux 1987). Government finance was meant to supplement and encourage private finance, and it is worth pointing out that the percentage of investment originating from the state declined quite significantly over time. According to Rioux (1987), it comprised half of the total in 1950, but only about a quarter by the time the Fourth Republic collapsed. Over time, then, planning's role in making connections, sharing information, and facilitating private finance took precedence over its role as a direct source of money.

In an official letter from Charles de Gaulle to Jean Monnet, dated January 10, 1946, the president of the provisional government laid out the agreed planning institutions to his new planning chief:

> The reconstruction of France involves not only the repair of wartime destruction but also the modernization of its equipment and methods of production . . . The French producers that should be the object of modernization studies will be determined by the Conseil du Plan. A modernization commission will be created for each group comprising representatives of the administration responsible for the sector, experts, representatives of business associations and labor unions, and other interested parties. . . . A representative of the Commissaire général [CGT] will sit at the heart of each commission as chair, rapporteur, or secretary to facilitate the coordination of work. The Commissaire général and its services . . . are responsible for the synthesis of the work of the diverse commissions.[8]

The letter also makes clear that the focus on the new CGP should be on increasing productivity:

> The essential notion under which the commissions should direct all of their work will be that of labor productivity. . . . When this backwardness [vis-à-vis other countries] appears significant, it [the relevant commission] should research the causes and propose methods for eliminating it: technical training of the labor force, mechanization, replacement of existing equipment, amelioration of organization, technical concentration and geographical decentralization, development of research services.[9]

Central to the French vision of indicative planning were the "modernization commissions" (Hackett and Hackett 1965, Bauchet 1962, Hall 1986, Eichengreen 2007). These commissions, made up of representatives of private interests and the state, cooperated with the French planning bureaucracy to set the broad guidelines for the economy, especially during the 1940s and 1950s. The First Plan contained twenty-four commissions, divided between so-called horizontal commissions that dealt with economy-wide issues such as research, and vertical commissions dealing with specific industries (Mioche 1987).[10] These commissions remained part of future plans, only increasing in number, though as we will see their importance, and the importance of planning in general, declined during the Fifth Republic.

To give a better sense of how the Fourth Republic's pluralist, or micro-upgrading, system functioned, it is useful to take a closer look at the membership of one of these modernization commissions. The commission on steel was chaired by Roy, the director-general of Steel Plants of Longwy, the vice chair was (the well-named) Bureau, director of steel production in the Ministry of Industry, and the rapporteur was Latourté, an engineer with a grand cadre of the state, the Corps des mines. So, the heads of the commission included a business leader, a senior ministry official, and a government technical expert. Beyond these three, the other members included five business leaders, three representatives of syndicates, two members of government cadres, two experts, and three administrators.[11] Altogether, according to a letter from Monnet dated January 1947, some 1200 people from across the French state and economy would take part in the modernization commissions.[12]

Critically, the pluralist modernization commissions mostly represented business interests at the sectoral level, rather than at the peak level as would be expected of a more corporatist arrangement (Estrin and Holmes 1983,

Hackett and Hackett 1965, Bauchet 1964).[13] Labor union representation was also present, though the CGT pulled out of the process in 1947, and the other unions largely felt marginalized (Nord 2010). The primary planning relationship, then, embodied a complex series of agreements between an influential state, which was ideologically committed to planning, and a large number of firms and sectoral level business associations. We will discuss the planning process in more detail later in the chapter.

An excellent summary of the functioning of the Monnet Plan is provided in the introduction to the first meeting of the Conseil du Plan:

> The execution of a plan for economic reconstruction is only possible if all of the interests, industries, workers, farmers, and engineers give to the government and to the public administration their active cooperation and participate closely in the decision-making as well as in the execution.
>
> It is to establish this permanent cooperation that the government has decided to create the Conseil du Plan and the Modernization Commissions.
>
> The Conseil du Plan is presided over by the president of the government [prime minister] and composed, on the one hand, of all of the ministers interested in the modernization and reequipment of France and, on the other hand, of 18 persons representing workers organizations, industry, agriculture, overseas territories, and scientific research. Its mission is to give directives to the modernization commissions, to study the results of their work, and to submit a selection of concrete propositions for the reequipping and modernization of the country.
>
> The modernization commissions are composed, according to the same formula, of representatives of the administration and of everyone interested in the activity of an agricultural or industrial sector. They are charged with elaborating for their branch a plan of modernization and equipment taking into account the general directives formulated by the Conseil du Plan.
>
> The Commissariat général du plan furnishes them the means to work and coordinates their activity. It must present to the Conseil du Plan a first draft of the plan after a delay of six months.
>
> During its first session, the Conseil du Plan, under the chairmanship of M. Félix Gouin, took note of a report . . . [presenting] the work accomplished up to now by the modernization commissions and by the commissariat. It gives a general summary of the French economy,

> the objectives to attain, the obstacles to surmount, and proposes for the approval of the council a certain number of production levels and immediate measures for the fundamental sectors.
>
> After a general discussion, the council adopted a group of resolutions that constituted the basic instructions from which the modernization commissions must pursue their task. They concerned coal, electricity, wood, interior transport, and the exportation of labor.
>
> Everything was targeted to attaining as rapidly as possible a goal which could be summarized by this formula: repair, modernize, produce.[14]

With Monnet leaving to concern himself more with the development of cooperation in Europe, the Second Plan was conceived and implemented under the leadership of Étienne Hirsch. The planning process began in 1953 and the plan itself ran from 1954 To 1957 (Rioux 1987, Sheahan 1963, Shonfield 1965).[15] While the Second Plan was clearly the progeny of the First, it also differed in a number of important ways. First, the CGP was moved out of the prime minister's office to the Finance Ministry, effectively demoting its power in the bureaucratic hierarchy. More significantly, perhaps, the new plan rested on a more sophisticated modeling framework than had its predecessor and was more conscious of the macroeconomic implications of a concerted economy. It expanded its concern beyond the five industries of the First Plan and shifted its attention away from reconstruction and more explicitly toward upgrading (Rioux 1987).

The third and final plan of the Fourth Republic continued the trend toward more sophisticated modelling, broader reach, and greater focus on upgrading that its predecessor had started. Planning began in 1956 and implementation in the following year, which coincided with the signing of the Treaty of Rome, the landmark agreement that gave birth to the European Community.[16] While the European Community would limit some forms of industrial policy, especially those using the tools of trade protection, it left significant leeway for industrial policy to continue functioning. Using that leeway, the Third Plan focused on increasing investment and productivity as well as balancing the national accounts (Howell 1992). It was also the first plan to use input-output tables and to rely on a modern system of national accounts (Estrin and Holmes 1983).

None of this modernization of planning, however, undermined the pluralist approach that the Fourth Republic took to planning. Indeed, Bauchet (1962) counts nineteen modernization commissions that took part in the planning process, with a total of 612 members. Of these, 136 were government officials, 206 were business leaders, 82 came from farmers organizations or trade unions, 13 from the financial world, and the rest were technical experts and representatives of other professions (Bauchet 1962). Another nearly 2500 people participated in planning through the more specialized working parties and other institutions. But the Third Plan's efforts were interrupted early as the crisis over Algeria gathered steam, ultimately resulting in the collapse of the Fourth Republic and the coming of the Fifth.

Planning is not the only area where the pluralist structure of industrial policy during the Fourth Republic is visible. Indeed, Kuisel (1981) points out that private interests were represented on fully 5000 different state consultative committees in the 1950s, facilitating state-private cooperation in nearly all policy areas. Pluralism can also be seen in the system of *pantouflage*, where senior French administrators, especially members of the elite Corps d'état, would leave their public role to take leadership jobs in the private sector (Vinen 1995, Suleiman 1974). The similar social background of senior state and business leaders made multiple, uncoordinated bargains between specific industries and specific state ministries possible. More than that, there is strong evidence that businesses and business groups wielded tremendous power in the National Assembly, not least in their ability to provide campaign funding for politicians (Ehrmann 1957).

Industrial Policy and Planning in the Fifth Republic

French planning continued under the Fifth Republic, but in an altered form. The state had centralized, as discussed in the previous chapter, and so found itself in a position to dictate terms to business and labor, leading to statist industrial policy. President de Gaulle and most of his advisors were ideologically committed to planning and focused even more than the Fourth Republic on encouraging intensive, high productivity growth (Balassa 1981), though as we shall see their efforts did not always meet with success.

With the European Economic Community opening markets, the Fifth Republic was also much more concerned about enhancing France's international productivity under the strict rules of the treaty (Keeler 1981a, Loriaux 1999, Hall 1986). In this context, a 1960 ministerial note highlighted the need to accommodate the newly created institutions in designing and implementing the Fourth Plan, but it also made clear that the French government would find a way to implement its preferred policies:

> The Commissariat du Plan will place an emphasis on the necessity of harmonizing the domestic political economy in the Europe of the Six as well as in the community. In the absence of such harmonization, considered as a non-negligible means of realizing the objectives of the plan, the Economic Council advocates the maximum utilization, within the limits permitted by the Treaty, of regulatory, fiscal, customs, and budgetary measures, or of credit.[17]

A good sense of the new regime's attitude to planning can be found in a discourse by de Gaulle, as quoted by his advisor Peyrefitte (2012):

> Nothing counts more than the Plan. The management of territory must be closely subordinated to it. Nothing is more important than the Plan. Neither the management of the district of Paris, nor the management of territory, outside the Plan. Neither the growth of salaries, nor the increase of vacation and the reduction of worktime, outside the Plan. The Plan always allows us to stay focused. Everyone agrees with its broad lines. Everyone must now stick to it. To every demand, we can respond: "Impossible, the Plan doesn't foresee it." We must create a mystique of the Plan. Do you hear, Peyrefitte? The Plan is salvation.[18]

The Third Plan—which had been created under the Fourth Republic—was revised by Jacques Rueff and his colleagues at the CGP and Finance Ministry, and it ran through 1961 (de Gaulle 1971). The Fourth Plan, which extended from 1962 to 1966, was the first to be articulated fully by the Fifth Republic. Contrary to what we might expect, the new plan continued to create modernization commissions, and indeed expanded their number, and it gave parliament the right to vote earlier on the plan.[19] That said, as the theory would predict, de Gaulle and his government took much more centralized control of the planning process, weakening the CGP and enhancing the role of the Ministry of Finance (Hall 1986, Aujac 1986, Vinen 1995). While the modernization commissions were expanded in number, their influence was limited while personal relationships between the state and specific businesses grew in significance. Moreover, as I discussed in the previous chapter, the French National Assembly itself had lost much of its authority under the new constitution, dominated as it was by the government. Seeking plan approval from that body is therefore a poor indicator of any increased power that the legislature might have enjoyed.

The Fourth Plan is often seen as breaking the mold of the first three plans, which is not surprising given the altered political and economic circumstances in which it was created and implemented. Among other things, the Fourth Plan shifted attention from France's basic industries and toward emerging areas of the industrial economy such as chemicals and electronics (Howell 1992). For example, the new prime minister, Michel Debré, noted in his memoirs (1984) that, as the Fifth Republic took power, he wanted to focus planning more on targeting strategic firms and industries, for example in nuclear energy, airports, and naval construction. This interest in high technology was also displayed during the early years of the Fifth Republic by the intensive discussions within the prime minister's office over how to grow the electronics industry in France.[20]

Moreover, the emphasis on maintaining the balance of payments became clearer as international markets opened and as the role of the Finance Ministry eclipsed that of the CGP (Schmidt 1996). Indeed, a letter from Prime Minister Debré to the President of the National Assembly, Jacques Chaban-Delmas, made very clear that the Ministry of Finance was in charge of developing the Fourth Plan.[21] The same was true for the Fifth Plan, which internal French documents describe as being created as follows:

> 1959/60: Preparatory studies made by the Commissariat General
> 1960: Initial directives of the government
> End of 1959: Opinion of the section of the plan from the Economic and Social Council
> End of 1960 to beginning of 1961: Establishment of the reports of the Modernization Commissions
> End of 1961: Arbitration and adoption by the government
> November 1961: Adoption by the Economic and Social Council[22]

Two new approaches were especially characteristic of the Fourth Plan and those that followed: (1) a new emphasis on firm-level rather than sectoral level interventions, and (2) an obsession with consolidation and mergers (Howell 1992, Balassa 1981). The Fifth Republic eschewed the more sectoral and cooperative strategy of the Fourth Republic, preferring instead to channel state support to a small number of large businesses in an effort to create "national champions" (Hall 1986, Zysman 1977, Schmidt 1996). For example, Prime Minister Debré (1984) mentions in his memoirs the monthly meetings he scheduled with key business leaders, highlighting the high-level one-on-one interactions with firms that characterized Fifth Republic efforts to create large, internationally competitive firms.

As the official planning document itself stated, "the Fifth Plan proposes . . . the creation, or the reinforcement where it already exists, of a small number of *corporations or groups of international scale* capable of confronting foreign business groups . . ."[23] I argue that this strategy, far from representing the influence of major corporations, indicated instead the ability of the French state to do whatever it wanted with industrial policy. Indeed, there were a sparse sixty mergers from 1950 to 1958, but nearly triple that number during the first seven years of the Fifth Republic (Howell 1992). And during the 1960s there was a 20% increase in firms employing more than 1000 people among medium and large enterprises (Balassa 1981).

The cohesion of state institutions, and the weakening of the National Assembly, meant that business associations were no longer able to wield as much power over the policies that affected them (Hall 1986, Zysman 1977, Schmidt 1996).[24] The CNPF lost influence, and the state, sometimes relying on personal connections between senior officials and business leaders, dealt more directly with individual businesses. This declining influence is reflected in the fact that business associations generally opposed mergers but were nevertheless forced to accept them. It can also be seen in the apparent decline in significance of the consultation institutions of planning. For example, although the Fifth Plan took regionalism more seriously than did prior plans, the Commissions du développement régional (CODER) created to facilitate decentralized consultation were ignored by the centrally appointed prefects to the point that the CNPF rarely took part.[25]

Individual businesses targeted by the state were not entirely without influence, of course, and there were cases where they resisted state initiatives that they disliked (Hayward 1986, Cohen and Bauer 1985, 135). But overall, it was the state which called the shots, as evidenced by the fact that many mergers orchestrated by government officials did not correspond with the existing market strategies of firms. For example, the state pushed Elf Aquitaine to diversify unsuccessfully into pharmaceuticals and chemicals, and it motivated Pechiney—an aluminum firm—to try dyes and chemicals. It also forced French firms into acquiring other French firms to avoid foreign takeovers, for example requiring CII to accept Alcatel as a major shareholder (Goyer 2008). In the final analysis, the state was able to select which firms to assist and which to ignore, something that would have been impossible if state institutions were more fragmented or business institutions more cohesive. As de Gaulle himself put it to his advisor Peyrefitte (2012):

> I've seen the union leaders. I've seen the representatives of business. Descamps, Bothereau, Villiers have all come to see me in their capacity as individuals, not as syndicalists or in the company of syndical-

ists, but alone and as individuals. These are people who know we are right. But they don't dare to speak nor act as if they are on our side. We can't count on them. We must take the decisions, explain them, and impose them.[26]

Industrial Policy: Assessing the Theory

As the theory would predict, French industrial policy and planning during the Fourth Republic took a pluralist form, with individual firms and industries cooperating with different state institutions to promote incremental upgrading. This pluralist structure can be observed both in the development of the plans and in their implementation.

Turning first to the planning process of the Fourth Republic itself, the first steps were undertaken by the CGP and, given the CGP's modest size, other state institutions such as the Ministry of Finance and the French statistical service, INSEE (Bauchet 1962, Hackett and Hackett 1965, Rioux 1987). These institutions would put together a broad outline for the plan, construct the macroeconomic model, and consider the sources of finance. The heart of the planning process would then shift to the modernization commissions. As discussed above, state administrators, business leaders, outside experts, labor representatives and others served on these commissions, which were formed to discuss the planning needs of specific industries and sectors. Each of the commissions created a sectoral plan which was, in its turn, incorporated into the national plan.

Once the CGP and the planning apparatus had produced a national plan, it was reviewed by the Conseil supérieur du plan, a national representative organization formed at the same time as the CGP to oversee and critique the plan. Nord (2010) highlights well both the influence and the broad members of the Conseil, which included, for the First Plan, most of the primary players in government and the private sector. These included, in addition to Monnet and the key government ministers, Jouhaux from the CGT, Ricard from the CNPF, Lamour from the CGA/FNSEA, and Gingembre from the CGPME. The plan was then reviewed and revised by the National Economic Council, another broadly representative group created to opine on economic policy more generally (see Mendès-France 1963), and ultimately (after the First Plan) by the National Assembly.

As discussed above, French planning followed the logic of an "économée concerté" rather than the logic of command as implemented in the Soviet context. For this reason, planning was indicative, using financial incentives and moral suasion to convince private actors to follow its dictates. Critical to this approach was the legal basis allowing the plans to be funded off budget, giving them considerable autonomy. Without these quasi-independent means of financing, ultimately embodied in the FDES, the careful, multilevel creation and implementation of the plans would have risked diversion by political interests (Bauchet 1962). Also critical to the successful functioning of the plan was the nationalization of France's major deposit banks, making it possible for the authorities to direct monies toward sectors of the economy earmarked in the plans for increased resources (Zysman 1977).

Both the formation and implementation of the plans during the Fourth Republic reveals a pluralist structure of decision-making, in accordance with the theory. The institutions of planning, as discussed above, were highly fragmented. There were multiple institutions at the sectoral level, including those represented on the influential modernization commissions, and there were also multiple power sources at the center, including the CGP, Prime Minister's Office, Ministry of Finance, Conseil supérieur du plan, Economic Council, and National Assembly. Moreover, each of these organizations were internally fragmented and could hardly claim to embody economy-scaled corporatist bargains.

The process allowed each of these stakeholders a role, to a greater or lesser degree, in the formation and implementation of the plans. This was especially critical because of the need for information sharing between business and the state, identified by Evans (1995) and other scholars as indispensable for success. This form of cooperation and information sharing happened at the sectoral level first and foremost, making structural adjustment less likely but aiding in the gradual upgrading of specific firms and industries. The state, in this system, was able to use the policy tools at its disposal to efficiently aid industry in moving up the value chain.

So far, I have focused primarily on the institutions of upgrading. These institutions, however, were backed by micro-coalitions of key stakeholders, though in the Fourth Republic context it can be difficult to separate the coalitions from the institutions. In general, members of modernization commissions were not formally representing their businesses, but they could count on the support of their businesses and business associations, at least most of the time. The same principle pertained to the representatives of the state. There was fragmentation across ministries, civil service corps, and political parties, but there were leaders in each of these institutions which stood behind the planning institutions, sharing their goals to ensure the upgrading of the French economy.

The Fifth Republic was very different. While the institutions of planning continued to exist and to function, real power had shifted to the executive branch. Fragmented business associations and firms, not to mention labor unions, were unable to influence the planning process as they had under the Fourth Republic. In other words, as power centralized in the state and especially in the executive, the nature of upgrading coalitions began to shift and cohere. With planning power in the hands of elite bureaucrats and politicians, most in the resurgent Finance Ministry, the traditional institutions of planning, though still present, lost their place as the locus of upgrading. The fact that they continued to operate is not as surprising as it may seem; the theory predicts a lag between transformations in the structure of upgrading coalitions and changes in the more formal institutions that carry out policy. With the end of the Fourth Republic, however, the upgrading coalitions had narrowed, and real upgrading would henceforth occur between the state and individual firms, a relationship that was very much unbalanced and statist.

In this section, I have laid out how upgrading coalitions and institutions in industry have evolved in postwar France as a function of changing patterns of state and interest group fragmentation. The historical evidence provides support for my theory, showing how the nature and outcomes of upgrading policy can evolve with the institutions that create it. More specifically, it is clear that industrial policy under the Fourth Republic was pluralist in form, with multiple representatives of the state and of business (and to some extent labor) cooperating at the sectoral level to create planning policy. These interactions occurred in formal institutions such as the modernization commissions, and they also occurred informally through a variety of other mechanisms. All of these efforts were themselves underpinned by the presence of informal micro-coalitions of powerful actors, some of whom were the very business leaders and civil servants acting in the formal institutions. By contrast, upgrading efforts in the Fifth Republic were considerably more statist, with the centralization of state institutions allowing the CGP and the ministries to dictate terms to individual firms. The state used these powers especially to encourage consolidation among firms in an effort to create "national champions," even when these consolidations made little business sense. In the next section, I turn to upgrading policy in agriculture.

Agricultural Policy in the Fourth Republic

The FNSEA, as noted earlier, was made up primarily of individual farmers, each of which was smaller than most of the businesses which formed the CNPF. Perhaps ironically, the small size of the organization's component groups may have made it easier for the FNSEA to speak with a single voice during the early postwar period. Individual farmers, especially smaller ones, largely understood that they would be powerless outside the context of a national agricultural organization, and so were more incentivized than individual businesses to coordinate with the FNSEA (see Wright 1964).

Another unifying factor for the FNSEA was the significant material services to farmers that it undertook through its extension programs. But more importantly, during the early postwar years, the FNSEA was able to keep its constituent units intact by focusing largely on keeping prices high and stable, something on which all producers could agree (Keeler 1987, Wright 1962). This strategy, as we will see, maintained the organization's cohesion, but did so at the expense of any significant efforts to modernize the agricultural sector. Such an approach was not available to the business community, at least after communism seemed to be less of a threat, ensuring that agriculture would remain significantly more cohesion than business.

With this in mind, the evidence indicates that French agricultural policy under the fragmented Fourth Republic was dominated by an effort to appease the country's highly organized agricultural interests in their demands for costly price supports (Keeler 1981a, Rioux 1987). The willingness of French authorities to ignore the need for land reform in favor of supports accords well with the theory's predictions of agricultural dominance.

Agriculture was not among the key industries in the Monnet Plan, though the related sector of agricultural machinery was included. This absence seems especially surprising given the general understanding in postwar France that agriculture was highly inefficient, that indeed France was facing a crisis of agricultural modernization (see Debré 1984). This crisis was especially acute in the South, where innumerable marginal farms struggled to make a profit. Indeed, while there were some highly efficient farms in the North of France and in the Paris region, modern techniques and especially mechanization were not very widespread (see Keeler 1987).

In this situation, state leadership would likely have been necessary to bring the industry into the future, at least in the most backward farming areas. Unfortunately, during the Fourth Republic, the state was too weak to force any difficult changes on agriculture that would have increased its productivity and upgraded it to higher efficiency. This is likely one reason that agriculture was largely neglected in planning, at least in its early years.

A French report delivered to the GATT in early 1959 (before the new Fifth Republic had time to change policy) described the agricultural policy of the Third Plan and the late Fourth Republic as follows:

> The main objectives of agricultural policy are to raise the standards of living of the farming population, and therefore, to increase income from farm holdings and to lower productions costs. The General Aims, as set out in the Third Modernization and Equipment Plan (1957–61) are further to expand agricultural production (20 percent in five years), to increase agricultural value added to gross national product (by Frs. 370,000 millions), to raise agricultural income, and to protect family holdings. . . . Price fixing and market organization are the main instruments for implementing agricultural policy.[27]

Along the same lines, another report to the GATT has this to say about Fourth Republic agricultural policy:

> By decree of 18 September 1957, a so-called "Four-Year Plan" was instituted for a number of basic agricultural products (such as wheat, barley, corn, industrial sugar beet, beef, pork, eggs). This decree contained specific provisions as to the scope and aims envisaged for fixing the prices of these items. In order to protect farmers against currency depreciation, it was provided that the prices for these products could be adjusted for fluctuations in accordance with an index based on 100 at 1 July 1957.[28]

The power of agriculture during this period is best demonstrated by its extraordinary influence over the National Assembly. The FNSEA formed what was by far the most powerful caucus in the National Assembly—the Independent Peasant Bloc—which counted some 130 deputies in 1951, when the leftist newspaper *Combat* facetiously proposed renaming the parliament "The National Peasant Assembly" (Wright 1964). The success of the agricultural lobby in the National Assembly was due in part to this strategy of forming a bloc rather than backing a particular party. In 1957, the FNSEA was even able to force the calling of a special session of parliament to consider a perceived crisis in agricultural prices (Wilson 1987). More to the point, the agricultural lobby was ultimately successful with its central demand of broad commodity price indexation, which it achieved in 1957, despite cost and inflation worries (Debré 1984, 75; Cleary 1989).

Another indicator of state capture during this period relates to European policy. A strong French motivation for the negotiation of the Rome Treaty and the creation of the European Community, a process which began in the closing years of the Fourth Republic, was to maintain agricultural price supports while reducing their cost to the French state (Gueldry 2001). The

Fourth Republic governments were well aware that the fiscal burden of maintaining commodity price supports would be very difficult to bear, but they also knew that they risked political suicide if they did not provide the farmers with what they demanded. The European Community seemed like a way out of the conundrum.

Agricultural Policy in the Fifth Republic

Things began to change during the Fifth Republic. The political strength of agrarian interests met its match in the newly cohesive power of the state, and neither the Fifth Republic nor the FNSEA was able to dictate its own terms to the other. France's new political leadership ended the indexation of prices and pointedly ignored FNSEA efforts to call a special session of the National Assembly (Debré 1984, Wilson 1987, Cleary 1989). Indeed, Prime Minister Debré's reaction to FNSEA's pressure on the parliament was to state that "we are no longer under the Fourth Republic."[29]

During the Fifth Republic, then, political leaders were in a better position to force changes in agriculture than they had been during the shifting coalitional politics of the Fourth Republic. As de Gaulle put it: "we must get our agriculture going in the way that our industry is already going."[30] That they chose corporatist cooperation with the FNSEA to achieve agricultural upgrading is in keeping with the matched cohesion of the public and private sectors (see Keeler 1981a and 1981b for the classic account of this choice). The cohesion of agricultural interest groups meant that even the stronger state of the Fifth Republic needed the assent of organized farming to carry out its upgrading policies. In particular, the executive institutions of the Fifth Republic, where power had shifted from the National Assembly, knew that any successful modernization policy would require agricultural cooperation to implement.

The new corporatism in agriculture was born out of a common interest in agricultural transformation shared by Fifth Republic planners and the progressive youth wing of the FNSEA, the Centre national des jeunes agriculteurs (CNJA) and the left reformist Jeunesse agricole catholique (JAC). The JAC was formed in 1929 by young farmers frustrated with the traditional, price-centered politics of the agricultural movement. These young farmers came principally from the middle peasant class and were motivated to effect more basic transformation of the countryside along social Catholic principles. After the occupation, they quickly made common cause with the like-minded CNJA, formed as the youth wing of the CGA in 1947 and then incorporated directly into the FNSEA. Indeed, many of the JAC activists joined the leadership of the CNJA, deepening their mutual role as the vanguard of agrarian reform (Cleary 1989, Wright 1964, Keeler 1987).

Realizing that the powerful FNSEA would need to be brought on board for upgrading to work, officials of the Fifth Republic reached out to the CNJA as a possible ally (Keeler 1981a, 1981b, 1987). The young agriculturalists, for their part, wanted to see syndicalism stand for more than price supports and saw cooperation with the state as a way to encourage but also cushion the changes needed in the countryside (Rioux 1987). Initially, the newfound cooperation between the state and CNJA was resisted by the leaders of the FNSEA, but they ultimately came on board with the new corporatist arrangements, especially once the CNJA leadership began to take power in the parent organization (Keeler 1987, Wilson 1987, Cleary 1989).

These new corporatist arrangements were the result of close negotiations between the state and the CNJA, and they would have been impossible without the commitment and buy-in of both parties. Of particular importance was the relationship between de Gaulle's new minister of agriculture, Edgard Pisani, and the head of the CNJA, Michel Debatisse (Pisani 1974). Indeed, Pisani's respect for the progressive young farmers was such that he noted in his memoirs (1974, 81–82) that "the agricultural youth perhaps constitutes today the most revolutionary force in France."

The new approach to agrarian reform was embodied in the Orientation Law of 1960 and the Complementarity Law of 1962, which created new institutions to oversee agricultural upgrading (Keeler 1981a, 1987). These institutions included (1) the Sociétiés d'aménagement foncier et d'établissement rural (SAFERs), which purchased new agricultural land coming onto the market and resold it to encourage the creation of larger farms, (2) the Services d'utilité agricole de développement (SUADs), which provided outreach and training in modern techniques to farmers, and (3) the Associations départementales pour l'aménagement des structures des exploitations agricoles (ADASEAs), created to oversee the increased subsidies being provided to agriculture. They also included the Chambers of Agriculture, elected bodies created under the Fourth Republic but given additional powers and funding by the Fifth Republic, which were almost always dominated by the FNSEA (Keeler 1981a, Keeler 1987, de Gaulle 1971, Cleary 1989). The cooperation between professional organizations and the state in agricultural planning is also clear from the numerous changes to the agricultural section of the 4th plan.[31]

It is notable that all of these new institutions, through which the Fifth Republic's new corporatist policy was implemented, were focused, in the end, on upgrading. The SAFERs consolidated land, ensuring the economies of scale needed for productivity, the SUADs provided access to modern farming techniques, and the ADASEAs and Chambers oversaw resources directed heavily at making the countryside more productive. This was an upgrading policy first and foremost.

The corporatist nature of the policy can be seen in the critical role played both by the state and by private interests. It was the state that created the upgrading institutions and financed them. As de Gaulle himself noted in his memoirs (1971), credits to farmers more than tripled, to 3 billion new francs, from 1958 to 1962. But it was the CNJA and its parent FNSEA which oversaw these new resources. Indeed, the FNSEA controlled up to 90% of the seats in the Chambers, and its control over the ADASEAs was so complete that Keeler (1981a) finds they were generally housed in the same building. The FNSEA also dominated the SAFERs and SUADS, in cooperation with representatives of the state (Keeler 1981a, 1981b, 1987). Clearly, as in classic corporatist systems, the state and private interests needed each other.

Over time, this system of "cogestion" made it difficult to distinguish between the powers of the state and those of the agricultural syndicate. This corporatist arrangement benefited the FNSEA by institutionalizing its power and giving it shared control over government resources, and it benefited the state by providing it a partner through which it could influence agricultural policy at the grassroots. Of course, the FNSEA lost some legitimacy among its members, as it gave up its freedom to protest and march against state policy, but its institutional power left farmers few alternatives but to cooperate with it (Wright 1964, Wilson 1987, Keeler 1981a, 1981b, 1987). Likewise, the state ceded some of its authority to the FNSEA, but in return the implementation of the modernization program was considerably smoother.

The ongoing power of the FNSEA despite the strength of state institutions in the Fifth Republic is best demonstrated in European policy. De Gaulle approved of the Fourth Republic's insistence on including agricultural subsidies in the agreements creating the Treaty of Rome and continued to view agricultural policy as a central pillar in the agreement. Moving subsidies to the European level ensured that French farmers remained somewhat insulated from market forces while sharing the fiscal burden of protection. In 1961, Michel Debré, the prime minister, put it this way in a statement to the National Assembly:

> after having very clearly specified that there exists an agricultural problem in France and, indeed, globally, it is true to say—bearing in mind the noted precautions—that the common market is crucial for France, crucial for the future solidarity of European nations, and that it must,

> in this sense, make its place as a common agricultural policy, as far as France is concerned—I repeat—because its neighbors are, by necessity, the first outlet for future surplus agriculture, and, as far as Europe is concerned, there will not be a sense of common economic prosperity if agriculture is left aside.[32]

French farmers, for their part, had by the 1960s come to value the European Community. For this reason, when they perceived de Gaulle as skeptical of the European project when he halted French participation as part of his demands to retain voting unanimity in the Council, farmers did not hesitate to punish him. A 1965 white paper of France's professional agricultural organizations stated:

> To leave unoccupied the place of France at the negotiating table is not a constructive attitude. Continuing on this path would put in question the Treaty of Rome, which was freely negotiated, freely signed, and freely ratified by France. Mandated by farmers, the agricultural professional organizations have fought for a European Community where problems can be better resolved by a common agricultural policy. They must affirm that any prolongation of the crisis in Brussels would be at the same time disruptive for agriculture and for all of the French economy.[33]

Indeed, this "policy of the empty chair" was a key reason that de Gaulle, to his shock, was forced into a second round in the election of 1965 (Moravcsik 2000, Nord 2010). Overall, however this form of corporatist cooperation was beneficial to both actors and to French agricultural transformation more broadly.

Agricultural Upgrading: Assessing the Theory

The historical analysis bears out the theory quite well. During the Fourth Republic, the state was fragmented while agricultural interests were cohesive, resulting in a captured upgrading policy. Agriculture was largely excluded from planning during this period, meaning that there were essentially no upgrading institutions in the sector. Rather, despite the backward nature of much of French farming, state policy was oriented toward financial support rather than transformation. Price supports, and ultimately indexation, were the primary components of state policy, an approach that is not surprising given the power of the FNSEA in the National Assembly and over the government. In other word, upgrading coalitions were absent, as the powerful agricultural sector used its influence to extract rents.

By contrast, when the state centralized during the Fifth Republic, a cohesive state now interacted with the cohesive agricultural interests, resulting in a corporatist upgrading policy. The French state began to work through the progressive youth wing of the agricultural sector, which was itself committed to modernization and upgrading. Eventually members of this youth wing took over the FNSEA parent organization, implementing upgrading policy on behalf of farming interests.

Agricultural upgrading was corporatist in form because it was decided and implemented by an upgrading coalition of farming interests and state actors at the national level. This centralized coalition oversaw the complex institutions that were created to ensure that upgrading was effective and smooth. It is true that there did not exist a single institution charged with upgrading in agriculture, and that this task was overseen rather by organizations dedicated to specific elements of the task. This remains, however, compatible with the theory, given the room it makes for specialized upgrading institutions under corporatism, as long as they are overseen by cohesive upgrading coalitions.

The key point, then, is that the core national coalition of state and FNSEA stood behind all of the institutions and oversaw their activities. While the state was more involved in constructing and financing these institutions, and the CNJA and FNSEA in overseeing them and carrying out their mandates, upgrading was very much a cooperative enterprise. In other words, as anticipated by the theory, the dual cohesive structure of the state and interest groups in Fifth Republic agriculture led to a corporatist approach to upgrading. The next section will address the relative success of industrial and agricultural policy during the two periods.

Comparing the Success of Industrial and Agricultural Policy in France

How does the evidence from this chapter accord with my predictions about which configurations of state-interest relations are most effective for promoting economic upgrading? Because of the complex causation that underlies economic outcomes, historical case studies may not be the best format for testing this portion of my theory. For that reason, I provide a quantitative test of success in Chapter 8. Nevertheless, a few observations are in order. My framework predicts that pluralist industrial policy under the Fourth Republic and corporatist agricultural policy under the Fifth Republic will prove more successful than the interest capture of Fourth Republic agrarian policy and the statism of Fifth Republic industrial policy.

These predictions are largely borne out by the evidence, though the case is stronger in agriculture than in industry. Industrial transformation proceeded at a rapid clip during the 1950s, when France had the fastest growing productivity levels in Western Europe. Indeed, the country's ability to come back from the stagnation of the interwar period and the destruction of World War II to produce such substantial growth in productivity and capital stock was quite extraordinary. There is good reason to believe that the fragmented cooperation between the state and major economic actors was a large part of the reason why (Kuisel 1981, Vinen 1996, Sheahan 1963, Estrin and Holmes 1983, Shonfield 1965). By the end of the Second Plan, total output had risen by nearly a third from just three years earlier (Hackett and Hackett 1965). Interestingly, industrial production rose a full 46%, greatly outstripping the planning target, while agriculture underperformed slightly, only achieving 19%. This is consistent with the theory's expectation that industrial policy should outperform agricultural policy under the Fourth Republic.

Further, as the theory would expect, the most success during this period came not from any fundamental structural transformation of the French economy, but rather from the incremental upgrading of existing industries. This success was born, at least in part, from the information sharing and coordination that occurred through the decentralized planning apparatus. The dual fragmentation that characterized the period ensured that stakeholders—operating at the sectoral level and coming from both the state and private interests—were able to coordinate effectively and take the actions necessary for upgrading.

By contrast, the less cooperative industrial policy of the de Gaulle years, while it did enjoy some successes, also saddled the French economy with a series of large, unproductive firms. Indeed, many scholars, among them Adams (1989), Eichengreen (2007), Hall (1986), Schmidt (1996), Zysman (1977), Cohen and Bauer (1985), and Berger (1981a), have emphasized the weak results of the national champions policy. Notable examples of the failure of the policy to yield benefits include the chemical (Cohen and Bauer 1985) and computer (Zysman 1977) industries, where the state intervened to compel changes in the market strategies of specific companies. In neither of these instances did this intervention produce products capable of success on international markets. At particular risk of failure were firms created from forced mergers, which often put together two or more companies with little inherent compatibility (Cohen and Bauer 1985). One well-known example of this dynamic is the computer firm CII, which was created by the French state under the 1966 Plan Calcul. As Zysman (1977) and Fasteau and Fletcher (2024) show, state backing for new computer firms was driven primarily by an ideology of national greatness and a desire for France to become a leader in the newest and hottest industries. Unfortunately, CII (which later merged with Bull), despite some successes, never became a leader in computer technology and was ultimately sold off.

The fundamental problem with upgrading policy during this period emerged from the ability of state actors to enforce their policy preferences, which were often ill-informed, over business objections. The idea that creating large industries was a desirable outcome in its own right, apart from any specific efficiencies that size might generate, took hold among the Gaullist elite (see Berger 1981a). Unfortunately for the French economy, forced consolidation often backfired. In many cases consolidation was merely financial, and therefore did not produce any gains in productivity. In other cases, targeted firms were forced to expand outside of their core competencies into areas where they possessed little experience and knowledge. In the worst cases, the policies of the Fifth Republic prevented industries from moving into niche areas where they could compete globally. Instead, as in computers, the state insisted on French companies making high profile goods rather than the less "exciting" products where they could flourish.

This study formally ends in 1968, but it is worth considering for a moment later efforts in industrial upgrading associated with the statist Fifth Republic. To correct the problems that had come before, each of de Gaulle's successors as president—the Gaullist Georges Pompidou, the liberal Valéry Giscard d'Estaing, and the socialist François Mitterrand—developed distinct approaches to industrial policy. Pompidou developed the "plans sectoriels," focused on rescuing French competitiveness in declining sectors such as textiles and steel (Fasteau and Fletcher 2024, 211). Giscard, with his more pro-market orientation, reoriented policy toward a "politique des creneaux" (Adams and Stoffaës 1986). The idea was to zero in on niches where success could be had, rather than to attempt to rescue declining industries. And Mitterrand, whose victory as leader of the Socialist Party was a watershed for French history, adopted a "politique des filières" focused on developing the links between upstream and downstream industries in French industrial policy (Fasteau and Fletcher 2024, 215).

While it cannot be said that any of the three presidents followed their own strategies with perfect consistency, the political economy of this period does point to an effort by each administration to learn from the mistakes of the past. In other words, while the structure of statism, as defined by the theory, remained relatively constant, industrial policy varied. This dynamic continued during the 1990s and after, when the increasing integration of the European Union and of global markets more generally put pressure on French leaders to make their upgrading policy more market-conforming. Indeed, an early sign that defying the market might pose dire consequences came during the first years of Mitterrand's presidency, when a backlash forced the socialist leader to abandon and partially reverse his policy of nationalization (Schmidt 1996). More recently, however, Macron, while conforming his policy to market pressures, has refocused French policy on upgrading to a degree unseen since the 1960s. I provide a brief summary of this new orientation in the conclusion.

Contrary to what the theory might expect, French industrial policy also enjoyed a number of successes during the Fifth Republic. Some of these owe their origins to our period of study but only came to fruition later, while others were products of later administrations. Perhaps the most extraordinary of these successes was the growth of the French nuclear industry, first after de Gaulle's rejection of NATO and accelerating in the wake of the 1973 oil shock (Peyrefitte 2012, Fasteau and Fletcher 2024). France is now recognized as a key global innovator in nuclear energy and ranks as one of the world's leading exporters in the sector (Loriaux 1999). The 1970s also saw the birth of France's most successful national champion, Airbus, which would become one of the world's two major producers of airliners. It was born as part of a cooperative arrangement between the French, West German, and British governments, though France has long been the larger player (Zysman 1977, Fasteau and Fletcher 2024). A third triumph of Fifth Republic industrial policy was high-speed rail, where France finds itself consistently among the top global providers (Fasteau and Fletcher 2024).

How can we explain this variation in approach and success, given the ongoing statism of industrial policy in France? What does it mean for the theory? First, the structure of upgrading in Fifth Republic France has remained consistently statist, as predicted. Changes in policy are driven not by corporatist bargains or business initiative but by state action. Moreover, as discussed above, industrial policy during the period did indeed produce many inefficient firms and extend the life of many others. But the French experience also shows that French policymakers were capable of learning from their mistakes (at least sometimes) and of incubating success. The structure of policymaking complicated industrial policy, but it could be overcome at times to yield success.

The story for agricultural is more straightforward. Agricultural policy under de Gaulle succeeded in promoting upgrading in a way that Fourth Republic agrarian policy was not able to do (Keeler 1987, Wright 1964, Cleary

1989). The interest dominance of the Fourth Republic led to an agrarian policy focused on price supports, but which ignored the underlying problems of French agriculture, especially the surfeit of small, unproductive farms. The FNSEA had little interest in bearing the costs of a tough adjustment, and its power over the state gave it little incentive to do so. Productivity did grow during the Fourth Republic, but many small and inefficient farms remained (Rioux 1987).

The advent of the Fifth Republic put a strong state in power that was able to force upgrading by aligning with, and ultimately empowering, progressive interests within the agricultural movement. The FNSEA became a partner in successful transformation, helping to tackle the problems of the countryside while softening the difficulties that come with change. As de Gaulle noted (1971), the first five years of the Fifth Republic saw agricultural output rise by nearly a third at the same time that the number of farms declined from 2.2 million to 1.9 million. In this sense, as the theory would expect, transformation in the agricultural sector was broad and deep, representing real structural change. This outcome would likely not have been possible with a cohesive, corporatist form of state-interest group relations.

Conclusions from the French Case

Upgrading in postwar France has provided a powerful opportunity to test the theory and its causal mechanisms across all four structures that it predicts. The historical evidence, as we have seen, largely supports the expectations of the theory. Industrial policy during the Fourth Republic was pluralist, with a fragmented French state cooperating effectively with fragmented business interests to promote recovery from the ravages of war and ultimately a huge leap in efficiency. As predicted, this upgrading took the form of microcoalitions of specific state and private actors, manifested through the fragmented upgrading institutions, and in particular modernization commissions, that were created as part of the planning process. Upgrading during this period was not primarily about restructuring the French economy as a whole, but rather concerned with incremental upgrading in existing firms.

Fifth Republic industrial policy was different and less effective. It was characterized by a statist system, with a newly cohesive government apparatus confronting a still fragmented business elite. In this environment, while the institutions of upgrading remained, the coalitions backing them were replaced by state power. The information sharing and beneficial trade-offs that had characterized industrial policy during the Fourth Republic gave way to a state-dominated policy of mergers in an effort to create national champions. As we have seen, while this policy could boast some successes, it was largely inefficient. Firms were often forced to make decisions by state officials that made little sense economically.

Agricultural upgrading was the reverse—ineffective during the Fourth Republic and much more successful during the Fifth. In the immediate postwar years, the fragmented state confronted a cohesive front of agricultural interests. As a result, policy was captured and focused on providing rents to farmers through price supports rather than much needed modernization. Both upgrading coalitions and upgrading institutions were largely absent.

By contrast, during the Fifth Republic, the state had become cohesive and could interact with the powerful agricultural lobby on equal terms. This balance led to corporatist arrangements in agriculture, with central state officials and leaders of the CNJA and ultimately the FNSEA cooperating in a mutual effort to transform the countryside. This centralized upgrading coalition oversaw a new series of upgrading institutions, financed largely by the state and controlled largely by agricultural interests, which effectively restructured farming in the country.

In the final analysis, then, the structures of the state and key interest groups combined to inform both the structure and success of upgrading policy, as anticipated by the theory. In the next chapter, we turn to the case of India across time to evaluate the utility of the theory in a very different environment.

FIVE

India

Upgrading and the "Tryst with Destiny"

In this chapter and the next two, I explore the theory's utility in a developing country case.[1] India is ideal for this purpose because, from its independence in 1947 to the present, the country has evolved from a low-income to a middle income country, dealing with the growth problems particular to both along the way. Moreover, India is a major country to understand in its own right, accounting for more than 15% of the world's population. India was also among the first post-colonial countries to implement comprehensive central planning, an approach which it largely (though not entirely) abandoned in the 1990s due to stagnant growth rates. If the theory can be found to illuminate India's development trajectory, it will buttress the argument considerably.

Both the sources of India's past economic failure and its current economic success have generated a great deal of debate, and indeed disagreement, among scholars. To take two prominent examples, Kohli (2004) classifies India as a "fragmented-multiclass" state, one where social and political divisions impede the achievement of development goals. By contrast, Evans (1995) emphasizes India's failure to fully achieve "embedded autonomy," where a strong state is nevertheless enmeshed in myriad productive linkages to the private sector. In these chapters, I will argue that both scholars are correct for different periods of India's political and economic life.

My hope is that the case study will serve to highlight how the complexities of the real world might, or might not, fit with the expectations of the theory. After all, no intellectual construct can explain everything that happens on the ground in a real-world political environment, especially one as multifaceted as

India. For that reason, it is critical to dive deeply into the details of a particular case to evaluate the strengths and weaknesses of the theory.

My focus in this chapter and the next two is on exploring the theory's explanatory power for India's development in industry and services, excluding a deep discussion of agriculture for reasons of space. More specifically, I examine India across four periods in its post-independence life. Across all of these periods, I argue, India was characterized by fragmented business and labor interests, meaning that the driver of change in upgrading was the structure of the state. This structure, although remaining constant on paper, varied considerably over time.

As we will see, India from 1947 to about 1969 was governed by a fragmented and decentralized dominant party—the Indian National Congress, or Congress Party. In 1969, several years after the death of Jawaharlal Nehru, his daughter Indira Gandhi, then serving as prime minister in her own right, split the Congress Party. She walked away with the loyalty of its parliamentary delegation, leaving the Congress Party organization as a separate entity. After winning the elections that year, she governed through a now centralized and cohesive (though institutionally weak) state apparatus, drawing on personal appeals to remain in power. This strategy reached its apotheosis with the brief period of authoritarian "Emergency" government from 1975 to 1977, and continued (apart from a short time of opposition rule) under Indira Gandhi and her son Rajiv through the late 1980s.

This period of centralized and cohesive Congress rule collapsed after the party lost power in 1989. When it returned to office two years later, with Narasimha Rao in the prime minister's chair, the Congress was forced to rule as part of a minority government. From this point until the 2014 landslide election of a Bharatiya Janata Party (BJP) government under Narendra Modi, the current prime minister, India was governed by coalitions led by three different parties or party groups. Government therefore became considerably fragmented vis-à-vis what it had been during the period of Congress dominance under the Gandhi family. This fragmentation, however, had different roots from that during India's early years, resulting not from a decentralized dominant party but rather from the absence of a dominant party altogether.

The fourth and current period began in 2014 with the election of Narendra Modi and the return of the BJP, this time in a much more dominant position than it had enjoyed during its earlier years in power. This dominance only increased in the 2019 elections, with the BJP able to win an astonishing 55% of seats in the Lok Sabha, or Indian Parliament. Moreover, the BJP has succeeded in extending its control to many of India's largest state governments, most notably that of Uttar Pradesh. At the moment, therefore, the extent of BJP control has begun to rival that enjoyed by the Congress Party before the 1990s.

How did these changing political winds influence the structure and success of upgrading policy in India? The earliest period was characterized by a dominant but fragmented Congress Party interacting with fragmented private interests. Upgrading policy from 1947 to 1969 was conducted through the "Congress System" (Kothari 1964), where state and local party elites bargained over the form and distribution of government development benefits. In particular, the Second Five Year Plan, a comprehensive approach to industrializing India, was created and implemented during this period, and it was overseen by a "National Development Council" made up of state and national elites. While India's economic policy was characterized by a fair degree of clientelism during this period, economic growth was also quite high, at 4.4% (Das, Erumban, and Mallick 2021). As expected, therefore, upgrading policy during these early years can be classified as pluralist and, within certain bounds, successful.

Once the Congress Party centralized under Indira Gandhi, economic policy became a top-down affair. State and local officials lost their influence, and the system began to focus less on development and upgrading and more on pure clientelism, which had become a necessary part, in the absence of grassroots party institutions, of Gandhi's efforts to remain in power. The system, then, was one of statism, and the economy suffered as a result, with annual economic growth declining to an average of 3.0% per annum (Das, Erumban, and Mallick 2021).

The fragmentation of the Indian political system that occurred in the late 1980s and early 1990s brought with it pluralist economic policy once again, though with a more interparty character than had existed before. Though non-institutional factors also played an important role, the 1990s were the decade of India's economic take-off, with growth accelerating to an annual average of 6.4% between 1992 and 2014 (World Bank 2021). More than that, India's high-value-added software industry, which was nurtured in the 1980s, also became globally competitive, a sure sign of success in upgrading.

Since the advent of BJP dominance in 2014, it appears that India's new cohesive and centralized form of government has not been able to practice corporatism in an efficient way, due to the weakness of private interests. Instead, while it is still early to draw any definitive conclusions, we are likely witnessing the return of a statist approach to upgrading policy. More than that, the current Indian government is focused much more on questions of national identity and religion than it is on economic development, and its strength and cohesion allows the issue of upgrading to be deprioritized.

Notably, since 2015, with the exception of a 2021 bounce-back, growth in India has experienced a downward trajectory (World Bank 2021).

The Structure of Private Interests: Fragmented

Throughout the history of independent India, business and labor interests have been fragmented—to greater or lesser degrees—in approaching the state. While it is certainly true that the history of lobby groups in India is not one of stasis, and that there is variation over time in the degree and nature of fragmentation, the fundamental reality of interest group weakness has remained.

Among business interests, a significant impediment to interest group cohesion has been India's competing "Houses." These Houses are essentially family dominated conglomerates which have traditionally exhibited reluctance in following the lead of business associations. In the early years of India's independence, for example, the powerful Tata family, leading a group of industrialists based in Bombay, opposed Congress dominance and backed the creation of an opposing free-market party, Swatantra (Herring 1999). By contrast, the Birla family took the opposite position, seeking to accommodate the Congress Party and influence economic policy from within the existing power structures.

Another source of division within India's business community tracks the divisions within Indian society itself. Historically, just as Indian businesses had tended to form around family "Houses," they have also been very much structured around caste, community, and language. As Wanjari (2022) has shown through a meticulous study of business connections in various parts of India, the traditional association of particular castes with particular employment, while certainly not determinative in modern India, still matters. Links between individuals of the same caste are mutually reinforcing in the business world, as the added trust generated by such connections encourages deeper economic relationships. The same is true for businesspeople from the same religion or linguistic group. Though, consonant with India's economic and social development, these traditional linkages matter less to business activity than they did in the past, they are nevertheless very much present. And, while caste, community, and language can unite, they can also divide, making it more difficult for firms with similar political interests to join together in approaching the state.

These divisions, as well as others such as business size and type, are reflected in the structure of India's business associations. The Federation of Indian Chambers of Commerce and Industry (FICCI) is historically India's leading association of firms. The FICCI was founded in 1927 and represented the major indigenous businesses during the British Raj. It co-existed with the Associated Chambers of Commerce and Industry (ASSOCHAM), which took its direction in the immediate post-independence period from British-owned businesses concerned that the new dispensation would be antagonistic to their interests. A third major business association, the Confederation of Indian Industry (CII) was formed in 1991, though its origins go back to the late nineteenth century. During the 1980s, CII's immediate predecessor came to be associated with the growing technology industry in India, and more generally with export-oriented businesses. This orientation continued with the 1991 reforms, as CII slowly grew to partially eclipse the traditional dominance of FICCI (see Kochanek 1974, 1995).

It is worth noting that each of these business associations amalgamated numerous local and sectoral associations and chambers (see Damodaran 2018). In this sense, the divisions across these associations are only one part of the story; internally, they were often not able to reconcile their differences to come to a single position (see Murali 2019). While there are exceptions, this dynamic also includes certain of the more recent and more specialized business associations such as biotech's AIBA (Athreye and Chaturvedi 2007). In general, therefore, Indian business interests have split along the lines of size, region, and industry, diluting their ability to communicate with the state as a single entity.

Labor interests in India have fared no better. The challenge to cohesion in working class representation arises first from the traditional association of unions with particular ideologies and political parties (Agarwala 2019). India's unions have often focused on politics more than the specific material interests of the working class, and each of the country's major political parties has an associated union. For example, the All India Trade Union Conference (AITUC) is affiliated with the Communist Party of India (CPI), the Indian National Trade Union Conference (INTUC) is an arm of the Congress Party, and the Bharatiya Mazdoor Sangh (BMS) has connections with the BJP. It is true that these unions are at times capable of taking an independent and unified stance against government actions, for example privatization programs (see Jenkins 1999, Varshney 1999, and Agarwala 2019). Nevertheless, partisan loyalties, not surprisingly, have severely compromised the independent influence of unions as an interlocutor of the state.

That said, internal divisions and political loyalties are not the only challenges faced by unions, and indeed by business associations, in India. About 93% of Indian workers remain in the informal, or "unorganized," sector.[2] Workers in this sector include small agriculturalists, operators of food stands, rickshaw drivers, cleaners, and many other professions. These individuals have never been successfully organized by an interest group, including those in the agricultural sector. For this reason, some scholars have considered even labor unions as representing a higher stratum of Indian society, those working in the formal sector who are therefore protected by labor laws. The large bulk of the Indian workforce enjoys, essentially, no representation in the councils of state beyond, perhaps, their elected politicians.

In the final analysis, therefore, India's business associations and labor unions can generally be characterized as fragmented. India's interest groups are divided by industry, region, caste, and other cleavages, both internally and across organizations, and they are also often politically committed and unable to speak independently for the constituencies they represent. Moreover, the informality of a vast portion of the Indian economy means that, even in the best of circumstances, only a small portion of economic actors can be considered organized. As we will discover later in the chapter, however, there is some variation in the effectiveness of interest representation, notably in the technology sector, and this has had important implications for India's development. Moreover, as many scholars have pointed out, there is reason to believe that Indian business associations became more influential in the wake of the 1991 reforms. As we will see, I argue that this development was not the result of stronger interest group cohesion but rather of state fragmentation and the introduction of what Kochanek (1995) called "pluralism" and Sinha (2019) named "the porous state."

1947–1969: Fragmented Congress Dominance and Successful Pluralist Planning

While the structure of private interests has remained largely fragmented, the structure of the state has evolved over time. I begin with the first twenty-two years after independence, when the Congress Party was dominant but was itself fragmented and decentralized, an amalgamation of the state and local elites who had driven the independence movement and now wanted a role in governing the country.

India had become independent from Britain in 1947, a momentous development which presented the country's nationalist leaders with a number of difficult questions. What form should India's government take? What economic policies should the country adopt to pull the millions out of poverty? How should the Indian National Congress, the center of the national struggle for independence, transform itself into an organized political party able to contest elections in the new India? How should it relate to a national government elected from its ranks?

Virtually all of India's nationalist leaders agreed that two centuries of British colonial rule had crippled the country's economy, relegating India to the periphery of the imperial economic system (Corbridge and Harriss 2000). As the Congress manifesto for the provincial elections of 1945 put it, "India, under British rule, has been progressively ruralised, many of her avenues of work and employment closed, a vast mass of the population thrown on the land, which has undergone continuous fragmentation, till a very large number of holdings have become uneconomic."[3] India's new leaders inherited a country afflicted by massive poverty, with an average life expectancy of only 40 years.[4] Broad recognition of the extent of India's economic problems, however, did not translate into a consensus on how to address these problems. Instead, three competing visions of India's economy emerged.

In keeping with his ideas about a decentralized state, Mohandas Gandhi advocated a village economy based on local industry and productive capacity. Sardar Patel, a powerful rival to Nehru in India's first cabinet, favored the private sector and supported a market-based approach to development (Frankel 1978). Jawaharlal Nehru, by contrast, preferred a policy of centralized planning and import substitution. Influenced by the Soviet experience, Nehru believed India would achieve social equality and economic greatness only through the development of heavy industry (Brass 1994). The economy would be driven by the state, which would see to it that India's developing economic strength was used to benefit the poor. Nehru's vision triumphed, quickly achieving broad support among the country's elite. An India based upon the principals of democracy, secularism, and socialism—with Nehru at its helm—was born.[5] And this India would prioritize industrialization and the upgrading of the economy from one dominated by low efficiency agriculture to one that could compete with the industrial powerhouses of the day. In its attempt to achieve this goal, as we shall see, it would make use of a particularly rigorous form of industrial policy.

A key question confronting the Congress leadership at the dawn of independence was how the party should transform itself to effectively contest elections in free India. As a congressman noted on the eve of the first general election in 1952, "the work of administration is not the same as the work of agitation" (Mahtab 1951/2). Before independence, the party contained a highly disparate mix of groups, all united in their desire to see the British go. As Myron Weiner (1967) argued, the Congress was widely aggregative from its origins, channeling the views of an extraordinary array of interests into its policy decisions. After the departure of the British, however, it was debatable whether any party could maintain the support of communists and capitalists, Brahmins and Dalits, urbanites and farmers. For the Congress to become a political party in a self-governing India, would it not have to develop a specific, cohesive ideology and expel those who objected?

Ultimately, despite its adaptation to Indian independence, the early post-independence Congress would remain ideologically heterogeneous and would continue to aggregate the disparate preferences of numerous local and state elites. It continued, in a sense, to function as a mass movement even as it contested elections as a political party. It was this Congress Party and this Congress government that moved the country toward a planning approach to upgrading.

In his waning years as prime minister, Jawaharlal Nehru came under increasing criticism for his handling of India's economic affairs. Observers were more and more united in their judgment that economic planning had not been the success that everyone had hoped (Corbridge and Harriss 2000; Frankel 1978; Rai and Pandy 1971). At the same time, the Congress System that had integrated and mediated conflict across India for the last decade was beginning a long, slow decline. New communal, class, and regional interests were starting to resist the power of local and state elites and the national party, and factional struggles within the Congress organization had accelerated (Frankel 1978, Kochanek 1968). A proposal launched by Kamaraj, the chief minister of Madras and future Congress president, to inject new life into the declining party organization was only partially able to arrest this decline (Corbridge and Harriss 2000; Frankel 1978; Kochanek 1968; Rudolph and Rudolph 1987; Rai and Pandy 1971).

After Nehru suffered from a stroke in January 1964, he tapped Lal Bahadur Shastri as his preferred successor as prime minister of India. Kamaraj and a coalition of other powerful party leaders, who would come to be known as the "Syndicate," backed Shastri as well, and their influence assured his election after Nehru's death in May (Frankel 1978; Kochanek 1968; Rudolph and Rudolph 1987; Rai and Pandy 1971; Corbridge and Harriss 2000). In the years that immediately followed, the Congress Party and Indian politics became even more decentralized and fragmented than they had been under Nehru. The party organization, always a source of power, grew in its influence over the government to the point where some have spoken of a Shastri-Kamaraj duumvirate (Rai and Pandy 1971). Shastri was a consummate conciliator, and during his time as prime minister, decisions were made cooperatively in the cabinet and the Congress Working Committee (Frankel 1978; Kochanek 1968). In economic policy, Shastri began to push the country toward greater openness. He was under pressure from the international aid donors who provided the foreign exchange vital to the plans, and he himself was not convinced that Nehru's approach to development had been successful. Additionally, Shastri and the Syndicate based their support on conservative rural landholders and other local elites who were opposed to agrarian reform (Frankel 1978). During his tenure, Shastri weakened the Planning Commission, supported more investment in agriculture (a move that would lead to the "green revolution"), and backed a larger role for the private sector (Frankel 1978; Corbridge and Harriss 2000; Chibber 2003).

Shastri's unexpected death in 1966 brought his tenure as prime minister to a sudden end. The vote to determine his successor pitted Indira Gandhi, Nehru's youthful daughter and a leftist cabinet member, against the senior conservative Morarji Desai. Kamaraj and the Syndicate, loath to see the independently powerful Desai as prime minister, were convinced that they could easily control the relatively inexperienced Gandhi. As a result, they supported her candidacy and engineered her election as India's third prime minister (Frankel 1978; Kochanek 1968; Rudolph and Rudolph 1987; Rai and Pandy 1971; Corbridge and Harriss 2000). It was Gandhi, as we will see in the next section, who would centralize the Congress Party—creating cohesive, national party structures—and lead India toward a statist, and considerably less effective, economic policy trajectory.

A Fragmented Dominant Party

During the Nehru era, the Congress Party dominated Indian politics, winning every federal election and controlling almost every state. The party sprawled across India's political scene, aggregating the views of local and state elites from Punjab to Madras and providing the country with direction and stability.

The 1950s saw the heyday of the so-called Congress System.[6] During this period, the Congress, while contesting free elections, met with little effective opposition from minority parties. India's democracy was preserved less through parliamentary elections than through the organization of the party itself. The preferences of sub-national elites across the country were aggregated into policy within the Congress structure, and the party possessed great legitimacy and deep organizational roots among the electorate. It served as the primary integrating institution in the country, building consensus through mediation, and support through the distribution of patronage. Opposition parties sought to influence policy through sympathetic groups within Congress rather than by contesting elections.

During the Nehru era, then, the Indian National Congress was dominant but decentralized and fragmented, giving voice to local and state as well as national elites. This fragmented structure was reflected in, among other things, the formal party organization. On paper and to a significant extent in reality, the Congress was a bottom-up organization.[7] The Congress was a mass party composed of both primary members and active members. To join as a primary member, a citizen had only to pay a small fee and refrain from joining another party. After two years, a primary member, upon additional payments and pledges, was then eligible for active membership and advancement in the party.

At the base of the party were the Mandal Congress Committees (MCCs), largely chosen by the party's primary members and responsible for a population of at most 20,000 people. Above these local committees were the District Congress Committees (DCCs), of which there were about 430 in the mid-1960s (Kochanek 1968). The DCCs comprised officials elected from the party's primary members as well as MCC presidents, members of parliament, members of the state legislative assembly, presidents of local legislative bodies, and leaders of important institutions in the district. In practice, the DCCs were often the smallest organizational units of the party to meet and take action on a regular basis.

The Pradesh Congress Committees (PCCs) occupied the next highest level in the Congress organization, overseeing the party's activities in each of India's states and union territories. Some PCC officials were elected by the party's primary membership, while others were guaranteed membership. These committees and their presidents were generally quite powerful in Congress decision-making.

At the national level, members of India's PCCs elected the president of the party and chose one-eighth of their number to constitute the All India Congress Committee (AICC). Although the AICC was formally the highest policy-making institution in the party, the Congress Working Committee (CWC) was generally considered the most important body in the national Congress. The CWC comprised members elected by the AICC and others appointed by the Congress president. In practice, Prime Minister Nehru, even when he did not hold the office of Congress president, exercised tremendous influence over the composition of the CWC.

Under Nehru, this organizational structure had real weight, and the national party leadership, while firmly in control, based its power in the consent of the party's local and state units.[8] As Weiner famously pointed out in his grassroots study of the party, Congress dominance was founded not on mobilization but on mediation and broad-based aggregation (Weiner 1967).

The decentralized party structure was a conduit for passing the preferences of sub-national elites and, to a lesser extent, the rank-and-file up to the PCCs and the CWC (Kothari 1964, Manor 1988, Chhibber and Petrocik 1990, Weiner 1967, Rudolph and Rudolph 1987, Brass 1994). As described above, each level of the party was chosen from the leadership of the level below it. Further, even the primary membership had some influence in choosing the party leadership.

The national party leadership thus could not ignore the demands of sub-national elites with independent power bases in state and local government (Sirsikar and Fernandes 1984, Kochanek 1968, Hanson 1966, and Weiner 1967). The Indian constitution delegated certain key powers to the states, and officials in state Congress governments derived their power largely from the party base rather than from the national leadership. As we will see, they were able to leverage this influence at the national level through both party and state institutions.[9] Further, with the introduction of panchayati raj in most states during the later 1950s and early 1960s, district party leaders acquired a similar independent power base in government.[10] Panchayati raj, a system of elected local councils based on traditional patterns of Indian governance, had long been advocated by Gandhians in the party. Under this system, citizens elected a village panchayat, or council, which in turn chose the members of a council at the block level, which then selected a council at the district level. The national and state governments devolved important powers, including influence over the local development apparatus, to these elected councils. As a result, village and district Congress officials, when the party controlled these councils (as it usually did), acquired significant administrative powers. Like party leaders at the state level, they were able to transform these powers into influence within the Congress system.

The formal organization of the Congress was not the only important factor in creating the party's decentralized structure. Factional struggles also strengthened sub-national Congress elites vis-à-vis the national leadership, ensuring that the party would remain decentralized. At the party base, Congress supporters were divided along factional lines. In fact, the role played by factions in Indian politics was so great that one prominent scholar referred to them as "the basic unit of the Congress Party."[11] Factions are political coalitions based on personal ties of affection and dependence that are formed to advance the self-interest of their members.[12] Factional struggles were not ideological but personal, and they could often be quite vicious. Faction leaders provided patronage to their followers, who in turn pledged their political support.

With independent local factions competing for patronage and influence, domination by the central party leadership was impossible. The chief concern of powerful factional leaders was to provide benefits to their supporters; following the national party line was a secondary issue at best. For example, H. C. Heda, a Congress member of the Lok Sabha, India's lower house of parliament, lamented the role of factional conflicts in undermining voting discipline among Congress legislators (Heda 1958).

Factional struggles also provided a strong incentive for the mobilization of voters at the grassroots level (Kothari 1964, Brass 1965, Sisson 1972). To capture local and state Congress institutions, factions had to compete for adherents, expanding party support among the electorate. When in ascendancy within the party and the government, faction leaders would then provide their supporters with patronage. Typically, key factions shared influence over District and Pradesh Congress committees, panchayati raj institutions, and state ministries. In this way, the preferences of faction members and the broad electorate were aggregated through party institutions to the party and government leadership.

The national leadership, primarily through the Congress Working Committee, mediated factional struggles within the party. Factional leaders were vital to the success of the party. Their support ensured the Congress not only their personal votes, but also the votes of their dependents (Manor 1992). The CWC sought to prevent any faction from achieving complete control over party or government institutions in a particular locale (Kochanek 1968, Kothari 1964, Brass 1994, Brass 1965). They hoped to use the factional struggles to mobilize supporters for the Congress without alienating any powerful groups. Through its role in mediation, the central party leadership remained connected to the concerns of party members and sub-national elites.

The Congress's decentralized and fragmented structure was also visible in its candidate nomination procedures. Control over candidate nominations is among the most important tools that central party leaders can wield. When citizens, general party members, or the candidates themselves control nominations, the central party leadership is usually less able to enforce its will on the party. While the Congress nomination process was not characterized by a general primary or free access to the party name, it was significantly decentralized compared to most parties and to the Congress under Indira Gandhi.[13]

When the party sought potential candidates for state and national elections, it first solicited the views of the Mandal and District Congress Committees. The state-level Pradesh Congress Committee (or the Pradesh Election Committee) might, for example, send representatives to constituencies to interview potential candidates and to speak with MCC and DCC members. Local knowledge and advice was vitally important to assess the likelihood of any individual to win. Determining the competitiveness of a potential candidate required a detailed knowledge of factional, caste, and religious divisions within a constituency, something that could not be evaluated from New Delhi or even from state capitals.

The views of the Mandal and District party leadership generally weighed heavily on the decision at the state level. After considering carefully the views of these local party leaders, the PCC would make candidate recommendations to the Central Election Committee (CEC). The CEC, drawn from the Congress Working Committee, would then consider the recommendations and produce the final list of candidates.

In states with fairly stable Congress governments, the CEC generally left the nomination decision at the Pradesh level (Kochanek 1968). When state parties were particularly faction-ridden and unstable, the CEC would involve itself more deeply in the nomination procedure. Even then, however, it was a mediator or arbitrator among competing state factions, not a central organization imposing its will on subordinates.

Clearly, then, the Congress Party under Nehru was a broadly decentralized and fragmented organization. Sub-national elites maintained independent power bases in party factions, loyal electoral support, local governing councils, and state ministries. Their preferences were aggregated up through the party apparatus, and the central leadership provided broad policy guidance while acting as a mediator of local and state interests.

1947–1969: Economic Upgrading and the Second Five Year Plan

Although the language of upgrading was not used at the time, the Congress Party leadership recognized that the Indian economy would have to undergo a fundamental transformation if the nation was to achieve true autonomy and prosperity. For most Congress leaders, not least Nehru, industrial policy, and in particular national planning, would have to form a critical part of India's post-independence economic policy.

Indeed, the Congress Party leadership began to consider a planned Indian economy at least a decade before independence. Planning advocates argued that private enterprise alone would be unable to pull India out of poverty and underdevelopment. They felt the private sector, driven by the profit motive and limited in its ability to mobilize investment, would be unable to drive rapid economic growth without the aid of the state. As Nehru himself later put it in a 1956 speech to the Lok Sabha:

> The essence of planning is to find the best way to utilize all resources—of manpower, of money and so on—and the essence of free enterprise

> is to leave these things more or less to chance. Well, if chance is a more satisfactory way of dealing with the problems of life than carefully thought out methods, then, of course, there need be no planning at all. . . . For an underdeveloped country particularly, planning is essential. It may not be so necessary in developed countries; they can perhaps do without it. But there is no other way but planning in an underdeveloped country like ours.[14]

Nevertheless, for all the influence of the Soviet Gosplan over Nehru and his supporters, they held fast to their beliefs that planning in India must be carried out democratically and that it must not involve complete state ownership of the economy. Writing to India's Chief Ministers, the highest executives at the state level, Nehru put it this way:

> Thus far we see a full-blooded socialism, if that is the right term, working in Communist countries, together with an accompaniment of authoritarian control and an absence of the democratic approach. . . . Certain economic results are undoubtedly obtained this way, but the price paid is heavy.[15]

Planning in India was to be democratic in process and result in a mixed economy.

With the ascendance of Nehru, the First Five Year Plan was inaugurated in 1951. The primary responsibility for drafting the First Plan and its successors fell to the Planning Commission, an organization with both political and technical characteristics. The First Plan was essentially a collection of projects and possessed a more liberal bent than later plans. Its focus was primarily on agriculture and infrastructure, and the sums of investment distributed through the plan, while significant, were much smaller than those allocated in future planning efforts (Hanson 1966). Export and import policy under the First Plan remained quite open, and the role of the private sector in development was clearly recognized as central. Nevertheless, the First Plan required the public sector to expand dramatically and subjected private enterprise to the tight licensing regulations established under the 1951 Industries (Development and Regulation) Act (Frankel 1978).

Only with the Second Five Year Plan of 1956 to 1961 was Nehru's vision for planning and development fully realized. The Second Plan, unlike the First, focused on heavy industry and committed India to the development path of import substitution industrialization (ISI). Under ISI, India closed its markets to the outside world and attempted to industrialize by substituting imports with domestically produced goods. The protection of high tariffs and tough import licensing, the country's planners believed, would allow India to leverage its domestic demand to improve the standard of living for all its citizens.

Many of India's leaders found ISI attractive for two reasons (Bhagwati and Desai 1970). First, widespread export pessimism existed among the country's elite, many of whom were skeptical of India's ability to compete on world markets. Second, elites believed that foreign competition would rob India of any prospect of developing its own industries if it remained committed to an open economy (Ahluwalia 1985).

The Indian strategy of import substitution, inaugurated with the Second Plan, differed in a key respect from similar ISI approaches adopted in East and Southeast Asian countries (Agrawal et al. 2000). The Second Plan emphasized the industrial production of capital and intermediate goods rather than the production of consumer goods. India would make "the machines that make machines," thus increasing its consumption and reducing its dependence in the long run. As the Planning Commission put it, "India believes . . . that its own stability, both internally and as a free, independent nation, depends on the degree to which it develops industries to produce for the nation and its people."[16]

As summarized by the Planning Commission, the Second Five Year plan was organized around four stated goals:

> (i) a sizeable increase in national income so as to raise the level of living in the country;
> (ii) rapid industrialization with particular emphasis on the development of basic and heavy industries;
> (iii) a large expansion of employment opportunities;
> (iv) reduction of inequalities in incomes and wealth and a more even distribution of economic power.[17]

The Second Five Year Plan represented a significant increase in investment financing over the First Plan. Much of this money was distributed by the federal government (usually called "the Centre") to be spent on a variety of projects, although significant sums were collected and spent by the state governments. The planners also set targets for the production of a wide variety of commodities. To ensure that India's resources were used in keeping with plan priorities, they developed an extensive system of industrial licensing. Under this system, private enterprise was forced to obtain government permission before any significant expansion, and entrepreneurs required a license before they could begin a new undertaking. Economic efficiency aside, this system of controls was necessary to ensure that investment responded to plan priorities rather than market incentives (Bhagwati and Desai 1970).

Did the Second Five Year Plan represent an effort to achieve economic upgrading? That term was not in regular circulation during the 1950s, and the plan embodied a number of goals, not least national independence and economic redistribution. It was also heavily oriented toward extensive growth through the mobilization of investment. Nevertheless, elements of the plan were clearly oriented toward upgrading, directing finance and effort away from inefficient agriculture and toward higher-value-added industries. All of this leads to two critical questions. First, how were upgrading policies formulated, given the structure of the state and private interests, and second, how successful were these policies?

Formulating Upgrading Policy: Effective Localized Upgrading Coalitions

A window into the fragmented decision-making of the time is provided by tracing the process through which the Second Five Year Plan was created and implemented. Decisions about which regions and industries would receive the all-important plan rupees were the product, along with the plan itself, of a complex, multi-level process.

At the center of this process was the Planning Commission, formed soon after the adoption of India's constitution in 1950. The Commission's purpose was:

> to assess the nation's resources, draw up a plan to use them with proper priorities and allocation, determine the conditions, machinery and adjustments needed to make the plan succeed, appraise the progress of the plan from time to time and make any recommendations necessary to facilitate it.[18]

The Planning Commission is sometimes viewed, incorrectly, as a purely technocratic body, dictating plan priorities and endeavoring to hold firm against the economically inefficient demands of politicians. In fact, the Commission embodied a mix of technical and political perspectives. During the 1950s, the Planning Commission was chaired by Nehru himself, and also included a varying number of cabinet ministers, among them the Finance Minister and the Minister for Planning. Non-ministers, including senior administrators, prominent business leaders, and well-known experts, were also represented on the Commission. Answering to these Commission members was a medium-sized staff of technical experts who drafted and redrafted the plans. The presence of the prime minister and several key cabinet ministers on the Planning Commission aimed to ensure that the ambitious national plans would not be ignored (Hanson 1966). It had the additional effect, however, of building political considerations into the planning process from the start.

Central government ministers were not the only politicians deeply involved in the planning process. In 1952, the cabinet established a body, the National Development Council (NDC), to represent formally the views of India's state governments. The Indian government hoped that endorsement of the Second Plan by state chief ministers in an official government body would add to the legitimacy of their economic program. However, the creation and structure of the NDC reflected quite clearly the organization of the Congress and would have functioned quite differently had the Congress been centralized. As we shall see, state chief ministers, and through them village and district elites, exercised tremendous influence over disbursements under the plan.

The NDC comprised the members of the Planning Commission as well as each of India's chief ministers, or heads of state government. The cabinet resolution creating the NDC gave the body such a key role that planning scholar A. H. Hanson has called it, "an advisory body which could be said to rival the Planning Commission itself in importance."[19] The NDC served as a forum through which powerful sub-national elites could influence the plan and advocate for the interests of their states. The input of the NDC often concerned the broad orientation of the plan, but also frequently consisted of state leaders applying pressure to win government finance and protected industries for their constituents.[20]

The formulation of the Second Plan began as early as 1954, more than two years before its final adoption. During the early planning stages, a series of debates were held within the Planning Commission, the cabinet, and the NDC over the broad outline of the plan. At the same time, state, district, and even village governments were in the process of formulating their own plans to be incorporated into the national document (Hanson 1966). The planning process in India, while coordinated at the national level, was carried out, to one degree or another, in cities and villages across the country. At the lowest level, it involved the formulation by elected village councils, or panchayats, of basic plans for their constituencies. Plans were also developed at the district level, generally by District Development Councils, made up of the district administrative officer, local members of the national and state legislatures, and leaders of service agencies and farming cooperatives, among others (Planning

Commission 1958). The efficacy of village and district level planning varied dramatically across the country. Often, local plans were in fact developed by state officials to satisfy New Delhi's demands for grass roots involvement. Sometimes, however, village and district officials formulated the local plans themselves and pressured state officials to advocate their projects to the Planning Commission (see Hanson 1966).

While village and district plans were being developed across the country, the states themselves were working to formulate their own plans. Caught between the plan guidelines developed in New Delhi and the demands of village and district authorities and interest groups, their task was not a trivial one. The processes through which Indian states developed their plans also varied quite significantly, with some incorporating more local and interest group consultations than others. After consultations, each state government generally submitted its draft plan to the state assembly for consideration. Despite significant variations across states, the development of state plans and the incorporation of village and district plans (when they were in fact formulated separately) frequently involved a process of logrolling among state ministries and lobbying by various powerful interests. In fact, state plans often included requests for significantly more federal money and federally financed industries than were likely to be forthcoming. State requests were inflated in part to provide chief ministers with more bargaining leverage in the NDC and in part to satisfy a seemingly endless number of local demands (Hanson 1966).

Local elites and demand groups with influence over state plans seem to have traded favors, producing documents full of requests for the central government. In the state of Andhra Pradesh, for example, the consultative Advisory Board raised the suggested total money to be spent under the plan from Rs475 crores to Rs482 crores.[21]

In July 1955, the Planning Commission and the NDC began to consider how the state plans would be incorporated into the national effort. Thus began a round of logrolling and negotiation among the state chief ministers, each advocating for the expansion of protected industries and the provision of finance to his state.[22] The state plans were so inflated that nearly two-thirds of proposed financial allocations had to be cut to meet the plan investment target (Hanson 1966). Indeed, the finance minister called into question the fiscal solvency of the plan in the NDC by arguing that foreign assistance had been grossly overestimated in plan projections. This problem, he argued, was exacerbated by the refusal of the states to raise taxes to a level sufficient to meet their component of the plan's investment finance.

No doubt in a centralized and nationally cohesive system the financial allocations incorporated into the plan would have been reduced, but in India's decentralized and fragmented system the Chief Ministers would have none of it. They blocked the efforts of the Finance Minister and the Planning Commission to cut financial outlays under the plan, and at the same time initially refused to increase taxes. If the proposals in their state plans had to be cut, they likely reasoned, at the very least they would not be cut more than was absolutely necessary. Even after the final version of the plan was published, interest group pressures on the Planning Commission forced it to increase public investment even beyond the already unrealistic target (Hanson 1966).

While the NDC was working to revise the state and national plans, the powerful Congress Party organization was holding its own discussions. On August 14, 1955, for example, the president of the All-India Congress Committee issued a circular to prepare members for a wide-ranging discussion of the plan:

> You perhaps know that the Plan Frame and the question of resources were discussed by the Standing Committee of the National Development Council on which are represented some of the Chief Ministers who are also in their political capacity our leaders. . . . Our leaders in the government are in a better position to study these questions. . . . Apart from this, I would not set any limit to constructive suggestions. . . . Nor would I like to set any limit to suggestions for the more efficient and economical implementation of the Second Five Year Plan.[23]

While the party's organizational leadership showed a willingness to defer somewhat to their colleagues in the government, they were still determined to have their say. Members of the party's influential governing body brought with them concerns about how the plan would influence their home villages, cities, and states. These views would have been aggregated up to the party leadership that controlled the future of the plan.

After six months of discussions, the Commission published the Draft Memorandum for the Second Plan, and, one month later, the Draft Outline. The Draft Outline contained the Planning Commission's first recommendations for the general shape of financial allocations under the plan. Its release began a national debate over the details of the plan, a debate carried out in the NDC, the cabinet, the Lok Sabha, the Congress Party, and numerous less official forums. In its explanation of the planning process, the Commission put it this way:

> With the approval of the [National Development] Council, the Draft Outline is published as a document for the widest public discussion

> and consideration. Comments are invited from all sections of opinion. State governments arrange for the Draft Outline to be discussed at the district level by District Development Councils and other bodies.[24]

The central and state governments consulted again with influential local elites and pressure groups, absorbing their views for the final session of logrolling before the publication of the final plan document. Meanwhile, the Congress Party met in Amritsar and used the opportunity to discuss the Second Plan draft. It passed a resolution endorsing the broad principles of the plan, and reminded the government that, "the claims of social justice, both in its individual and regional aspects, should always be kept in view and should be made through changes in economic organization and suitable administrative and fiscal measures."[25]

The upper and lower houses of the national parliament also debated the Draft Outline. As the Planning Commission put it:

> . . . at the national level, both Houses of Parliament arrange for discussion of the Draft Outline, first in a general way for a few days at a time, and then in greater detail through a series of Parliamentary Committees which individual Members are free to join. . . .[26]

The Draft Outline of the Second Plan elicited significant interest among the MPs, leading to additional demands for changes. Member comments ranged from questions about the broad structure of the plan to concerns over its effects in their constituencies (Hanson 1966).

Taking all these views into consideration, the Planning Commission, still working in consultation with state Chief Ministers on the NDC, produced the final plan document. Even this "final" document was not, however, final in any true sense, but was subjected to constant review and criticism over the plan's five years. The Lok Sabha debated it several times, and the NDC considered proposed changes, including a dramatic increase in agricultural production targets. Indeed, as already noted, the Planning Commission caved to pressure groups by increasing plan outlays to a number of economic sectors. When 1957 saw the severe balance of payments crisis made almost inevitable by unrealistic plan expenditures, the NDC again considered serious revisions to the plan. It initially rejected attempts by the Planning Commission to reduce plan expenditure from Rs4800 crores to Rs4500 crores. No chief minister wanted to sacrifice hard-bargained allocations to his state. Only Nehru's personal intervention persuaded the NDC to approve a division of finance payments into Rs4500 crores of priority outlays and Rs300 crores of less urgent outlays. Even in the midst of a foreign exchange crunch state officials and central ministers were able to continue successfully their effort to expand disbursements under the plan. As the crisis worsened, however, the Planning Commission and the finance minister pushed for a further reduction of investment to Rs4200–4300 crores. Once again, the NDC balked, but finally agreed that total outlays would stand at Rs4500 crores. In the end, the government spent Rs4600 crores during the Second Five Year Plan (Hanson 1966).

Applying the Theory

In applying the theory to this case-study, let us begin at the beginning and ask whether planning and industrial policy under Nehru can be called upgrading policy at all. As I discussed in Chapter 1, some forms of industrial policy may be oriented less toward moving up the value chain and more toward alternative goals such as promoting economic security or protecting sunset industries. Of course, most major economic interventions have multiple goals, and certainly multiple effects. In the case of early post-independence India, it is clear that upgrading was among the critical goals of India's policymakers. As the case study makes clear, Nehru and his allies were specifically dedicated to growing India's international competitiveness and, with it, India's autonomy. While they may have used the language of modernization and development, upgrading was a critical part of the plan. Without more efficient usage of India's factors of production, improving the country's international competitiveness would have been impossible.

What, then, can we say about how well the theory describes economic, and especially upgrading, policy during this period? As I have shown, the state itself was fragmented, with power shared between the government and the party apparatus; the national, state, and to some extent local governments; elites at the various tiers; and officials of the planning commission and the powerful central ministries. At the same time, interest groups and civil society in India are, in general, fragmented and weak. If the theory is correct, these organizational dynamics should have led to a dual fragmented system, one in which the formation and implementation of upgrading policy could be characterized as pluralist.

Going a bit deeper, the theory anticipates that we should observe multiple upgrading coalitions at the industrial and local level, and that these should stand behind (and possibly be integrated into) a multitude of upgrading institutions. In addition, we would expect the country to be less effective at centralized transformation of the economy but better at detailed upgrading of existing industries. Is this in fact an accurate characterization of early post-independence India?

An immediate objection is that India did indeed have a centralized plan, one developed by a single national planning commission. Is this not a classic example of corporatist or perhaps even statist upgrading policy? It is fair to say that the Planning Commission and the national plan are not anticipated by the theory, which might instead expect a more obviously pluralist upgrading system to function like the one in the United States, discussed in Chapter 8. The American system has no national planning commission, no national plan at all, but rather numerous federal agencies interacting with numerous business and private organizations in a multitude of different ways.

But, upon closer inspection, is upgrading policy in early post-independence India really that different from how the theory would anticipate dual fragmented systems to behave? Is it centralized in reality or just on paper? I argue here that in fact, this first portion of the Indian case comports fairly well with the theory's expectations. While there was indeed a national plan and a national planning commission, the actual planning process was bottom-up rather than top-down. The most important upgrading coalition comprised the state chief ministers and the prime minister who sat on the NDC, and this was incorporated into the most critical national planning institution, the planning commission. But numerous other, more local and specific upgrading coalitions existed throughout India. These were more informal and comprised local officials (state ministers, district magistrates, and so on) along with the leaders of specific firms. Their insights were incorporated into the national plan. More than that, due in part to the planning commission's relatively small size, other organizations acted as effective upgrading institutions. These included portions of the central ministries dedicated to particular industries, as well as state-level institutions.

Of course, the national plan in India, as elsewhere, was impacted by a particular governing ideology, and the development of this ideology represents an important part of the history of this period. In addition, as noted above, there was an element of rent seeking in the fragmented process, as private interests and actors at different tiers competed for more funding. Nevertheless, within the context of rent seeking and a belief that the state should take the lead in the industrialization process, institutions continued to matter a great deal. Indeed, even if the administrative process had been centralized on paper, without the NDC and lacking state and local planning, a decentralized Congress would have ensured a decentralized plan. When local and state Congress members have independent power bases, they demand a role in the process, whether formal or informal.

But was the upgrading process during this period more successful at economic transformation, as the theory would anticipate for a dual cohesive system, or did it excel at more detailed upgrading of existing industries? Indeed, was upgrading policy under Nehru a success at all? This is a complicated question, to be sure, and I will not be able to provide a complete answer to it here. There is no doubt that the intension of the Nehru government was a fundamental transformation of the Indian economy, from agrarian to industrial. Many of the industrial policy tools used by the Indian government, including the ubiquitous industrial and import licenses, were focused on this goal. And, indeed, much of the criticism that the Nehru government has since received from market-friendly thinkers—that it wasted national resources in creating uncompetitive industries at a time when India should have focused on reinforcing its comparative advantage—focuses on the dangers of (socialist) central planning.

It is true, then, that the Nehru government engaged in "central planning" oriented toward industrialization, though, as I argue above, it was a uniquely decentralized and fragmented form of central planning. It is also true that a number of industries created during this period, including of course the steel plants on which the prime minister rested so many of his hopes, did not do well in the international marketplace, at least initially. So, upgrading policy in this period could not be termed a resounding and unequivocal success.

At the same time, however, many scholars are reevaluating the long-term effects of Nehru's upgrading policy. For example, Balakrishnan (2007) revisits economic data from the period to argue convincingly that planning under Nehru promoted growth and set the stage for innovations to come. Likewise, Felipe, Kumar, and Abdon (2013) point out that India's bundle of exports is considerably more capital intensive than would be expected given its economic and demographic characteristics. This they attribute to industrial policy in the country's early years. Indeed, the average annual growth rate in India's first twenty years of independence was 4.4% (Das, Erumban, and Malik 2021), very respectable indeed if a bit shy of recent numbers.

So, scholars are beginning to recognize the benefits that industrial policy brought to India during the 1950s and 1960s, despite its drawbacks and failures. It really did increase the capital intensity of economic production in the country while deepening the knowledge base of the citizens. But efforts to transform the economy fully toward industry were not entirely successful, and newly created industries were more likely to suffer from low levels of efficiency. Greater success was had in existing industries, such as textiles, where state direction of finance allowed deeper investment than would likely have occurred in free market conditions. As a result, the evidence does support, at least partially, the hypothesis that upgrading policy during the Nehru period followed the expected dual fragmentation pattern. It was formulated in a decentralized and fragmented way, despite the presence of a national plan, and it was broadly successful. The portions of upgrading activity that were most successful and least costly were precisely those which focused on the detailed upgrading of existing industries, rather than on the creation of new industries out of whole cloth. In the next chapter, we will turn our attention to the period of central dominance ushered in by Indira Gandhi.

SIX

India

Party Centralization, State Dominance, and Industrial Policy

In Chapter 5, I showed that India has generally been characterized by fragmented interest groups and civil society organizations, and so the structure of its upgrading process has been largely driven by the changing organization of state institutions. These institutions, while remaining the same on paper, varied dramatically in their actual levels of cohesion and centralization. During the early post-independence period, the Congress Party was dominant but was also fragmented and decentralized, giving rise to the famous "Congress System." I argued that, despite the seemingly centralized nature of upgrading policy in the 1950s and 1960s, complete with a national plan and a planning commission, in practice it was quite fragmented. Multiple upgrading coalitions and institutions existed at the local and industrial level, and local plans were incorporated upwards into the national plan.

Economic policy from this period is often criticized as having set India on a dirigiste path which ultimately resulted in stagnation, at least until the market reforms of 1991 (Panagariya 2010). But the truth may be more complicated, as suggested by the scholars who are reevaluating the period and finding much to appreciate (Felipe, Kumar, and Abdon 2013, Balakrishnan 2007). It would appear that the harmful dirigisme that slowed India's growth was more a product of the years that followed, when Indira Gandhi centralized authority under the prime minister's office. This created a statist approach to upgrading, one where, as the theory would predict, inefficiencies ran rampant and clientelism took a front seat.

1969–1989: Centralized Congress Dominance and Failed Statism

In her early years as prime minister, Indira Gandhi followed largely in the footsteps of Shastri, her predecessor as prime minister, according a prominent place to the Syndicate and the state-level party organization in decision-making and continuing her predecessor's economic reforms (Frankel 1978). Indeed, upon taking office she was immediately confronted with a severe balance of payments crisis, largely the result of droughts and crop failures in 1965 and 1966 and the 1965 war with Pakistan (Joshi and Little 1994, Bhagwati and Srinivasan 1975, Planning Commission 1969). Unfortunately for the Congress, the resulting devaluation and liberalization package—endorsed by Gandhi—met with a profoundly negative reaction among Indian voters. Many believed that she had buckled to foreign pressure, and perceived the reforms as imposed by the United States, the World Bank, and the IMF.

As a direct result, Indira Gandhi and the Congress leadership received a severe shock at the polls in India's 1967 general election. The party, while still maintaining a relatively slim majority in the Lok Sabha, lost almost 5% of the popular vote, and, more ominously, was forced to cede control of several states to opposition parties (Mitra and Singh 1999). Voters had taken the opportunity to punish the Congress for its obsession with factional struggles and its perceived inability to address the country's severe economic woes (Chhibber 1999).

The 1967 election signified more, however, than a simple rebuke to the Congress. Opposition parties had succeeded for the first time in pulling class, communal, and regional cleavages out of latency and transforming them into a political force (Kohli 1990; Corbridge and Harriss 2000; Kothari 1975). Further, the Congress organization was straining to bear the weight of increasing factional disputes within the state parties (Kochanek 1968; Chhibber 1999). Members of the Syndicate were unable to use the CWC and the Parliamentary Board to mediate these disputes, as Nehru had done, because their power was based in state politics and they had an interest in the outcomes (Chhibber 1999). Astute observers could now clearly see that the integrative, and elitist, politics of the Congress System might not last forever.

After the disaster of the 1967 elections, Gandhi became more assertive in her dealings with the Syndicate and the party organization. She found herself in a stronger position, as many powerful Congress leaders (including Kamaraj himself) had failed to win seats in the Lok Sabha. Confrontation between the prime minister and the Congress Party's organizational leadership was in the air, and it culminated in 1969 with a complete split. This split, which I discuss in more detail in the next section, left Indira Gandhi as the sole master of the new party, the so-called Congress (R). With the support of the parliamentary party, she could now move to mold the party in her own image, free of the interference of its organizational leaders.

By 1975, an increasingly wide gulf had developed between Gandhi's socialist rhetoric and her deinstitutionalized party's ability to implement its promises. A severe crisis in Indian democracy was in the making (Corbridge and Harriss 2000; Rudolph and Rudolph 1987; Kohli 1990; Brass 1994). On June 26 of that year, the president of India, at Gandhi's insistence, declared a State of Emergency. The prime minister ordered the arrest and imprisonment of her political opponents, suspended the 1976 elections, and introduced authoritarian government for the first time since independence. She declared that Emergency government was necessary to quell unrest in the country and promised that she would use her new authority to benefit the poor. However, even Gandhi's dictatorial powers could not substitute for a functioning party organization. The government was unable to mobilize support for radical change, and the Emergency period is notable for largely preserving the social and economic status quo (Corbridge and Harriss 2000; Rudolph and Rudolph 1987; Kohli 1990).

Two years after she had introduced authoritarian government in India, Gandhi decided, quite unexpectedly, that the time had come to call elections. Many observers argue that, due to lack of an effective local party organization, Gandhi imagined the Emergency to have been popular among many voters (Corbridge and Harriss 2000). In any case, the Congress suffered its worst electoral defeat since independence, gaining a mere 28.4% of seats in the Lok Sabha. In a clear statement of support for democracy, Indian voters punished Gandhi for the Emergency and the rampant corruption in politics. For the first time in its history, the Congress Party was forced to cede power to the opposition.

The Janata Party, which took the reins of power in 1977, was an opportunistic collection of parties tied together by a loose Gandhian ideology, a distaste for Indira Gandhi, and a desire to win power (Rudolph and Rudolph 1987). After gaining power, however, such a diverse collection of parties led by independently powerful and indeed stubborn men, found the business of governing to be quite difficult (Corbridge and Harriss 2000). Factions within the Janata party began to surface, and Charan Singh made a move to replace Morarji Desai as prime minister. The Janata government collapsed into bickering and factionalism, necessitating a new round of elections in 1980. While it did initiate some limited economic reforms, the Janata had lacked the internal party cohesion to serve as clear competitor to Gandhi's bruised but cohesive Congress.

The 1980 elections produced a startling comeback for Indira Gandhi and the Congress Party. Faced with a choice between Gandhi, who had been working to rebuild her position, the constituent parties of the Janata, and the ever-present communists, the voters once again opted for Indira. Her popularity with the poor remained strong, and, indeed, there was little viable alternative to Congress government. Nevertheless, the electoral support of Gandhi's new government was more tenuous than ever, and the Janata had shown that the party of Nehru was not invulnerable (Corbridge and Harriss 2000). Gandhi and the Congress had to ensure that they could capture the support of backward castes and other "awakening groups" against appeals from the Lok Dal, BJP, and others.

In her new (and final) tenure as prime minister, Gandhi continued and even expanded her centralizing tendencies, and the Congress remained largely an instrument of her will. Additionally, she made little effort to rebuild the party organization, ensuring that the linkages connecting the Congress with its electoral base would remain unstable. Populism remained the watchword of Indira Gandhi's style of governance.

That much of the business community had enthusiastically embraced Desai's government was an issue of grave concern for the Congress. In response, the prime minister liberalized India's import constraints in uncontroversial areas and dropped industrial licensing requirements in several industries (Kohli 1990). Economic policy was not the only area where a shift to the right was discernable in Gandhi's policies. To confront the growing threat from the Jana Sangh / BJP, the prime minister began to incorporate Hindu nationalist rhetoric into her speeches. She took tough positions on the Kashmir dispute, and violently repressed Sikh separatists in Punjab (Kohli 1990).

This was the immediate legacy left by Indira Gandhi when, just before the 1984 election, she was assassinated by Sikh bodyguards who objected to her actions in Punjab. The mantle of the Congress Party and the Nehru-Gandhi family was passed to Gandhi's oldest son, a former professional pilot named Rajiv.

Riding a wave of sympathy, Mr. Gandhi captured 76.6% of the Lok Sabha for the Congress, a greater percentage than even Nehru had achieved at the height of his standing. Rajiv, a relative newcomer to politics, was determined to leverage this massive victory to achieve his twin goals of re-institutionalizing the Congress and bringing India into the world economy (Kohli 1990; Corbridge and Harriss 2000; Brass 1994; Rudolph and Rudolph 1987). Foreign educated, modern, and distrustful of the traditional Congress elite, the new prime minister depended on a small coterie of technocrats to carry out these broad goals.

Even Rajiv's unprecedented electoral victory was not, however, sufficient to overcome the constraints imposed by his unstable electoral base. The weakness of the Congress party organization left Rajiv Gandhi's government at the mercy of particularistic interests that opposed his economic reforms. A series of scandals tarnished the prime minister's image as "Mr. Clean," weakening his shallow, populist support and undermining his political capital.[1] As Atul Kohli has argued, Rajiv exercised extraordinarily centralized control over the Congress and the government, but was powerless to effect significant change (Kohli 1990). He succeeded in reducing trade protection in capital goods to some degree and in loosening moderately India's industrial licensing scheme, but was sidetracked before his government was even two years old.[2] Gandhi's efforts to reinstitutionalize the Congress Party were no more successful, and his plans for party elections were put on indefinite hold by 1986 (Kohli 1990).

Indian voters, disgusted with the corrupt and ineffective rule of the Congress, dealt the party a defeat in 1989 that was as stunning as the party's victory in 1984. The commanding majority in the Lok Sabha that the Congress had enjoyed under Rajiv was replaced with control over barely more than a third of the parliament's seats. The Janata Dal, a combination of the Janata and the agrarian Lok Dal, formed a government under V. P. Singh with the support of the communist parties and the emergent BJP.

From Fragmentation to Cohesion: The Centralization of a Dominant Party

Any explanation of the Congress Party's transformation under Indira Gandhi must credit significant importance to the party's acrimonious 1969 split. In the wake of this historic event, Indira Gandhi centralized the Congress under her direct control and, after her stunning electoral victory in 1971, never rebuilt a strong local party organization. Her Congress was centralized but decoupled from the strong party organization that had supported the party under Nehru. Its appeals were personalistic and were targeted at individual voters across India, giving the party unstable linkages to a large portion of the electorate.

Tension between the Syndicate and the prime minister whom they had initially hoped to control can be traced back to Gandhi's failure to consult the CWC before devaluing the rupee in 1966. It only worsened after the 1967 election debacle, and soon thereafter a new Congress President, S. Nijalingappa, was selected to ease the relationship (Frankel 1978). Despite this effort at reconciliation, Gandhi continued to ignore the Congress organization when making vital policy decisions, and the Syndicate (Nijalingappa included) continued to resent her lack of respect for those who had supported her election. Soon, both the prime minister and the Syndicate had mobilized support for their respective positions, and a serious factional struggle had developed at the apex of the party.

To strengthen her position within the party and the electorate, Indira Gandhi courted the left-wing of the Congress, painting the Syndicate as right-wing conformists who had hardened their hearts to the poor.[3] The dispute between Indira Gandhi and the Syndicate came to a head over the election of the Indian president in 1969. The Indian presidency, elected by a vote of both houses of parliament and the state legislatures, is a largely ceremonial position intended to replace the British monarch as head of state. The Indian constitution does, however, award the president substantial powers that he or she is expected to use on the advice of the prime minister and the Council of Ministers (Brass 1994). The Congress Parliamentary Board, with the prime minister's initial agreement, nominated for the office Sanjiva Reddy, a prominent member of the Syndicate with a power base in Andhra Pradesh. Between the nomination of Reddy and the actual election, however, Gandhi began to fear that the Syndicate intended Reddy to use his powers actively to weaken or even remove her as prime minister (Frankel 1978; Rai and Pandy 1971).

As a result, Gandhi threw her explicit support behind the right of presidential electors to exercise a "free vote," and her implicit support behind the independent candidate V. V. Giri. On the eve of the Presidential contest, the prime minister sent a letter to the party's electors:

> It has been said that this is a struggle for power and a clash of personalities. But to my mind the differences that have arisen in the party have much deeper significance and are based on the approaches to the problems and programmes facing the country today. . . . Let us then march forward, shoulder to shoulder, towards the new goals that we have set for ourselves in the service of our nation and our people.[4]

Two days later, Giri emerged victorious from the presidential election, having defeated Reddy by only a few votes. Indira Gandhi had achieved her first major victory over the Syndicate, but the confrontation was not yet finished.

Nijalingappa and the Syndicate, furious over the breach in traditional party discipline that had allowed Giri to win, removed two of Gandhi's key supporters from the CWC.[5] In response, the prime minister and her supporters, without the approval of the CWC, requisitioned a meeting of the All India Congress Committee to consider the issue. Ten days before this requisitioned AICC meeting was to be held, the CWC formally approved a resolution removing the prime minister from membership in the party. Somewhat naively, they forwarded the resolution to her office, informing her that she was no longer the leader of the Congress Parliamentary Party. The next day, the majority of Congress Lok Sabha members, in a deliberate snub to the Syndicate, reaffirmed their support for Gandhi as prime minister. Shortly thereafter, the requisitioned AICC, consisting of those party members who backed the prime minister, met in New Delhi and voted to remove Nijalingappa from the Congress presidency. With this act, two Congress Parties were effectively created; one, termed the Congress (R) for "requisitioned," supported Gandhi, and the other, labeled the Congress (O) for "organization," backed the Syndicate. Speaking to the plenary session of the Congress (O) in December, Nijalingappa interpreted the year's events this way:

> The Congress is split and the country's political stability endangered by the actions of Smt. Indira Gandhi. . . . Smt. Gandhi's technique was clear. Through nationalisation of the banks she drew to herself an aura of radicalism. . . . She made herself the sole focus for a shift in allegiance of Congressman. It was a brazen-faced assertion of personality cult organised with the full panoply of her vast authority in the government.[6]

While Nijalingappa's assessment of Gandhi's motivations was undoubtedly partisan and extreme, his belief in the populist nature of her appeal was to be proven correct in the coming years.

When the dust had settled, Indira Gandhi had retained the support of most Congress parliamentarians, but was forced to seek votes from the Communist Party of India (CPI) and other smaller parties to remain prime minister. More importantly, she had lost much of the party organization to the Congress (O). Although the Congress (R) followed the letter of the party constitution and formed such institutions as the AICC, the CWC, and the Pradesh and District Congress Committees, it was the Congress (O) that inherited most of the party's preexisting organization (Frankel 1978; Kohli 1990; Chhibber 1999). Still, despite these sacrifices, Gandhi was now in complete control of the Congress (R).

While Gandhi's interest in centralizing power was visible before the split, it was only after she had broken with the Syndicate that she could truly dominate the party apparatus.[7] From 1969, power in Gandhi's Congress was concentrated in her hands and in the hands of her closest associates (Mitra 1994; Kochanek 1976; Manor 1992; Kohli 1990; Chhibber 1999; Frankel 1978; Rai and Pandy 1971; Singh 1981). This centralization of control was only expanded after the prime minister's triumphant 1971 election victory, in which she secured fully 67.9% of seats in the Lok Sabha, performing significantly better than had the united Congress in 1967 (Mitra and Singh 1999). No longer dependent on the CPI, the Syndicate, or the Congress left-wing for her position, Indira Gandhi exercised a level of power that her father never could have imagined.

No doubt thinking of her recent confrontation with the Syndicate, Gandhi moved quickly to establish her control over the Congress Working Committee, the Parliamentary Board, and the Central Election Committee (Kochanek 1976). Never again would the prime minister allow herself to be challenged by independently powerful party leaders at the apex of the Congress. To that end, she ensured that all Congress presidents would be close associates and unlikely to criticize her openly. Indeed, after her strength was reinforced by the successful 1971 elections, Gandhi made sure that holders of that high office would have no political base and would be totally dependent on her largess. Further, to prevent any future Congress president from transforming the position into a source of independent power, Gandhi ensured that no one would hold the office for long. Five different individuals held the presidency between 1969 and 1975 (Kochanek 1976). In 1972, the prime minister pushed one of her closest associates, Jagjivan Ram, out of the Congress presidency and replaced him with D. Sanjivayya, a party leader with no independent base. Although Ram had proven his loyalty by co-writing the letter accusing Nijalingappa of negotiating with rightist parties, Gandhi very likely perceived his strong base among Dalits as a threat (Kochanek 1976).

With her control of the Congress presidency ensured, Gandhi could select one-half of the members of the Congress Working Committee quite directly. She also exercised great influence over the remaining members, who were elected by the AICC, by regulating the selection of candidates (Kochanek 1976). With the CWC in her pocket, Gandhi was also in effective control over its associated organizations, the Parliamentary Board and the CEC. She used her power over the party's apex bodies to turn the organization on its head. On paper, and to a considerable extent in reality under Nehru, officials at each level of the Congress organization derived their power from the primary membership and from the level below. Some members of the District Congress Committees, for example, were elected by the primary membership, others were presidents of Mandal Congress Committees, and still others were local MPs and MLAs. Pradesh Congress Committees were comparably constituted.[8]

By contrast, Gandhi adopted the practice of using the powers of the Parliamentary Board and the CEC to appoint members of Pradesh Congress

Committees by fiat. These members would be personally loyal to the prime minister and would generally not have an independent power base that could challenge her in the future. These centrally-appointed PCCs would often be charged with selecting members of the DCCs who fit the same criteria. PCCs that opposed or threatened her Gandhi would simply dissolve and replace with ad hoc bodies that operated under her personal direction. Gandhi and her Congress president postponed the 1970 party elections and suspended those scheduled for 1972. Further, in 1969 the Congress president assumed the authority to nominate two representatives on every Congress Committee (Frankel 1978; Kochanek 1976; Rudolph and Rudolph 1987). Gandhi had transformed a party organization that had derived its power from the political base into a top-down institution, and she had done it without changing the letter of the party constitution (Kochanek 1976; Manor 1992).

In addition to expanding her control over the new Congress Party organization, Gandhi moved to dominate the process of selecting candidates for the Lok Sabha. In Nehru's time, the Central Election Committee had generally allowed bodies at the state level to select candidates, only intervening in the decisions of faction-ridden states. By contrast, Gandhi used the CEC to, as Stanley Kochanek put it, "restructure state legislative elites from above" (Kochanek 1976, 100). Through the CEC and the Parliamentary Board, the prime minister appointed and removed state Chief Ministers and members of Pradesh Congress Committees and Pradesh Election Committees. She refused to re-nominate state politicians whom she opposed, replacing them with creatures of New Delhi selected for their loyalty to the prime minister rather than their base in the state (Corbridge and Harriss 2000; Rudolph and Rudolph 1987). On the eve of her success in the state elections of 1972, for example, Gandhi forced out the powerful chief ministers of Andhra Pradesh, Assam, Madhya Pradesh, and Rajasthan (Kochanek 1976).

The prime minister's power to intervene in state politics through candidate selection, while great, was limited by the continuing strength of factional bosses. Although the influence of factions had been in decline since the arrival of mass politics in the 1967 and 1971 elections, they remained a force in the states. Many of the weak chief ministers appointed by Gandhi were unable to exercise power or even remain in office in the face of entrenched factional opposition (Mitra 1994). In addition, factions continued to control significant numbers of voters, forcing Gandhi to consider their preferences when deciding who should run for office. She was not, therefore, completely free to restructure the party in her own image (Kochanek 1976; Frankel 1978). As we have seen, however, her personal power over candidate nominations was very significant.

Because the Congress Party dominated Indian politics, its centralized and cohesive structure was grafted onto the government. Without any visible changes in form, the same federal and state institutions that had functioned with significant independence under Nehru became vassals of the new prime minister. As I have already noted, Gandhi exercised tremendous influence over state government elites, including chief ministers, through her use of the party apparatus. The increased role of the central government and the prime minister vis-à-vis the states is indicated by a decrease in the number of voters who could name their chief ministers (Mitra and Singh 1999). In those states where factional conflict prevented the establishment of a stable government, or where non-Congress parties held sway, Indira Gandhi often exercised president's rule. Under the constitution, the president of India, acting on the advice of the prime minister, can assume direct control of state governments when necessary. Nehru and Shastri resorted to President's rule only ten times during their tenures in office, whereas Gandhi (plus the 1977–80 Janata government) made use of it fully seventy-two times (Chhibber 1999).

Another sign of Gandhi's centralization of power was the federal government's increased proportion of public non-defense expenditure. Indeed, the prime minister extended her control over government finance by redefining the tax code so that the states would receive a smaller proportion of tax revenues to spend at their discretion. Further, as we will see in the next section, Gandhi nationalized India's major commercial banks and expanded her influence over the Finance Commission (Chhibber 1999).

At the federal level, Gandhi concentrated power in the prime minister's secretariat. The secretariat had been created by Shastri to strengthen his hand in dealing with the party organization and was beholden only to the prime minister (Frankel 1978). Under Indira Gandhi, it took on a new identity as the center of power in the Indian government. As long-time civil servant Nitish Sengupta put it:

> Interestingly, PM's secretariat became a miniature central secretariat. Some of the Joint Secretaries or even Deputy Secretaries would only deal with the Ministers or Secretaries of other departments and would zealously guard their authority. The PM's secretariat became, for all practical purposes, the most important Ministry in the Government of India between 1970 and 1977. It had the power to veto any proposed activity.[9]

In the process of strengthening her own secretariat, Gandhi weakened considerably the cabinet. In an effort to prevent the growth of any potential rival to power, the prime minister endlessly shuffled MPs in and out of the cabinet, and from position to position (Kochanek 1976). Perhaps the most notorious example of this approach was the prime minister's removal of her most senior supporters Y. B. Chavan, Jagjivan Ram, Swaran Singh, and F. A. Ahmed from their strong positions in the cabinet. This major cabinet reshuffle, which took place in June 1970, was intended to eliminate any potential power rivalries in the central government (Rai and Pandy 1971).

Finally, after her confrontation with the Syndicate over the Indian presidency, Gandhi ensured that whoever held that exalted office was clearly under her influence. In 1974, she prevented V. V. Giri from serving a second term, and instead appointed F. A. Ahmed to become President. Ahmed, for his part, did not raise an objection when the prime minister asked him to declare a state of Emergency in 1975 (Kochanek 1976).

Formulating Upgrading Policy: Failed Statism

Indian economic policy during this period was characterized by failed statism, as a cohesive government interacted with fragmented private interests. As predicted, the upgrading coalitions that had developed during the Nehru period collapsed under centralized power, and the government's economic resources refocused on political rather than economic goals. To strengthen the patronage networks necessary to maintain her broad but unstable voting coalition, the prime minister expanded state regulation of the economy. Further, by centralizing the Congress Party, she personally directed the strategic distribution of economic benefits to build and maintain electoral support.

More to the point, the political exigencies that Gandhi faced made a serious effort at upgrading impossible. The cohesive state had little reason to engage with weak and fragmented private interests and was able to impose its will, economically efficient or not, on the economy. Indeed, during this period, economic policy was composed with little regard for economic upgrading and development, but rather with an eye toward stabilizing the government's hold on power.

Indira Gandhi's power, based in a cohesive and centralized Congress Party, was all encompassing but fundamentally shallow. This reality meant that Gandhi not only had little incentive to cooperate with relevant private interests to promote upgrading, but that she and the Indian state likely lacked the strong institutions necessary to implement complex upgrading policies in the first place.

Instead of trying to build such institutions, Gandhi accumulated an extraordinary array of additional sources of patronage. For example, she created an increasingly stringent import and industrial licensing process and established greater state control over the financial resources used to create and expand protected industries. The Congress System soon gave way to an Indira system, in which populist rhetoric and shallow voter support produced extensive—but inefficient—government intervention in the economy.

Gandhi used her new sources of patronage to influence elites and to elicit support from voters. Gandhi's Congress, devoid of a functioning party organization and obliged to campaign across a vast country with limited media access, depended heavily on donations for its electoral success. Most of these campaign donations originated from the private sector, many as a result of government coercion or reciprocal promises (Kochanek 1974; Sengupta 1995; Weiner 1989; Rudolph and Rudolph 1987). Gandhi used her control over vital economic and trade resources to establish her influence over Indian businesses, to punish industrialists who had supported the Syndicate in 1969, and to ensure her access to financial support.[10] She also distributed government finance and food aid to state governments to influence their elections, and provided jobs, farm subsidies, and other economic benefits to voters to encourage their support for her party (Bardhan 1984; Chhibber 1999).

The focus of government policy therefore came to center on clientelism rather than on upgrading, something that is especially prone to occur when private interests are fragmented and weak. In these circumstances, government officials are free to use the government's resources to shore up their political position. Unconstrained by coordinated interest group representation, they can play private groups off one another with targeted benefits and can woo voters with large and visible state-financed projects. This is essentially what came to pass in the India of the 1970s and 1980s.

At the end of the 1960s, Gandhi restored India's stringent import licensing, raised tariffs, and reintroduced export subsidies.[11] No doubt the prime minister's decision to revert to import substitution was driven in part by her socialist rhetoric and her dependence (until 1971) on the CPI. However, the restoration of strict import controls also provided Gandhi with a key source of patronage to help shore up her shallow voting coalition, and she soon distributed licenses and export subsidies to benefit friends and punish enemies.[12] Further, Gandhi expanded the number of tariff exemptions available to businesses, allowing her to "cherry-pick" the importing firms that would receive her largess. Her power was not, therefore, restricted by the need to apply preset tariff lines to specific categories of commodities. Very likely, the prime minister also used her power to ensure the protection of import-competing political allies.[13]

Gandhi's political dependence on trade protection was further revealed by her reaction to India's 1973 balance of payments crisis. This time the prime minister did not even attempt liberalization; instead, she introduced more stringent controls from the outset.[14] While adopting firm measures against inflation, she increased the complexity of India's import licensing clearance process and further escalated tariffs. The prime minister's precarious hold on power depended on populism and socialist rhetoric, making her unwilling to risk a repeat of her experience in 1966.

In addition to increasing the state's regulation of trade and foreign exchange, Gandhi further tightened an already restrictive industrial licensing system. The prime minister based her expanded licensing powers on a new law, the Monopolies and Restrictive Trade Practices Act of 1969, designed to prevent economic concentration. In stark contrast to Nehru, she centered decision-making for major industrial license requests in a special cabinet committee, ensuring that each application would require her personal approval. In doing so, she gained new powers over which firms would enjoy the benefits of import substitution, powers that she used to protect her position in the face of shallow electoral support.

By the mid-1960s, government studies had made it clear that industrial licensing, which was intended in part to encourage the growth of small firms, had in fact allowed larger enterprises to force them out of the market (Sudhanshu 1986; Kochanek 1974; Stone 1994). As the Fourth Five Year Plan put the problem:

> The largest corporate groups are the most advantageously placed to seek and obtain foreign collaboration and to expand or to initiate a number of large and new activities. . . . In the process there is inevitably an increase in the concentration of economic power.[15]

In 1967, ostensibly reacting to this unintended consequence of licensing, Gandhi and her party introduced in parliament the Monopolies and Restrictive Trade Practises (MRTP) Bill. Under the new bill, small and medium enterprises would be freed from the need to obtain a license for industrial projects that cost less than Rs1 crore. By contrast, India's largest business houses would always need to seek government approval to establish or expand their factories. Further, the major houses would be forced to direct their energies toward industries requiring massive investment, generally of more than Rs5 crores. Any sizable federal loans received by these big business houses would also allow the government to convert its investment into equity, introducing the potential for partial government ownership over the new project (Kochanek 1974; Frankel 1978; Sudhanshu 1986).

Needless to say, the major business associations adamantly opposed the new law, seeing in it a risk to their future existence. The Associated Chambers of Commerce and Industry (ASSOCHAM), when asked for its views by the government,

> . . . expressed apprehension that, if implemented in its present form, the Bill could have very far reaching and unforeseen effect which could be gravely deleterious to the future economic development of the country.[16]

Despite the objections of large businesses, parliament passed the MRTP Act in 1969, and it entered into force in 1970.

The same year that the MRTP Act went into effect, Gandhi decided to require government approval for major expansions in every industrial sector (Frankel 1978). She therefore revoked all forty-one license exemptions then in place. Further, through revised industrial policies introduced in 1970 and 1973, as well as through the Foreign Exchange Regulation and Control Act of 1973, the prime minister continued to expand her government's tight regulation of the economy (Sengupta 1995).

It is interesting to note that Gandhi's new industrial licensing policy began in 1969–70, during and immediately after the Congress Split. Nitish Sengupta, a deputy secretary charged with implementing the MRTP Act, put it this way:

> . . . it was really during the years of the late 1960s and early 1970s that the central government took upon itself the vast powers of intervention and regulation. . . . The central government came to occupy a decisive role in relation to the country's industrial and industry-related developments.[17]

The prime minister's new powers over industrial licensing formed one of her most important sources of patronage, allowing her to reward friends and to punish enemies (Stone 1994; Sengupta 1995; Bardhan 1984; Chibber 2003). Through industrial licensing, Gandhi was able to harness the financial power of the private sector to aid her in sustaining her precarious voting base. For example, in one notorious case, Gujarati oil barons funded the Congress Party's 1974 election campaign in Uttar Pradesh in exchange for industrial deregulation (Frankel 1978). Similarly, a 1988 government study (published when Rajiv Gandhi, who adopted much of his mother's approach, was prime minister) found that the government had used industrial licenses to dissuade private industry from investing in non-Congress states (Chhibber 1999).

Gandhi's centralized control over the Congress Party also allowed her to centralize industrial licensing decisions in her office. She had little fear that lower echelons of the party would object to her new powers. While Nehru had played little role in allocating industrial licenses, Indira Gandhi ensured that no major projects could be approved without her personal agreement. Under the MRTP, a committee of ministerial representatives would review the license applications of large business houses. Any proposals that the committee approved it would send to the Ministry of Industrial Development, while any questionable or complex proposals it would forward to a semi-independent Monopolies Commission (Frankel 1978; Sengupta 1995). In reality, however, decision-making had become so political that the Commission was often shut out of the process. In 1972, its members complained to the parliament:

> The Commission cannot help feeling that there is some incongruity in that sometimes cases not involving any major issue were referred to the Commission while other which would prima facie involve important considerations are not so referred.[18]

From 1970, the ultimate decision-making authority over industrial licenses lay neither with the Monopolies Commission nor with the ministries, but with the prime minister and her secretariat. All major applications had to be forwarded to the Cabinet Committee on Economic Coordination, a body chaired by Gandhi and essentially a part of her office (Frankel 1978; Sengupta 1995). As Nitish Sengupta, a civil servant heavily involved in the licensing process at the time, has written:

> No worthwhile project could be cleared without the Prime Minister's approval. Those who managed to get industrial licenses also managed to see to it that others did not. This was done by money, influence, and political muscle power.[19]

Industrial licenses had become largely an instrument of patronage to be doled out by the prime minister to shore up her political position.

Gandhi also made strategic use of the four primary sources of government finance: the Planning Commission, the Finance Commission, the central ministries, and the nationalized commercial banks. The money allocated through these government bodies was used for a variety of purposes, including the establishment and expansion of protected industries. The prime minister's centralized control of the Congress party allowed significant influence over the decision-making of each of the institutions (with the partial exception of the Planning Commission, as we shall see). As a result, she was able to use government outlays as a source of patronage to build her support base among both state governments and private actors.

Immediately before the Congress split, Gandhi moved to consolidate her control over India's credit markets. In July 1969, as part of her ongoing struggle with the Syndicate, the prime minister nationalized the country's fourteen largest commercial banks. In doing so, she extended an unprecedented level of government control over the distribution of investment in India, gaining for herself a powerful new source of patronage just as her party's linkages with the electorate were destabilizing.

Gandhi's decision to nationalize the banks, a possibility that had long been debated in the Congress, was first and foremost an effort by the prime minister to strengthen her socialist credentials vis-à-vis the Syndicate (Frankel 1978; Patel 2002). Finance Minister Morarji Desai, a vocal opponent of nationalization, had previously elicited an agreement within the government and the CWC to try bank regulation first. When the prime minister decided to move ahead with nationalization, she first removed Desai from the Finance portfolio, taking the job for herself. I. G. Patel, a secretary in the Finance Ministry, has described what happened next:

> Without any fanfare, she [Gandhi] asked me whether banking was under my charge. On telling her it was, she simply said: 'For political reasons, it has been decided to nationalize the banks. You have to prepare within 24 hours the bill, a note for the Cabinet and a speech for me to the nation on the radio tomorrow evening. Can you do it and make sure there is no leak?' There was no pretence that this was not a political decision, and the message was clear that no argument from me was required.[20]

The prime minister wanted nationalization to come as a surprise for maximum political effect, and she decided to implement it through presidential decree rather than to wait for the slow legislative process. This approach had the added benefit of implying to the public that bank nationalization had been effected solely on the initiative of the prime minister and over the objections of the Syndicate (Frankel 1978). Gandhi's decision was greeted with jubilation by the Indian masses and indeed by many members of the Congress Party. It played an important role in hastening the split and, very likely, in creating the progressive image that the prime minister exploited so effectively in the 1971 election.

The nationalized banks served as sources of credit for a wide variety of protected economic ventures across India, providing Gandhi with tremendous leverage over India's private sector. Her leverage was further increased by the banks' insertion of clauses into certain loan contracts allowing the government to convert its investment into equity.

Departing from the practice of other countries with nationalized credit systems, Gandhi extended direct political control over loan distribution. Representatives of the Congress were placed on the governing boards of nationalized banks, and non-market criteria made their way into allocative decisions. Because Gandhi exercised highly centralized control over the Congress Party, she was able to intervene in investment decisions through these representatives. Gandhi and her associates used this new source of patronage to coerce the backing of Indian industrial and farming interests, providing loans at low interest rates to supporters. India's credit system became increasingly politicized, loans were awarded based on non-market criteria, and defaults mounted.[21] Corruption ran rampant among loan offers and loan applicants, as schemes multiplied to take advantage of the arbitrary rules governing access to credit (Sengupta 1995; Bardhan 1984).

It is also likely that the prime minister made used of disbursements by the Finance Commission and the central ministries as sources of political influence. The Finance Commission was created under Article 275 of the constitution and is charged with determining the distribution of fiscal resources between the Centre and the states. In carrying out its duties, the Commission recommends the level of government disbursements to each state under tax sharing and grants-in-aid programs (Bhargava 1984; Thimmaiah 1985; Chhibber 1999). Even in Nehru's time, the Finance Commission was never truly independent of the government's wishes (Frankel 1978). Beginning around 1967, however, the Finance Ministry expanded its role in the Commission's decision-making process to a new level (Chhibber 1999). When Gandhi centralized her power over the Congress Party and its members in the cabinet, she also gained significant influence over government disbursements through the Commission. She very probably used this influence to target financial resources strategically to consolidate her political influence over state governments.

Gandhi's personal control over the Congress MPs in her cabinet also translated into influence over another major source of government financial outlays. Significant resources were transferred every year to the states from India's central ministries, and the prime minister also likely used these transfers as a source of political influence. Further, Gandhi probably used central outlays under the Fourth Five Year Plan to build political support, but broadly retained prior constraints on the central government's ability to determine the allocation of funds.

Applying the Theory

As the preceding section demonstrates, any decentralized upgrading coalitions that had been formed during the Nehru years were irreparably broken after his death. The centralization of party and state authority under Indira Gandhi, combined with the ongoing fragmentation of India's private interests, produced a system of unbalanced state cohesion and ineffective statism. The prime minister and India's key leaders were empowered to make economic policy with little regard for interest groups and civil society, and therefore had little incentive to engage in the give and take with the private sector necessary to make effective upgrading policy.

As I noted in Chapter 2, a cohesive state, by my definition, does not imply a high-capacity state. While India during this period was by no means a failed state, it nevertheless lacked the capacity, as well as the incentive, to carry out effective upgrading. Much of this low capacity, vis-à-vis the early post-independence period, resulted from the Congress Party's loss of its grassroots organization.

As the theory would predict, the government focused its economic policy not on upgrading but rather on staying in power. While the Planning Commission continued into the Indira Gandhi period, and five years plans continued to be developed, the authority of national planning had eroded. Under Nehru, planning had been much more fragmented in reality than it appeared on paper, but it was nonetheless a genuine and effective exercise. Under Gandhi, by contrast, economic policy came to be focused on delivering clientelism and staying in power. And, while private businesses held some influence over the government through their role in financing campaigns, the evidence shows that their interests could be ignored when the government saw fit.

In the final analysis, therefore, the historical record largely matches the theory's expectations. When the party and state centralized, economic policy became more centralized and less effective, and it oriented less toward upgrading and more toward clientelism. What can we conclude from all of this about the effectiveness of economic intervention during the Indira Gandhi period? While our focus in the qualitative analysis is on the structure of decision-making rather than the effectiveness, it is worth considering the growth rate during the period. Interestingly, growth during the period of Gandhi's leadership hit an average level of 4.3%, just shy of the level achieved during the Nehru years (World Bank 2021). On the face of it, this is not a terrible record of growth, though likely less than what might have been achieved under other circumstances. One thing to note, however, is that the level of volatility was extremely high during the period, with the Indian economy see-sawing from high peaks to deep troughs. It is also true that the Green Revolution, which hit its peak during this period, undoubtedly contributed to agricultural growth during the period, partially offsetting slower industrial growth (Varshney 1998). In the next section, we will explore the policy consequences of the growing fragmentation in Indian politics that began with minority and coalition governments at the end of the 1980s.

SEVEN

India

Political Change, Multiparty Politics, and Upgrading

In the last chapter, I argued that the period of dominance by a cohesive Congress Party, which extended roughly from 1969 to 1989, was characterized by inefficient statism in industrial policy. In this chapter, I explore the succeeding period in India's political economy, ranging from roughly 1989 to 2014, when the country's party system fragmented and coalition governments became the norm. During these years, I argue, dual fragmentation reemerged and the quality of upgrading policy improved, evidencing greater cooperation between state and private actors. I conclude the chapter with a brief discussion of the current period in India, which I date from 2014, the year of the Bharatiya Janata Party's (BJP) stunning victory at the polls. This victory, which brought Narendra Modi to power and was further consolidated by a 2019 electoral landslide, has allowed the party to govern essentially alone. These successes, combined with BJP victories in a number of key Indian states, suggest that we may be witnessing a return to less efficient statist economic policies.

1989–2014: Fragmented Coalition Politics and Economic Reform

As the 1980s came to a close, the twin issues of "Mandal and Mandir" rose to dominate Indian political discourse.[1] On August 7, 1990, Prime Minister Singh announced that his government would implement the recommendations of the 1980 Mandal Commission on Backward Castes. The Indian government would set aside 27% of all central government jobs for members of the backward castes, in addition to the existing reservation of 22% for scheduled castes and tribes. Unsurprisingly, this new policy enraged forward caste members across north India and increased the role of class cleavages in Indian politics.[2]

Competing with this caste-based politics was the communal logic of the Mandir. In the same year that Singh adopted the recommendations of the Mandal Commission, BJP leader L. K. Advani led a movement to replace the historic Babri Mosque in Ayodhya with a Hindu temple. This movement served to mobilize Hindu nationalist sentiment, injecting a powerful dose of communalism into Indian politics. When Singh moved to arrest Advani for his role in inciting Hindu-Muslim violence, the BJP removed its support from him and forced his removal as prime minister. He was replaced by Chandrasekhar, who, with outside support from the Congress, led an essentially caretaker government until the 1991 elections (Corbridge and Harriss 2000).

On May 21, 1991, the Congress Party and the country received a tremendous shock when Rajiv Gandhi was killed by a bomb during a campaign appearance. Riding another sympathy wave, the Congress Party—this time led by Narasimha Rao—emerged from the elections as the plurality, though still not majority, party in the Lok Sabha. The Congress had garnered a smaller proportion of the popular vote than it had two years before but had nevertheless managed to increase its seat share. Still in the minority, the Congress was able to govern only with the implicit blessing of the left parties (Varshney 1999; Brass 1994). As we shall see, despite this weak political position, the Congress Party under Rao was to revolutionize the Indian economy.

Rao succeeded in holding his fragile coalition together for six years, perhaps, as Varshney (1999) has argued, due to the fear of the BJP from the left members of the coalition. Whatever the case, the increasingly tottering Congress government was finally removed from office in 1996 by the electorate, which handed the plurality of seats for the first time to the emergent BJP. Government by the Hindu right was short-lived, however, as the United Front coalition, which included regional parties along with remnants of the 1970s Janata government, was able to collect enough votes to install two prime ministers and to govern until elections were called in 1998 (Guha 2008).

This time the BJP secured a much firmer lock on the Lok Sabha, winning a majority of votes through their coalition, the National Democratic Alliance (NDA). Atal Bihari Vajpayee was sworn in as prime minister and held power for nearly seven years, before giving way to the Congress-dominated United Progressive Alliance (UPA) in 2004. In that year, because the Italian-born Sonia Gandhi, Rajiv's widow, declined to run as the Congress candidate for prime minister, the respected economist Manmohan Singh took the office. Singh, who had presided over the reforms of the early 1990s as Rao's finance minister, continued to support economic liberalization but was often sidelined by his weak position vis-à-vis his coalition and the Congress hierarchy (see Baru 2014). His ten years in office, however, were marked by extraordinarily high rates of growth, as we will see.

The Rise of Fragmented Government

As noted above, from 1991 the period of Congress dominance had given way first to minority government and finally to multiparty coalitions in which no single party could control enough seats in the Lok Sabha to rule on its own. The rise of the BJP as the Congress Party's primary national competitor, along with the increasing salience of regional parties, ensured that government during the period from 1991 until the BJP's landslide victory in 2014 would be fragmented, this time due to the party system rather than the organization of the dominant party itself.

Indeed, the Congress that provided the political backing for Rao's reforms was not significantly different from the Congress of Indira Gandhi. While the party did undergo a number of changes on the margin, it remained fundamentally centralized and cohesive but weakly institutionalized. This centralization was based on several levers of control held by the party chiefs, not least of which was their power over the procedures of appointment and nomination. In the ten years following Gandhi's death, both Congress prime ministers attempted to decentralize and institutionalize these procedures. When Rajiv Gandhi came to power in 1984, he promised to build an effective Congress organization and to hold the party's first internal elections since 1972. However, his grand plans to recreate, in effect, the party of Nehru came up against several insurmountable obstacles. As the elections neared, for example, local party leaders began to register false party members to ensure their future positions. Factional conflict, always present within the Congress, threatened to boil over and damage party loyalty. Moreover, as Rajiv Gandhi's popularity with the electorate declined, the threat arose that elected party officials might threaten his position as Congress leader. In other words, Mr. Gandhi risked becoming the first victim of a stronger and more decentralized organization. As a result, the prime minister abandoned his plans for internal elections and maintained his centralized control over the organization.[3]

When Narasimha Rao took over as party leader and prime minister, he also resolved to hold party elections. Those elections were successfully held in 1992, and it appeared that the Congress might finally shed the centralized legacy of Indira Gandhi. However, when the prime minister found that he disliked the outcome of the elections, he quickly reasserted his central authority by nominating party officials himself.[4] The Congress remained under the thumb of the prime minister and the national party bosses.

Not only did Rao enjoy the continuing power to nominate party officials, but he also inherited from Rajiv Gandhi a useful tool for controlling Congress MPs. In 1985, under Mr. Gandhi's leadership, the Lok Sabha had enacted a law banning defections by parliament members from one party to another.[5] The law strengthened the ability of the prime minister and the Congress leadership to control party votes in the parliament. Such authority was particularly vital in light of the government's minority position within the parliament and may have played a role in maintaining support through the reforms to come.

The continued cohesion of the Congress Party was manifested clearly in the selection of Rao as prime minister and, in turn, in his selection of cabinet ministers. When Rajiv Gandhi was assassinated immediately before the 1991 elections, a shocked Congress leadership was faced with the difficult choice of a successor. Recognizing the continued populist orientation of the Congress (discussed below), the leadership at first requested that Sonia Gandhi, Rajiv's Italian-born wife, take his place. When she refused, a debate ensued over whether Rao or Sharad Pawar should take the leadership position. A "coterie" of party leaders soon selected Rao and maneuvered to have him appointed without resorting to an internal election (Singh 1991). As a result, the decision was made at an apex level, and local party elites were shut out of the process.

For his part, Narasimha Rao, while enjoying a much lower profile than his predecessor, was known within the Congress as a strong, even "dominating" personality.[6] Upon taking office, the new prime minister worked successfully to achieve the unity that the party would need to form a stable minority government (Chakravarty 1991). In selecting his cabinet ministers, Rao scrutinized each candidate for personal and party loyalty. He appointed Margaret Alva to the coveted post of home minister for her history of strong personal support and respect for party discipline. By contrast, the prime minister refused to select the party's chief in the Rajya Sabha, P. Shir Shankar, for the cabinet because of his support for Sharad Pawar as Mr. Gandhi's replacement (Devadas 1991). During the economic reforms, therefore, Narasimha Rao was in firm control of the government and the Congress party apparatus.

While the Congress Party may have remained quite centralized, India's overall system of government had fragmented significantly. For the first time in its history, the Congress was forced to govern as a minority or as part of a coalition. Indeed, India had accumulated only a grand total of six previous years of coalition or minority government before Rao took office, all of it under various unstable factions of the Janata movement. The remainder of

India's post-independence history was led by a dominant Congress. In this sense, 1989 was a watershed for Indian politics, the year that Congress was no longer able to govern the country alone and the beginning of a new system that would see two national parties—the Congress and the BJP—compete at the helm of enormous, fragmented coalitions made up primarily of newly ascendent regional parties.[7]

These two coalitions—the United Progressive Alliance (UPA) led by the Congress and the National Democratic Alliance (NDA) headed by the BJP—gave the semblance of a two-party system to India's national politics, at least until the BJP under Modi swept elections in 2014 (Guha 2019). This was to some extent a fiction. The two coalitions that the national parties had to manage were unwieldy in the extreme, and the regional parties especially felt free to switch alliances if denied the policy and material concessions they demanded. For example, during Singh's first term, the two communist parties, the CPI and the CPI(M) left the UPA coalition over the nuclear deal with the United States. On the BJP side, the ruling party of Bihar, the JD(U), has moved in and out of the NDA coalition depending on specific policies and local advantage.

As noted above, after the Congress lost power in 1996, it was replaced very briefly by the BJP, with Atal Bihari Vajpayee as the prime minister. The coalition supporting BJP government, however, turned out to be fragile, and Vajpayee was soon replaced with two old stalwarts of the Janata Dal, first Deve Gowda and then Gujral. Their hold on power was, however, weak, and 1998 ushered in a more sustained period of BJP rule, with Vajpayee holding the prime minister's chair for a full six years before the Congress was able to take it back under the leadership of Sonia Gandhi and Manmohan Singh. This period of Congress leadership, again dependent on the support of coalition parties, proved relatively stable and lasted until 2014, when the electorate, as we will see in the next section, tossed out a Congress that it had come to consider complacent and ineffectual (Baru 2014).

Cabinet fragmentation—consistently high during this period—is particularly relevant to economic policy, as it reduces the ability of the national leadership to dictate a centralized economic policy. This form of fragmentation meant that different parties controlled different key economic ministries, and it also meant that the political leadership was less able to dictate terms to the elite bureaucrats of the Indian Administrative Service (IAS). During Rao's time in office, for example, critical ministries such Agriculture, Corporate Affairs, and Railways were held by non-Congress politicians.

Moreover, government power was further fragmented by the increasing success of regional parties in capturing power in India's states. According to

Ziegfeld (2012, 69) "between 1991 and 1999, regional parties increased their vote share from 26 percent to 46 percent, and the number of regional parties represented in the lower legislative house increased from 19 to 35." State governments are critically important in India's federal system, and though the Centre remains dominant in the making of industrial policy, they hold some key levers of economic policy. We can therefore conclude that India's government from 1989 to 2014 returned to fragmentation, this time due not to the cohesion of the Congress Party but rather to coalition governments, the rise of the BJP and regional parties, and the growing strength of the states.

Setting the Stage for Pluralist Upgrading: The 1991 Reform Process

The loosening of the so-called "license-permit raj" which the Congress had built during the Nehru and Gandhi years was a necessary first step to the creation of more effective pluralist upgrading. It is important, as I have argued, not to conflate liberal reforms with successful industrial policy. Liberal reforms are about reducing the state's role in the economy and letting the market function more freely, while effective industrial policy results from specific types of state-business relationships. Nevertheless, it is true that irrational and rigorous state control over the private sector can make upgrading, and in particular the pluralist form of upgrading, extremely difficult to implement. In India, the multiple tools possessed by the state, as we have seen, tended to create a statist form of industrial policy, one that was highly inefficient. In order to promote more productive and balanced relationships between the state and private sector, these controls first needed to be loosened. Simple liberalization, then, can sometimes be a necessary condition for effective upgrading, though it is never sufficient.

With all of this in mind, it is important to discuss briefly the unprecedented process of reform set in motion by Rao and his government at the beginning of the period under study. When Narasimha Rao took office as prime minister in June of 1991, India was facing one of the most severe balance of payments crises in its history. Profligate spending during the late 1980s, particularly on politically motivated subsidies, had forced the government into significant debt. This problem was only exacerbated by the Gulf War, which had simultaneously raised oil prices and reduced remittances from Indians living in the oil rich principalities.[8] India's foreign exchange reserves had dwindled almost into non-existence.

The Congress had not been elected on a platform of radical economic change. Its official manifesto for the 1991 elections had promised to:

> tackle the problem of the present foreign exchange crisis by pursuing vigorous export promotion, effective import substitution, establishing an appropriate exchange rate mechanism and increasing productivity and efficiency in the economy.[9]

Faced with this looming crisis, however, the Rao government hesitated only briefly before introducing the first of a series of reforms that would go far beyond the immediate demands of economic stabilization. Over the course of its five years in office, the Rao government would establish India as an emerging economy with a newfound, if incomplete, belief in the free market. Under the leadership of Finance Minister Manmohan Singh, it would introduce reforms far more dramatic than those attempted by Rajiv Gandhi in the 1980s, with the final effect of moving India away from its historical state-driven pattern of development.[10]

More specifically, between 1991 and 1996, the Rao government introduced significant policy changes in three critical areas. To rationalize the relative prices of Indian goods, it devalued the rupee by 24%. More strikingly, it almost completely abolished licensing restrictions for the importation of capital and intermediate goods, reducing the share of manufacturing value-added covered by non-tariff barriers from 90% in 1991 to 36% in 1995 (Panagariya 1999). As a result of these policies, tariffs came to constitute the primary means of import protection for capital and intermediate goods. Even these tariffs, however, were targeted for reduction by Manmohan Singh, and India's average import duty was slashed from 87% immediately before the reforms to 25% in 1996–97 (Ahluwalia 1999). In addition, tariff lines were simplified and rationalized, easing the interpretation and implementation of Indian trade law.

While these external sector reforms were both extraordinary and unprecedented, they stopped short of truly radical liberalization. Although the Indian economy was much more open in 1996 than it had been in 1991, it remained among the most protected in the world. An average tariff of 25%, while strikingly low by Indian standards, is quite steep in comparison to most other countries (Jenkins 1999). Further, while liberalization proceeded at a rapid clip for capital and intermediate goods, it moved at a snail's pace in consumer goods. India's import licensing regime remained very much intact for these goods, and tariff levels were also quite high. To protect its domestic industry from serious damage in the wake of liberalization, the Rao government introduced India's first provisions for anti-dumping duties (Panagariya 2003). Speaking to a 1992 party meeting, Prime Minister Rao explained his new economic policy this way:

> Our concept of self reliance so far has included an emphasis on building up basic industries within the country and on import substitution. . . . We believe, however, that the stage has now come when we could review our strategy. Import substitution cannot be an end in itself. . . . There is hardly any country in the world, however developed, which insists on making everything it needs. Not that it does not possess the capacity to do so, but it finds it more economical, in its circumstances, to buy a number of things from others who make them. . . . Therefore, while we are redefining self-reliance, we are not abandoning the basic principle.[11]

The Congress government did not limit its impressive economic reforms to tariff and quota reductions. It also loosened India's stringent industrial regulations, allowing private firms considerably more freedom of action than had been permitted since Nehru. Among its first reforms, the Rao government limited industrial licensing requirements to only eighteen industries, a number that was further reduced to nine by 1998 (Jenkins 1999; Varshney 1999). In all other industries, Indian firms were free to create or expand business ventures free from government control. Further, the architects of reform abolished the Monopolies and Restrictive Trade Practices Act, an important source of state control under Indira Gandhi. As Prime Minister Rao put it: "the State must conserve its resources by withdrawing from various areas where private enterprise can effectively replace it."[12]

Nor did the Rao government leave untouched India's much criticized policy of reserving important industries for the public sector. By 1998, the Congress government, and the Janata governments that followed, had opened to private investment twelve of the eighteen industries once the sole purview of state enterprises (Ahluwalia 1999). In addition, Rao's government moved to ease the availability of foreign capital to Indian businesses. It relaxed the Foreign Exchange Regulation Act, another staple of Gandhi's restrictive economic policy, to allow 51% foreign ownership of Indian firms in most industries (Ahluwalia 1999; Varshney 1999).

Even these impressive reforms did not sweep away all of India's restrictions. As already noted, a number of industries remained closely regulated by the Indian state. Additionally, the country's policy of reserving certain industries for small-scale enterprises was not significantly relaxed, hampering India's ability to compete with China in exportable consumer goods. And, while the Indian government moved to divest a portion of its equity in some public sector enterprises, it rarely agreed to relinquish majority ownership. Large-scale privatization was, therefore, not a characteristic of Manmohan Singh's new economic approach (Jenkins 1999; Varshney 1999; Ahluwalia 1999).

Finally, the Congress government adopted a number of reforms affecting the size and distribution of federal outlays. It sought to introduce more market incentives into the lending practices of public sector banks, which had operated under the thumb of the Indian government since their nationalization in 1969. The Rao government and its successor opened India's capital markets to more private and foreign banks, growing their market share from 10.6% before the reforms to 17.6% in 1996–7 (Ahluwalia 1999). The greater premium placed on profitability is reflected in a decline in the nonperforming assets held by public sector banks from 16.3% in 1992–3 to 8.2% in 1997–8 (Ahluwalia 1999).

Despite these important changes in the government's approach to allocating finance, the Centre continued to control the distribution of significant monies. As noted above, it retained its ownership over India's major banks, reserving 40% of loans for specific government-sponsored projects (Varshney 1999). Additionally, the large subsidies allocated by the Indian government were only marginally reduced. These subsidies grew overall by Rs. 12 billion over the first five years of reforms, a small reduction after accounting for inflation (Jenkins 1999). Further, the government's enormous food and fertilizer subsidies were not at all reduced over the course of the reforms.

Explanations for Reform

Did this reform program, either in its early "big-bang" phase or in its more gradual later manifestations, result from the fragmentation of power in the Indian state? Many scholars have noted that, where earlier prime ministers enjoying super-majorities in the Lok Sabha were unable (or unwilling) to reform, it was finally a weak, minority government which succeeded. As my concern is with upgrading policy, explaining this puzzling fact lies outside the scope of the book, though it is a related question that is worth considering. Much of the existing literature is concerned with identifying factors that made the liberalization program possible *despite* government weakness. Varshney (1999), for example, draws a distinction between mass and elite politics. He argues that the mass politics of Mandal and Mandir trumped the elite politics of liberalization, providing the Rao government with an opening to take action that in the past would have seemed too controversial. Furthermore, he could rely on the ongoing support of the left parties despite his policies due to their greater fear of the BJP coming to power.

A more common argument points to ideology, which shifted in an important way before these events.[13] By 1971, economists were beginning to question import substitution as a development strategy, but it had yet not been broadly discredited. While Mrs. Gandhi's advocacy of a closed economy may not have been the result of ideological conviction, the intellectual climate of the 1960s and early 1970s facilitated her pursuit of such a policy. By 1991, however, most reputable economists were advocating trade liberalization as a vital step toward development and import substitution had become passé. More importantly, Indian policymakers had witnessed the rapid rise of the so-called Asian tigers (Sharan and Mukherji 2001). South Korea, Taiwan, and other formerly poor states had leveraged competitive exports into extraordinary economic growth during the 1980s. By contrast, few success stories of import substitution could be readily identified. India's growth since the 1960s had been steady but broadly disappointing, and Nehru's goal of genuine self-sufficiency and the eradication of poverty remained elusive. As a result, increasingly urgent voices both at home and abroad were clamoring for liberalization.

Perhaps the most common explanation for the reforms, however, points to the severe balance of payments (BOP) crisis confronting India in 1991. Many observers have argued that, faced with a serious shortage of foreign exchange, the Indian government had little choice but to liberalize trade policy. With its program of liberalization, they point out, India was able to increase export competitiveness and improve its current account.

While the BOP crisis was undoubtedly important in encouraging reforms, its role has often been overstated. Governments may respond in at least two ways to a severe shortage of foreign exchange. They may liberalize their trade policies to improve exports, or they may further close their economies to reduce imports. There is nothing that makes the choice of freer trade inevitable, and indeed Nehru increased protection during the crisis of 1957. During his first weeks in office, moreover, Rao's commerce minister Chidambaram moved to restrict imports in an emergency effort to conserve foreign exchange.[14] The immediate reaction of Indian observers to the crisis in no way indicated a belief in the inevitability of the liberalization that was to follow. Further, even if reforms had been inevitable, Rao's program went far beyond the general requirements for stabilization and quickly entered the realm of structural adjustment.[15] Put differently, the temporary BOP crisis, while severe, could have been addressed without resorting to fundamental economic restructuring.

Still, the role of the crisis cannot be completely discounted. When combined with the ideological shift, it provided the motivation and opportunity for the Indian government to take action. With the discrediting of import substitution, Prime Minister Rao was not likely to react to the foreign exchange crunch in the same way as Nehru.[16] Indeed, Rao's own finance minister, Manmohan Singh, was a noted economist with a strong dislike for India's traditional development approach.[17] His presence within the government may itself have played an important role in the liberalization. Finally, the BOP crisis forced the Rao government to seek financial support from the IMF, which imposed its usual conditionality requirements. While it seems unlikely that the IMF alone can explain the reforms, the external pressure on the new Indian government was strong.

Despite all of this, it is at least plausible that the fragmentation of government power can help explain the liberalization program. As Jenkins (1999) has noted, the fragmentation of power in the Rao government necessitated a "reform by stealth," through which the state strategically obfuscated what it was actually doing and played interests off one another. More than that, the increasing prospect of power passing to opposition parties may have introduced a motivation to reduce the scale of the interventionist state that had been created when Congress leaders believed they would never leave power. And increasingly, scholars such as Nooruddin (2011) and Gehlbach and Malesky (2010) have begun to explore the economic benefits of more fragmented government. Whatever the case, it is certain that the reform program, compounded by the political shift to minority and multiparty government, made possible a more efficient, "pluralist" form of upgrading policy. It is to this question that we next turn.

Applying the Theory

While the most important burst of economic policy change came at the beginning of the period, in 1991 and immediately after, gradual economic reforms continued to be advanced through at least 2014. As we have seen, the focus of much of the literature on Indian economic policy during the 1990s and 2000s has been squarely on pro-market reforms and the dismantling of the "license and permit raj." This approach, while not incorrect, conceals as much as it reveals. In reality, the state was changing the ways in which it related to economic actors, and some of this transformation was certainly in a pro-market direction. At the same time, however, India's leaders were rethinking not only *how much* the state should intervene, but also *how* it should participate in economic activity. More and more, state action fell into the realm of economic promotion and upgrading. Given the fragmented nature of state authority and of interest groups alike, India's industrial policy during this period is best understood as *pluralist*. And, as the theory would predict, much of it was successful.

It is worth pointing out that not all of India's industrial policy during the 1990s and 2000s was oriented toward promoting upgrading, and not all of it accomplished its goals. India's previous dirigiste approach had left a long hangover, and it took quite some time to dismantle. Even when this system of hyper-control was dismantled, state intervention was not necessarily effective.

Perhaps the best example of the weakness of Indian industrial policy can be found in steel (see the extensive analysis by Pinglé 1999). As I discussed above, steel production enjoyed an almost sacred status for Nehru and India's early leaders, symbolizing modernity and industrialization. For this reason, it was heavily financed for much of India's history, and indeed the state took over much of the country's steel production itself. State-owned industries such as Hindustan Steel Limited, later the Steel Authority of India (SAIL), coexisted with private firms like Tata Steel. This is the context in which the steel industry entered the period of reforms in the 1990s. As in other sectors, the government reduced licensing and permitting in steel, allowing state-owned and private enterprises more control over their investment, production, and exporting decisions.

At the same time, the structure of state oversight, which mostly took place within the Steel Ministry, remained largely constant. Pinglé (1999) shows that the Steel Ministry was dominated by generalists from the elite Indian Administrative Service (IAS). While these administrators were undoubtedly intelligent and competent, they often only served a few years at each of their appointments, not enough to master the complexities of steel production. Moreover, the hierarchical nature of relationships within the Steel Ministry impaired the sort of flexibility that would be necessary for the effective promotion of upgrading. Leading administrators within the ministry generally considered their interlocutors in industry to be subordinate, which, as the theory would predict, made the give and take that should characterize industrial policy impossible. To use the language of Evans (1995), the Steel Ministry was autonomous enough from industrial interests not to risk capture, but not embedded enough for the necessary sharing of information and coordination of policy. All of this meant that the liberalization reforms of the 1990s, while they freed steel producers from certain onerous restrictions, nevertheless did not promote significant upgrading in the sector.

Conversely, the software and pharmaceutical industries are examples of upgrading success during this period. Neo-liberal scholars often point to the world-beating success of the Indian software industry as proof that absent government is good government. And it is true that the degree of control exercised by the Indian government over software was considerably less than in steel. Nevertheless, the more accurate comparison between the two industries is not *whether* but instead *how* the state was involved.

In the steel industry, as noted above, state control was well established from the early years of independent India, and this tradition was difficult to break. By contrast, the software industry only developed in the 1980s and the state agencies responsible for interfacing with it had to adjust to a rapidly changing environment. For this reason, and because Prime Minister Rajiv Gandhi was committed to promoting high technology industries in India, the government's relationship with software took a unique form. Rather than being managed by IAS officers working in a traditional ministry, the government formed an independent agency, the Electronics Commission (Pinglé 1999). This agency, which answered directly to the prime minister's office, was staffed by technical experts who remained in their positions for years, mastering the intricacies of the industry. More than that, relations between the industrial leaders and the state officials were cooperative and cordial, and the focus was less on regulation and more on increasing productivity and market share. The relationship between software companies and the state produced what Pinglé (1999) calls a "developmental ensemble," a portion of the Indian political economy that promoted success while other sectors failed. As a result, the software industry grew rapidly, both in market share and productivity (Arora and Gambardella 2005).

Further light is shed on the success of the Indian software industry by Vijayabaskar and Babu (2014). They argue that the phenomenal growth of this sector after 2000 was due in large part to learning and skill acquisition, which was in turn made possible by deep networks of research and training institutions, US-based Indian nationals, and, significantly, state institutions. The role of these institutions was, Vijayabaskar and Babu (2014) argue, absolutely critical to promoting knowledge acquisition and setting standards. These observations fit perfectly with my understanding of pluralist upgrading. Another example of success comes from the pharmaceutical industry where, in the last few decades, India has developed a competitive niche mass producing drugs for the international market (Chaudhuri 2013, Pinglé 1999).

What, then, does the weakness of the steel industry and other portions of the industrial economy, compared with the success of software and pharmaceuticals tell us about India's industrial policy during this period? How does it accord with the theory? First, pro-market reforms played a critical role in freeing Indian industry from onerous rules that restricted investment and impeded productivity gains. A more effective, flexible form of industrial policy would hardly have been possible in a system of top-down regulation such as characterized India for much of its post-independence history. At the same time, while the reforms were a necessary component of upgrading, they were hardly sufficient. Removing inefficient forms of state regulation is only the first step toward promoting upgrading; the more complex task is building more efficient forms.

I have argued that the Indian state became more fragmented during this period, aligning with the existing fragmentation of interest groups and producing an effective, pluralist form of industrial policy. This is indeed the case, but there is another way in which the changing relationship between Indian businesses and the state may have facilitated upgrading.[18] It appears that, when Rajiv Gandhi loosened India's industrial licensing constraints, he began a transformation in the form of private sector lobbying. Under strict industrial licensing, firms in the same industry were in direct competition for the government's permission to expand production. Not surprisingly, these firms tended to lobby government officials independently and in secret. With the liberalization of industrial policy and licensing, however, the interests of firms in the same industry were in closer alignment, allowing a more cooperative and open approach to interacting with the state. Put differently, a firm approaching the government individually may demand an industrial license, higher protection for its finished products and lower protection for its inputs, or a subsidy. When businesses cooperate in lobbying, however, they must subordinate their firm-specific interests in protection, subsidies, and monopoly status to improve their chances of achieving wider interests.

More than that, with firms resolving their differences before approaching the government, this may also have facilitated the growing institutionalization and openness of state-firm relations in India. Today, there are a number of official bodies through which the government openly seeks the views of the private sector on economic policy issues. While most of this institutionalization occurred after the onset of reforms, the broader trend of changing state-firm relations likely began before the reforms and accelerated with them.

It should be emphasized that none of this implies that private sector interests in India were cohesive or peak-level. As I have discussed, they remained divided along lines of industry and were split into a multitude of different associations. And indeed, India's primary business associations were internally divided among firms that generally supported the Rao reforms and those that were broadly skeptical.[19] Nevertheless, the reforms, along with the more fragmented nature of the state, encouraged a more open and coordinated form of state-business relations, one that remained fragmented but took on a more institutionalized and less particularistic character.

How, then, does this portion of the Indian case shed light on the process? Overall, our observations for 1991–2014 are clearly consistent with the theory. The effectiveness of industrial policy was indeed a function of the interactive structure of the state and private interests. During this period, power in the government became significantly more fragmented, and therefore interacted more effectively with the already fragmented structure of interest representation. This fragmentation, combined with the neo-liberal reforms, made possible more efficient approaches to upgrading.

An interesting feature of the Indian case, already highlighted by Pinglé (1999) and Hsueh (2023), is that efficient upgrading coalitions arose in some industries and not in others. The theory, of course, anticipates that matching fragmentation allows multiple, distinct upgrading coalitions to form at the sectoral level. In the Indian case during this period, we observe exactly that happening in software, pharmaceuticals, and other successful industries. At the same time, it is notable that such effective coalitions were absent in many industries, notably steel.

The Indian case thus highlights the fact that matching state-private fragmentation opens the possibility of upgrading micro-coalitions, but it does not make their formation inevitable in all sectors of the economy. Why, under matching fragmentation, do such coalitions arise in some industries and not in others? The precise reasons for this are outside the boundaries of the theory, but the case details point to some potential answers. In the software industry, for example, business interests were represented by a fairly effective business association, the CII, something that set it apart from other sectors of the economy. Moreover, the state institution that managed the relationship with software was clearly distinct from those which interacted with most industries. It was led by industry experts and open to information sharing and consultation with private actors. The key point from the perspective of my theory is that these sorts of industry and region specific upgrading micro-coalitions would have been difficult to achieve under mismatched forms of state-private organization.

Conclusion: The Return of Ineffective Statism?

In this chapter, I have explored how the structure of state and private actors in India has evolved over time and influenced the effectiveness of upgrading policy. The case study provides strong evidence for the ability of the theory to explain cross-temporal variation in a complex, developing country context.

It also highlights areas where more work could be done to improve our understanding of the processes that underly the formation of upgrading coalitions and the implementation of upgrading policies.

I have argued that, while the structure of private interests in the industrial sector has remained fragmented for virtually all of India's post-independence history, there was significant variation in its state institutions. India's government passed from a relatively fragmented period in the first two decades of independence, characterized by a dominant but decentralized Congress Party, to a cohesive period of Congress centralization that lasted from 1969 to 1991 (with the exception of 1977–79 and 1989–90). Beginning in 1991, Indian government became fragmented again with the arrival of coalition government, and this lasted until the stunning success of Narendra Modi and the BJP in 2014.

As the theory would expect, upgrading in India was more successful during the periods of state fragmentation (1947 to 1969 and 1991 to 2014) than during the long period of centralized government in the 1970s and 1980s. During these periods, the structure of government was matched with the structure of private interests, allowing for the formation of effective upgrading micro-coalitions. By contrast, the period of centralization was characterized by state dominance of the economy, which generally produced low growth and inferior economic outcomes.

All of this is supported, in a broad way, by the evolving macroeconomic indicators of the Indian economy. Indeed, average annual growth during the "pluralist" period of 1989 to 2014 jumped to 6.1% from an average of 4.3% in the earlier period (World Bank 2021). However, as noted above, one interesting observation to come out of the Indian case is that matched fragmentation does not automatically generate upgrading coalitions in all sectors of the economy. Rather, it sets the preconditions for such coalitions to form. Whether they do form depends on a number of factors that will need to be explored in future work, but which undoubtedly include the specific ways in which state and private actors interact in the sector. A second interesting observation from the Indian case is the role played by market reforms. The removal of inefficient state controls over economic activity undoubtedly helped propel the Indian economy forward during the 1990s. At the same time, however, the construction of more efficient forms of state intervention was more challenging and equally important.

Another important observation is that the institutions of upgrading that exist on paper may not reflect the actual distribution of power in the policy process. India possessed a Planning Commission and developed five-year plans throughout each of the three major periods covered here. Only during the current Modi government was the commission dissolved and replaced with a government thinktank, the NITI Aayog. But the role of national planning, whether fragmented or indeed nearly superfluous, was a function of the nature and strength of upgrading coalitions. It is not that upgrading institutions do not matter, but rather that observers need to be aware that some institutions are more important in the actual policy process than others.

Indeed, as I discuss in Chapter 2, the paradoxical role of planning in India can be understood through the lens of Thelen's (2004) categorization of institutional change. In the case of the Planning Commission, we can identify an element of institutional "drift," where the role of the commission has changed across time as it has adjusted to the changing power dynamics of the coalitions that undergird it. More recently, Modi "converted" the commission into the NITI Aayog, which plays more of a research role than did the Planning Commission. We can also identify elements of "displacement," where the role of upgrading was moved away from the commission and toward other micro-institutions.

What, then, can we say about the current period of Indian political economy? With Modi's victory in 2014, and especially with his stunning sweep in 2019, the BJP has been able to rule India unimpeded at the center. BJP victories in a number of Indian states, notably the gargantuan Uttar Pradesh, have cleared the way for BJP control at much of the sub-national level as well. Given the fragmented nature of interest groups in the country, the theory would predict a return to inefficient statism in India's economic policy. Has this come to pass? It remains too early to pass judgement, but there is reason to think that the answer is "yes." India's economy has struggled over the past few years, achieving an average growth of only 5.1% since 2015, though of course external factors may be to blame.

What is certainly the fault of the Modi government, however, is the demonetization program which took place in 2016. In a spectacular and sudden move, Modi announced that all money above a low denomination would be instantly unusable and would have to be replaced with new rupee notes. Long lines instantly formed at banks as individuals (the author among them) tried to exchange their money in a panic, and the economy took a major hit. The government asserted that drastic action was necessary to end financial corruption in India, but independent studies have questioned whether the policy achieved its goals and whether it caused significant damage in the process (e.g., Manor 2019). It seems likely that a more fragmented government would have been more in touch with key private actors who could have communicated the risks of demonetization in advance. There is also more recent evidence of problems with Modi's approach to industrial policy in the form of a high-profile debacle with subsidies to Hyundai (Mukherjee 2022) and criticism of government support for a Tata-Airbus deal (Sharma 2022). Whatever the case, India seems to have achieved more economic success when the structures of the state and private interests were matched. In the next chapter, we turn to a quantitative exploration of the theory along with a brief plausibility probe of the US case.

EIGHT

Extending the Argument

Upgrading Coalitions in the OECD and the United States

As the previous five chapters have shown, careful study of industrial policy in France and India confirms the major predictions of the theory. In France, upgrading in the agricultural sector was more successful when both the state and private interests were cohesive, resulting in a corporatist form of decision-making that made possible a difficult transition in the structure of land ownership. By contrast, during the Fourth Republic, the non-cohesive state apparatus was in thrall to the policy desires—predominantly related to commodity pricing—of the agricultural sector.

The most successful upgrading in the industrial sector took place when both the state and business were not cohesive, during the Fourth Republic. The matching structures during this period facilitated the creation of industry-level upgrading coalitions, expressed in institutional form primarily as the "modernization commissions" of the planning process. The centralization of the state under the Fifth Republic led to the creation of a few quasi-successful "national champions." But much of the state's energies were dissipated in the creation of "white elephant" corporations, impressive on paper but not well positioned to compete effectively on world markets. Without the need to cooperate with fragmented corporate interests, public actors overreached in ways that were anything but efficient.

The situation in India parallels that in France and highlights the theory's application in a critical developing economy case. In that country, where interest groups and civil society tend to be fragmented and weak, the vicissitudes of state centralization and cohesion have dictated the form of upgrading policy. This policy was most effective in the early post-independence years and again in the 1990s and 2000s, when the government was fragmented and forced to deal with relevant interest groups on a more balanced basis. When the Indian state has been able to dictate terms from on high, the quality of industrial policy has suffered, as occurred under Indira Gandhi and appears to be happening again under Modi.

A deep exploration of the French and Indian cases has the virtue of highlighting the causal mechanisms that underlie the theory, showing how it operates in the complex environment of real world policymaking. But can the dynamics observed in the case studies be generalized elsewhere? This is the question I take on in Chapter 8. I begin with a simple quantitative evaluation of the theory using data from the OECD, and the results suggest strongly that the dynamics I identify in my theory are present across a broader spectrum of countries.

This conclusion is further solidified by a brief plausibility probe of the United States, also presented in this chapter. The US is in some sense a hard case for my theory, since most American political leaders will adamantly deny that the country practices any industrial policy at all. But, as a number of recent studies have pointed out (e.g., Mazzucato 2015), the United States is no stranger to industrial policy, at least in its informal and pluralist forms. And, as I discuss more in the conclusion, the Biden Administration has been developing new forms of industrial policy in order to face what it sees as the challenges of the world's shifting economic forces.

Upgrading Coalitions in the OECD: A Quantitative Evaluation

In this section, I test the upgrading success component of the theory using a quantitative examination of state and interest group structures in the developed world. My models examine outcomes in sixteen countries from 1961 until 2015, contingent on data availability.[1] I look only at the industrial sector, as good cross-national data on agrarian organization is difficult to find.

I focus on the success of upgrading rather than on the process that underlies it in part because it is more straightforward to quantify. Identifying dependent variables to operationalize upgrading success is significantly easier than finding ways to test whether the upgrading process was pluralist, corporatist, statist, or captured. More than that, the qualitative studies of France and India already presented are much more suited to identifying process rather than outcome. A large-N study, by contrast, is the best way to explore whether certain forms of political and economic organization are more likely to promote upgrading than others.

While my quantitative analysis does focus on the developed world, upgrading remains a continuous challenge even for high income countries that wish to remain on the technology frontier. In addition, scholars of the developing world can learn a great deal from the experiences of developed economies, and in any case the data available to measure institutional structures in these economies is much more available.

If my theory is correct, we would expect economic outcomes to be better, other things equal, when both the state and business groups are either cohesive or fragmented. When their level of cohesion is mismatched, outcomes should tend to be inferior. To operationalize these outcomes, I make use of four different dependent variables, each of which reflects annual change in an economic characteristic related to upgrading. These four variables—*GDP per capita (% Growth)*, *Gross Capital Formation (% Growth)*, *Gross Value Added (Annual Change)*, and *Patent Applications by Residents (Annual Change)*—are taken from World Bank (2021) and summarized in Table 8.1.

On the right side of the equation, I make use of *Business Cohesion (Kenworthy)*—described in Kenworthy (2003)—to measure the relative cohesion of business interests. Since this variable changes very little from year to year, I use Kenworthy's (2003) cross-temporal average and extend it to 2015. To measure state cohesion, I adopt two different operationalizations—the *Political Constraints* variable from Henisz (2000), recently updated to 2016 and the *Checks* variable from the Database of Political Institutions (Cruz, Keefer, and Scartascini 2016).

In addition, I include three control variables in each of the models. The first of these is *Union Cohesion (Cameron)*, which comes from Cameron (1984) and Kenworthy (2003) and measures a concept which, although not my focus theoretically, is likely to have an important impact on economic outcomes. As with the previous measures of business cohesion, I use Kenworthy's (2003) average across time and then extend it to 2015. My final two control variables are *Logged Population* and *Logged GDP*, both taken from World Bank (2021). I summarize all of my dependent, independent, and control variables in Table 8.1.

To deal with panel heterogeneity, I adopt the panel-corrected standard errors (PCSE) approach of Beck and Katz (1995) for each of my models. When my dependent variable is percentage change, I include a correction for the first order autocorrelation present in the model. When my dependent variable is differenced (a procedure which also deals with the unit root present in the gross value added and patent data), I instead use a lagged level of the dependent variable in keeping with the error correction model approach (Baltagi 2000).

TABLE 8.1: Summary Statistics

Variable	Computation Method and Source	Mean	Standard Deviation	Range
GDP per capita (% Growth)	Annual percentage change in GDP per capita (Source: World Bank 2021)	2.15	2.32	−8.71 to 12.5
Gross Capital Formation (% Growth)	Annual percentage change in Gross Capital Formation (Source: World Bank 2021)	2.40	7.42	−28.2 to 23.8
Gross Value Added (Annual Change)	Annual change in Gross Value Added at factor cost in billions of constant USD (Source: Computed from World Bank 2021)	34.5	80.2	−400 to 510
Patent Applications by Residents (Annual Change)	Annual change in Patent Applications by national residents in thousands (Source: Computed from World Bank 2021)	483	4124	−34795 to 28487
Business Cohesion (Kenworthy)	Coded "1" when no peak business association exists, "2" when one exists but has few powers, and "3" when it exists and has significant powers. Averaged over time and extended to 2015. (Source: Kenworthy 2003)	2.06	.658	1 to 3
Political Constraints	Degree to which political systems are constrained by multiple veto gates, and the degree to which these veto gates are controlled by ideologically different parties. (Source: Henisz 2000)	.327	.335	0 to .894
Checks	Count of the veto gates that represent genuine constraints on political leaders (Source: Cruz, Keefer, and Scartascini 2016)	2.56	1.71	1 to 18
Union Centralization (Cameron)	Coded "0" when unions are decentralized and "1" when they are fully centralized. (Source: Cameron 1984 Kenworthy 2003)	.371	.256	0 to .8
Logged Population	Natural log of Population (Source: World Bank 2021)	15.96	1.56	11.69 to 21.04
Logged GDP	Natural log of GDP in constant USD (Source: World Bank 2021)	24.12	2.16	18.92 to 30.44

Results

I present my results in Table 8.2. Overall, the models provide strong support for my theory. The interactive variable is significant and in the expected direction in seven of the eight models, which is quite robust given the variety of outcome and state cohesion measures employed. Furthermore, in nearly all of the models, the two component variables of the interaction are also statistically significant.

The easiest way to evaluate my hypotheses is to look at the predicted values of the dependent variables, along with their 90% confidence intervals, at different values of state and business cohesion. I present these computations at the bottom of the table for each model in which the interactive variable is significant. To calculate these numbers, I set the two components of the interaction at their minimums and maximums, matching them in all four possible ways, and then set the other variables to their means.

In all of the seven models where the interaction term was statistically significant, matching levels of state and business cohesion (i.e., cohesive-cohesive and fragmented-fragmented pairs) produce better predicted outcomes than mismatched levels of cohesion (i.e., cohesive-fragmented and fragmented-cohesive pairs).

This level of consistency is notable and is made even more impressive by the fact that the sizes of the predicted benefits from matched levels of cohesion are so large for many of the models. For example, in Model 3, moving from state cohesion-business fragmentation to matched cohesion improves the predicted annual change in gross value added by $660 billion. Switching from state fragmentation-business cohesion improves the change in value added by the slightly more modest sum of $201.5 billion. Similarly, in Model 4, we can see that moving from state fragmented-business cohesive to matching fragmentation leads from a predicted annual reduction of 886 new patents to a predicted increase of 3,210. This is a difference of about 4,000 patents, or one standard deviation of the variable. The predicted shift from cohesive-fragmented to matching cohesion is even bigger—an improvement of a whopping 35,000 patents. Numerous other examples can be described. It is also notable that in seven of the models, the predicted outcome generated by at least one of the two matched pairs has no overlap in confidence interval with the predicted outcome of either of the mismatched pairs. And in two of these models, both matched pairs have no overlap in confidence interval with either mismatched pair.

Perhaps the clearest way of observing the effects of matching organizational cohesion on economic outcomes is graphically. Drawing on the results

TABLE 8.2: Results

	Model 1	Model 2	Model 3	Model 4	Model 5	Model 6	Model 7	Model 8
	GDP per capita (% Growth) (N=849, 16 countries)	Gross Capital Formation (% Growth) (N=719, 16 countries)	Gross Value Added (Annual Change) (N=702, 16 countries)	Patent Applications by Residents (Annual Change) (N=748, 16 countries)	GDP per capita (% Growth) (N=623, 16 countries)	Gross Capital Formation (% Growth) (N=623, 16 countries)	Gross Value Added (Annual Change) (N=621, 16 countries)	Patent Applications by Residents (Annual Change) (N=566, 16 countries)
Business Cohesion (Kenworthy) X Political Constraints	−6.22*	−23.0	−279***	−14.5***				
	(3.49)	(14.2)	(86.1)	(5.02)				
Business Cohesion (Kenworthy) X Checks					-.415*	−1.42*	−9.45*	-.480*
					(.218)	(.759)	(5.17)	(.278)
Business Cohesion (Kenworthy)	5.27*	18.0	222***	11.6***	1.88*	5.24	32.1	1.48
	(2.84)	(11.8)	(68.5)	(3.98)	(.972)	(3.39)	(22.0)	(1.16)
Political Constraints	11.9*	48.9*	608***	30.7***				
	(7.10)	(29.0)	(185)	(10.7)				
Checks					.924**	3.16*	22.1*	1.27**
					(.443)	(1.55)	(11.6)	(.649)
Union Cohesion (Cameron)	-.286	-.159	14.9**	1.56**	.038	-.569	8.55**	2.14***
	(.331)	(1.41)	(6.61)	(.666)	(.463)	(1.64)	(3.96)	(.776)
Logged Population	2.46***	1.15	27.5***	.896**	1.79***	1.16	17.8**	.502
	(.452)	(1.70)	(9.92)	(.408)	(.682)	(1.97)	(8.46)	(.399)
Logged GDP	−2.63***	−1.37	−21.3***	-.080	−1.95**	−1.57	−17.7**	.417
	(.513)	(1.91)	(7.31)	(.350)	(.808)	(2.27)	(7.74)	(.551)
Constant	22.1***	18.1	−367**	−37.9***	20.8*	14.3	105	−24.6**
	(7.37)	(30.7)	(170)	(14.8)	(11.0)	(30.7)	(138)	(11.9)

Predicted Values of Y (with 90% confidence intervals) when:								
State Cohesion + Business	7.69		210	10.6	3.09	6.27	53.0	.677
Centralized	(3.13 to 12.3)		(110 to 310)	(4.73 to 16.4)	(1.36 to 4.82)	(.432 to 12.1)	(22.0 to 83.0)	(-.914 to 2.27)
State Cohesion + Business	−8.12		−450	−24.2	−2.54	−9.46	−44.0	−3.77
Fragmentation	(−17.8 to 1.56)		(−700 to −210)	(−38.4 to −10.1)	(−5.80 to −.725)	(−20.8 to 1.88)	(−120 to 37.0)	(−8.28 to .739)
State Fragmentation +	1.70		8.50	−.886	−2.69	−13.5	−59.0	−2.28
Business Cohesion	(.905 to 2.49)		(−6.30 to 23.0)	(−1.75 to −.018)	(−7.72 to 2.33)	(−30.8 to 3.87)	(−150 to 34.0)	(−7.38 to 2.83)
State Fragmentation +	2.54		91.0	3.21	14.1	47.4	350	19.2
Business Fragmentation	(1.65 to −3.43)		(62.0 to 120)	(1.50 to 4.93)	(4.18 to 24.0)	(12.7 to 82.1)	(92.0 to 620)	(4.37 to 34.0)

***p<.01, **p<.05, *p<.10. All tests are 2-tailed. Standard errors are in parentheses. All models use panel-corrected standard errors with autocorrelation correction.

from Model 3, Figure 1 shows the impact of business cohesion on the annual change in gross value added when the state is cohesive. Figure 2 shows the same effect when the state is fragmented. As is clear from the graphs, the cohesion of business strongly improves outcomes when the state is cohesive but worsens them when the state is fragmented. This is because, I argue, cohesive business is beneficial in the context of a cohesive state, generating a corporatist approach to policy making. By contrast, it is harmful when the state is fragmented, leading to the capture of policymaking by private interests.

Can we say anything about whether the corporatist combination of matched state-business cohesion or the pluralist combination of matched state-business fragmentation produces better outcomes? Unfortunately, the answer to this question remains a bit ambiguous. It appears that the political constraint models tend to generate more favorable results for the corporatist pairs, while the checks models seem to favor the pluralist pairs. This difference in outcome is likely related to differences in measures of state cohesion, but more research will be needed to tease out the relationships here. Overall, my results indicate clearly the superiority of matched state-business structures, but do not point to corporatism or pluralism as the best arrangement. It is interesting to note, however, that the mismatch of a fragmented state with cohesive business interests appears to be considerably less harmful than the mismatch of a cohesive state with fragmented business interests, at least for some outcomes. This result may point to the particular risk of an overweening state.

Industrial Policy in the United States

In the previous section, I tested elements of the theory in a quantitative framework using data from the OECD. But to strengthen our confidence in the argument, and also to explore industrial policy in a vitally important case, I now turn my attention to exploring upgrading policy in the United States. My analysis of the US case is considerably less detailed than my analyses of France and India, and it is not meant to bear the weight of causal inference. Rather, what I present here is a plausibility probe of the sort described by Eckstein (1972). My modest goal is to evaluate whether the theory can plausibly shed light on—and potentially help explain—this critical case.

As I have already noted, the US is in many senses a "hard case" for my theory, given its role as the global embodiment of the market system. Indeed, successive American governments have long resisted labeling any of their initiatives as "industrial policy." In American political discourse, the term is often

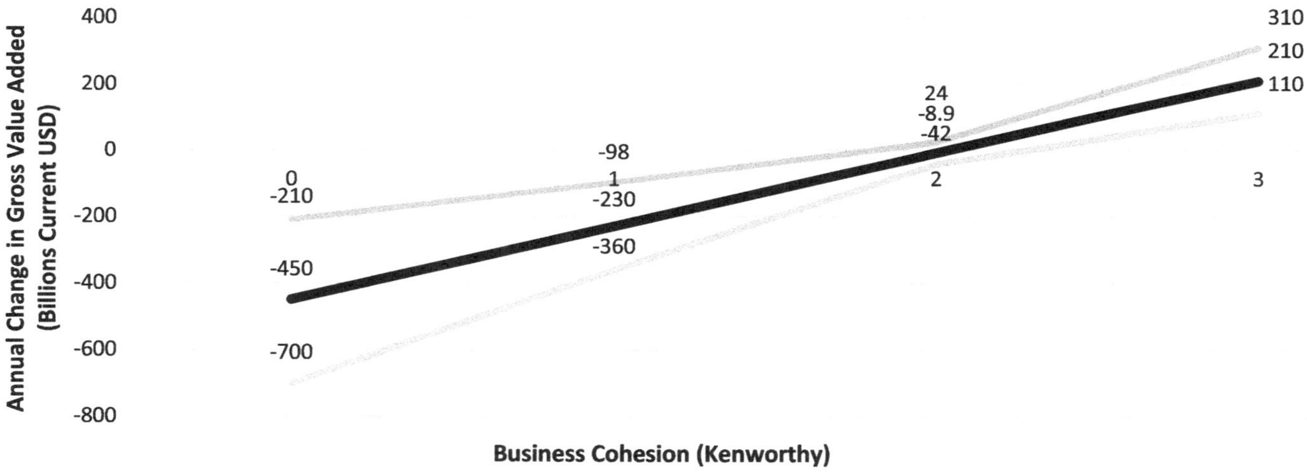

Figure 1. Predicted Annual Change in Gross Value Added at Different Levels of Business Cohesion When the State is Cohesive

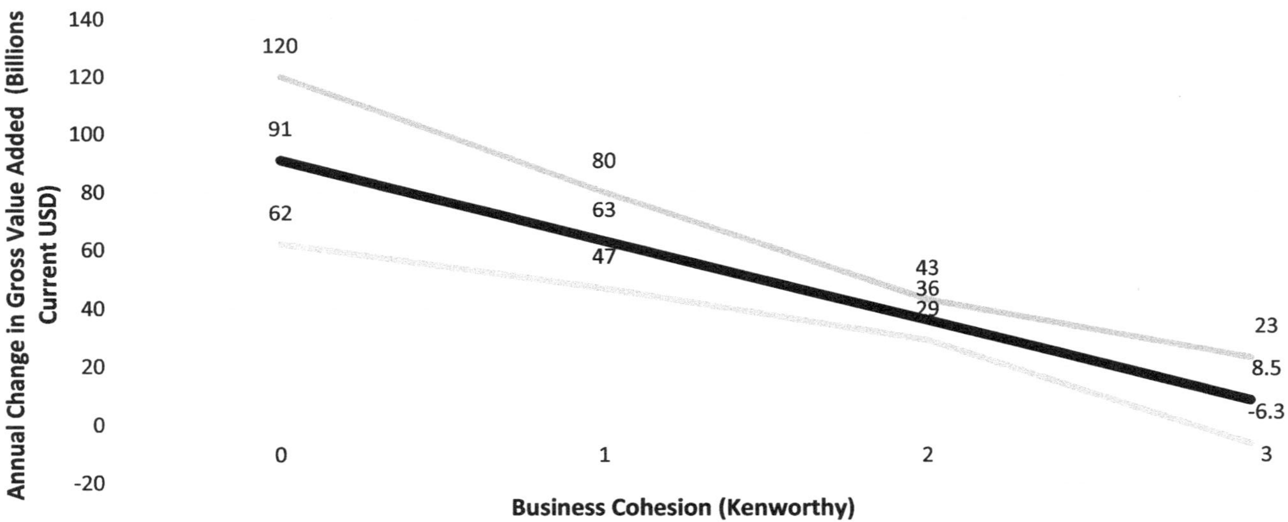

Figure 2. Predicted Annual Change in Gross Value Added at Different Levels of Business Cohesion When the State is Fragmented

associated with market skepticism and the explicitly interventionist policies of European social democracies. Worse, industrial policy, to the American ear, is inflected with the stigma of planning and with echoes of the Soviet system.

Nevertheless, the United States has always pursued an industrial policy to one degree or another. Indeed, Alexander Hamilton was one of the leading early thinkers on the subject, advocating for high tariffs and domestic preferences to build America's fledgling productive capacity. His disagreement with Thomas Jefferson's more agrarian and free market vision was among the most salient disputes of the early republic (Bingham 1998).

Over time, industrial policy in the United States has been most evident in certain sectors of the economy and at certain moments in history. First, the United States has intervened most heavily in defense related industries (Weiss 2014, Schrank and Whitford 2009, Ketels 2007). During shooting wars, and to a large extent during the Cold War, government purchases from private defense contractors have allowed Washington to stimulate the defense industry and, more precisely, to set the agenda for future innovation. But the US government has gone beyond mere purchasing. The National Science Foundation (NSF) and the Defense Advanced Research Projects Agency (DARPA) have used their resources to finance defense related research, and investments by the National Aeronautics and Space Administration (NASA) have often been connected to defense as well.

Outside of the defense industry, American industrial policy has been most evident in business development, infrastructure, and research (Schrank and Whitford 2009, Taylor 2016). In particular, as we will see in more detail below, the US government has encouraged upgrading in small and medium businesses, investments in economically marginalized locations, and research in high technology and biomedical industries. One could argue that such investments constitute the provision of a public good, but in many cases government support goes well beyond substituting for what the market will not provide (Mazzucato 2015).

Industrial policy has also been considerably more frequent during periods of economic anxiety and upheaval. The New Deal is perhaps the most well-known example, giving rise to formal government institutions such as the Works Progress Administration (WPA) and financing enormous infrastructure and energy investments. These efforts to combat the Depression soon gave way to an even broader national rearmament during the Second World War. Again, the US government's involvement was clear; while the bulk of armaments production remained in private hands, it was government decisions that determined what was produced and when (Siripurapu and Berman 2022).

However, direct government action of this sort is not a necessary component of industrial policy, and US actions have generally been more subtle. The growing postwar conflict with the Soviet Union meant the United States never shifted fully to a peacetime footing in the late 1940s, even if a quasi-dirigiste management of the defense sector was significantly less in evidence. Nevertheless, the explosion of defense funding and the rise of the national security state during the Cold War led to the consolidation of a large-scale US industrial policy, all justified by the communist threat (Weiss 2014). During this period, deep connections developed between the US Department of Defense, the Central Intelligence Agency (CIA), and other government agencies, defense related private industries, and research universities and institutions. Indeed, beginning at Los Alamos and Oak Ridge, where early nuclear weapons research was conducted, the US government created a series of well-funded national laboratories. These large research institutions, while mostly managed by universities, are financed by the Department of Energy and have created numerous technologies to be "spun-off" to the private sector (Ketels 2007).

During the 1980s, the rise of Japan sparked a debate about whether the United States should be adopting Japanese practices of state-private cooperation (Newfarmer 1984). Though such an approach was not amenable to the prevailing ideology of the time, serious commentators were explicitly defending the idea of a coordinated American industrial policy for the first time, and one that would extend well beyond defense. And, while these commentators failed in their attempt to create a Japanese style "developmental state," America's fragmented and largely under-the-radar industrial policy took another step forward.

More recently, the Bush Jr. Administration created a series of "manufacturing councils," which brought together representatives of key firms by sector (Ketels 2007). These councils, which can be seen as a formalization of the architecture of upgrading coalitions, brought out a series of policy recommendations in 2004. And after the "Great Recession" that began in 2008, the enormous bailouts backed by the Obama Administration took the form of industrial policy, with the US government taking partial ownership of such giant firms as General Motors.

Taking things to the present day, one of the most striking aspects of the Biden administration is its renewed commitment to industrial policy. This is evident in President Biden's embrace of more active, and costly, government measures to promote high technology sectors in the United States. All of this forms a critical component of Biden's "Build Back Better" approach to the economy, and it is explicit in a truly unique way in the recent White House policy document on supply chain policy, which I will address in more detail below (White House 2021a, 2021b).

An Industrial Policy of Matched Fragmentation

While the United States has implemented industrial policy since its founding, this policy has taken a very particular form. In this brief plausibility probe, I argue that this form is readily explicable through the application of my theory. From the historical overview above, it can already be seen that American industrial policy was highly pluralist and, while imperfect and spottily applied, generally successful. This outcome, I believe, is due principally to the fragmented structure of American political institutions interacting with the fragmented organization of industry, universities, and other critical actors. Far from an impediment to effective upgrading, this interaction—as theorized—appears to have contributed to America's ability to lead the world in innovation and technology.

Before exploring how matched fragmentation contributed to America's efforts to promote upgrading, it is important to establish how that fragmentation worked in practice. To begin with the organization of the state, it is well known that the US government is decentralized on multiple dimensions. First, of course, is the separation of powers, which allocates a fair degree of independence to the executive, legislative, and judicial branches.

US presidents are directly elected (through the electoral college system, of course), unlike executives in parliamentary systems, and cannot be removed by the legislature. This system gives presidents immense power and independence over their remit of carrying out and enforcing the law, but it limits their authority just as much. Prime ministers can generally depend on parliament to support their legislative initiatives since, without that support, they would not be in power in the first place. This is because prime ministers are generally the party leaders of the majority (or plurality) party in the legislature, and they can therefore use party discipline to compel backing on all but the most controversial issues (Huber 1996, Lijphart 1999).

By contrast, the United States, with increasing frequency, has been governed by a system of divided government, with different parties controlling the executive and at least one chamber of the legislature. In this case, presidents must rely primarily on executive powers and the bully pulpit to pursue their policy initiatives (Shugart and Carey 1992, Neustadt 2021 [1960]). Moreover, even when government is unified, America's weak parties, driven in part by the primary system which allows any candidate to seek a party nomination without the approval of party leaders, means that presidents cannot always set the agenda (Carey and Shugart 1995). And the US constitution, combined with law and tradition, gives Congress tremendous powers, more than legislatures enjoy in many systems. The budget process in the United States is the most obvious example of this phenomenon. Whereas in most of the world's democracies, the executive is the driving force behind nearly all spending initiatives, the "power of the purse" in Congress means that members play a much more active role in determining spending in Washington (e.g., Wehner 2010). Much of this power is expressed through the extensive committee system that has developed in both chambers, which allows members to develop expertise over policy issues of special interest to them.

The fragmentation of the US government does not, however, stop with the separation of powers. There is also the issue of federalism. Scholars of federalism generally classify the United States as among the most decentralized countries in the world, in the company of other exemplars of local autonomy such as Canada and Switzerland (e.g., Lijphart 1999). As is well known, the constitution gives the fifty states significant powers, and it also retains for them those powers not specifically enumerated for the federal government. Though over time the federal government has strengthened its position vis-à-vis the states, nevertheless, in many critical areas, including economic policy, the states cannot be ignored.

Finally, fragmentation exists within the federal executive itself. On paper, the president is the ultimate authority in this branch and can fire cabinet secretaries and the top tier of the federal bureaucracy at will. Indeed, compared to parliamentary systems where ministers are often members of parliament with their own power-bases, and sometimes also members of different parties from the prime minister, it would appear that, within its remit, the American executive is a strong and cohesive institution.

While this is true to some extent, it is equally the case that the executive is so large and complex, with competing power centers, that no president can truly control it (see Allison 1971). More than that, the senate must approve the president's nominations, and law limits the president's control over the bulk of the civil service. Often the Congress and the courts also set guidelines that limit presidential authority and that break up the executive into distinct, and sometimes competing, entities (see Farhang and Yaver 2015).

On the interest group and civil society side of things, the United States is also a well-known exemplar of fragmentation. In other words, the United States is the archetypical pluralist system, where numerous private actors compete for influence and act independently of state power. This is true among business associations, which are divided by size, region, and industry, and it is true of America's highly divided labor unions, which often disagree at the shop level. There are numerous geographical clusters of knowledge-based industries, and industry is notoriously unable to agree on such basic issues as trade policy. The broader civil society climate in America is just as fragmented. There are hundreds of separate universities, some private, some run by states, which perform industry relevant research. There are innumerable think tanks and government laboratories as well.

The pluralist relationship between state and private actors in the United States often takes the form of multiple relationships between individual government institutions and individual private interests. This dynamic occurs when a local business leader presses a member of Congress for a tariff (e.g., Schattschneider 1935, Hansen and Park 1995). It happens when county school systems seek extra funding from a federal Department of Education program. And it is to be seen in the thousands of competing interest groups that seek to influence election outcomes and policy on every issue.

How does all of this matter for industrial policy? Quite simply, the sorts of government-private interest relationships that are found across the American political economy are also associated with upgrading. Take, for example, the independent roles played by Congress and the president. Conflict between the two branches—along with the significant powers enjoyed by Congress—tends to complicate efforts to develop a coordinated top-down industrial policy for the United States. Congress is suspicious of allocating its constitutional powers to the executive but is unable to lead a program of industrial policy itself. The rapid turnover in House members also likely reduces the time horizons of the legislative branch, and members' relatively small constituencies make a national approach less likely (see McGillivray 2004). Without this legislative buy-in, the American executive is unable to sustain any sort of national coordinated planning, at least outside a crisis situation.

The same holds true when federalism is considered. Given the enormous fiscal and regulatory power enjoyed by the states, the federal government must consider state interests in upgrading policy. And each state has its own government with its own interests. Finally, the fragmented structure of executive power, under the president but made up of numerous cabinet departments and independent agencies, complicates coordination. Often such agencies are products of Congressional interest in one subject or another and continue to receive funding even when presidents might prefer to eliminate them (see Farhang and Yaver 2016).

Of course, America's pro-market ideology also matters for limiting the creation of a coordinated upgrading policy, but the institutions are clearly an important part of any understanding of US political economy. All of this fragmentation has led many scholars to argue that the United States is institutionally incapable of implementing an effective upgrading policy (e.g., Schultze 1983, Yoffie and Badaracco 1983, Lincicome 2021). A 1984 report to Congress puts it this way:

> Although its [industrial policy's] advocates deny that they wish to impose central planning on the American economy, without central planning industrial policy would be impossible. Industrial policy would vest in a small group of elite decisionmakers the authority to intervene in market allocation decisions. Without a central plan, this group would lack the necessary criteria for making nonmarket decisions. While the industrial policy advocates claim that a new panel is needed to coordinate government policy, they have never been able to demonstrate—and I doubt that it can be shown—that "the best and the brightest" are in Washington and that they can do a better job of making the economic decisions affecting our lives.[2]

Perhaps most prominently, scholars of the varieties of capitalism, as I discuss in Chapter 2, argue that a country's political economy is made up of interlocking institutions (Hall and Soskice 2001). Each of these institutions—which include business interests, state structures, financial institutions, educational entities, and the like—can only function to their optimal degree when in symbiosis with similar institutions. The United States, as the best example of a "liberal market economy" is simply not equipped to engage in industrial policy and other non-market forms of coordination.

This is a powerful theoretical argument, but the problem, as many scholars have already understood (e.g., Hufbauer and Jung 2021, Mazzucato 2015), is that there is plenty of evidence that the United States engages in upgrading policy and, moreover, that this upgrading policy has contributed tremendously to the country's economic and technological progress. For example, Hufbauer and Jung (2021) in their comprehensive analysis of US industrial policy since 1970, evaluate eighteen key interventions and find that, while not all were successful, many were. Failures such as steel and textiles and the recent, much lamented Solyndra episode were more than offset by stunning successes in everything from automatic assembly innovations to clean energy to biotechnology to the recent "Operation Warp Speed," which led to the rapid development of a COVID vaccine.

How can this be, if the United States lacks the ability to create and implement a consolidated industrial plan? The answer, contrary to Premus and Bradford (1984), is that industrial policy does not need to be centralized and does not require a national plan. And, indeed, American upgrading policy has not taken on the classic, centralized form that is sometimes expected. Rather, it is fragmented and complex but, for all that, no less effective. How, then, does US upgrading policy function in practice? In a word, it is fragmented. Numerous different federal, and to some extent state, agencies conduct actions that could fall under the rubric of industrial or upgrading policy.

The defense sector is probably the most prominent example of industrial policy in the United States, the only area where skeptical observers might concede significant government intervention. Even here, the forms of intervention are stunningly varied, as are the specific public-private relationships that are created (Weiss 2014). For example, the Department of Energy funds a series of national laboratories including such enormous facilities as Los Alamos, Oak Ridge, and Lawrence Livermore, which are in turn managed by other actors such as universities and corporations.[3] These labs produce government funded research in the defense sector, relating for example to nuclear stockpile stewardship and defense, but they also innovate in areas less traditionally seen as defense related. For example, Lawrence Livermore has been at the forefront of research into fusion energy, and the labs were also central to the creation of the internet. Innovations developed by these labs are spun off into the private sector and into education, and the tight relationships between government, universities, and industry are critical to their success.

No less important is DARPA (Rodrik and Sabel 2019a, Ocampo 2017, Bingham 1998, Weiss 2014). This institution within the Department of Defense (DOD) provides billions of dollars to universities and private firms for research activities, requiring that the fruits be shared. Rodrik and Sable (2019b) put the organization's contributions this way:

> Far from being a mere bystander, the state, acting through DARPA and related agencies, played, and continues to play, a fundamental role in organizing the research from which are hewn the building blocks of the information economy. Among its iconic contributions are the computer network protocols underlying the internet, precursors to the global positioning systems and fundamental tools and devices for microprocessor design and fabrication.[4]

DARPA's role, then, is not only research and development funding. It is also a critical builder of networks between researchers and business leaders who might never have interacted otherwise. This network building is a critical element of US industrial and upgrading policy, showing that "softer" forms of government intervention can be important. Apart from these two prominent examples, numerous other federal agencies finance research and development and encourage upgrading networks, including the DARPA spin-off ARPA-E, NASA (which also operates laboratories) and even the CIA.

Of course, a large element of the US Defense Department's influence on the American economy is through contracting. Some observers who recognize the critical role of contracting to the US technological economy think of it as simply another form of market interaction, but brief reflection shows clearly that this is just not the case. With its enormous budget, its specific needs, and its relative patience, the DOD is able to finance the creation of new technologies that the private market would never have created on its own. Once these technologies are created for military and defense purposes, they can then be "spun off" into the civilian marketplace. This specific government activity is an example of what Evans (1995) calls "husbandry," where the state provides the means for private businesses to bring forth new innovations and technologies.

Numerous examples of this dynamic exist, with the DOD and DARPA intimately linked to advances in the internet, nanotechnology, HDTV, and many other areas (Rodrik and Sabel 2019a, Ocampo 2018, Bingham 1998, Weiss 2014). As Rodrik and Sable (2019b) describe the process, DARPA and ARPA-E identify specific areas in a field where knowledge is weak and set out to find university and private-sectors partners who can fill in the gaps. Interestingly, they bring these partners together for regular interactions, creating networks, and they "discipline" their private-sector partners (as the developmental state literature would have it) by warning of project termination if key milestones are missed.

But US industrial policy is not confined to the defense sector. In the natural sciences, the National Institutes of Health (NIH) and the National Science Foundation (NSF) provide funding for a significant percentage of research innovations in the United States. As we discussed in Chapter 2, most scholars argue that good industrial policy does not replace the private sector, but rather does what the private sector is unwilling or unable to do. In this respect, the NIH and NSF are critical, as they finance the basic research which is difficult to marketize but which is indispensable for future innovation (Mazzucato 2015).

The Small Business Administration (SBA) is another federal agency that plays a critical part in America's industrial policy (Noman and Stiglitz 2017, Wade 2012, Ketels 2007). Through the approximately 5000 grants that the SBA distributes annually, it provides small and medium sized businesses with the capital they need to adopt the latest innovations to their production processes (Wade 2012). Indeed, the SBA highlights that upgrading policy is not only about financing basic science (as the NIH or NSF does), promoting public-private relationships for spinning-off of new technologies (such as seen in the national labs), or incentivizing the creation and application of new technologies (as done in DOD contracting). As I discussed in Chapter 2, equally important is adapting existing technologies or processes which are not new but are new to the business (Stiglitz and Greenwald 2015). It is here that the SBA contributes the most, though it also oversees regulations which require the federal government to purchase a certain percentage of goods from small and medium businesses. This approach helps ensure that federal efforts at promoting innovation are not limited to larger firms.

As I have already indicated, the federal government also plays a critical role in promoting network externalities between US businesses, universities, and government agencies. I discuss in Chapter 2 how scholars have identified networking and non-market links as a critical driver of innovation. One relatively recent institution devoted specially to promoting these networks is the series of Manufacturing Councils created by the George W. Bush Administration, already discussed. In addition, Wade (2012) points to SEMATECH as an especially instructive example of the benefits of networking in US industrial policy. The firm was set up, at the insistence and with the financial backing of DARPA, as a consortium of private companies working on semiconductors. It flourished and has helped to secure a place for the US in the global manufacture of these critical electronic components.

So, in the final analysis, how does the US experience accord with the theory? I believe very well. Both the state and private actors are fragmented. If the theory is correct, this arrangement should mean that upgrading coalitions exist at the industry or local level and that they in turn stand behind numerous upgrading institutions at those same decentralized levels. In other words, there should be no coordinating body or national plan, but rather many local and industry-specific interventions. The policy outcomes, for their part, should be especially effective at promoting detailed upgrading in existing industries.

As this brief plausibility probe has shown, there is clearly no national plan or single institution promoting upgrading, though presidential administrations have sometimes indicated a desire to focus government interventions in particular areas. Despite the absence of such national coordinating mechanisms, however, the United States has clearly implemented an extensive industrial policy, focused especially on the defense and biomedical industries, as well as on basic science, high technology research, and the upgrading of small and medium sized businesses. As a number of scholars have argued, there is also evidence that these interventions have been successful and have contributed to the country's ability to remain on the high technology frontier.

US industrial policy takes place at the level of individual industries and locales, and it is characterized by individual federal agencies interacting in multiple differentiated and complex ways with individual firms, laboratories, and researchers. These interventions take the form of research financing, contracting, incentivizing the creation and adoption of new technologies, supporting small businesses, targeting regulation, and supporting the creation of new networks. While the president and Congress certainly set broad policies and goals which influence the ways in which specific agencies act, much of the detailed work of promoting upgrading is left to experts at the lower level. All of this is in keeping with the predictions of the theory.

The theory also makes a distinction between upgrading coalitions and upgrading institutions. Upgrading coalitions are made up of influential individuals in government, business, and other fields who mutually support a cooperative approach to upgrading. Upgrading institutions, by contrast, are the specific government agencies tasked with implementing upgrading and industrial policies. Sometimes upgrading coalitions are incorporated directly into upgrading institutions (for example, in advisory councils) and sometimes they are informal and distinct.

How do these dynamics play out in the US case? Upgrading coalitions in America are very much informal and hard to identify, while upgrading institutions are generally part of a larger institution not expressly dedicated to industrial policy. For example, a number of critical upgrading institutions are located within the confines of the Department of Defense, though that enormous organization is not primarily dedicated to upgrading. The same is true for the Departments of Energy, Health and Human Services, and Commerce. Nevertheless, without these institutions, and without the informal coalitions that underlie them, upgrading policy in the United States would not be possible.

While the United States has consistently engaged in industrial policy for many decades, it is true, as I highlighted at the beginning of the case study, that the resources and support for such a policy vary over time. Under President Biden, it appears that industrial policy and state-promoted upgrading are experiencing a significant resurgence. The renewed commitment of the Biden administration to industrial policy was made clear in the recent White House report, led by national security advisor Jake Sullivan and economic policy advisor Brian Deese, on securing supply chains (White House 2021b). The report recommends a focus on four industries—semiconductors, large capacity batteries, critical minerals and materials, and pharmaceuticals. To rectify supply chain problems in these industries, it recommends six approaches:

1. Rebuild our production and innovation capabilities; . . .
2. Support the development of markets that invest in workers, value sustainability, and drive quality; . . .

3. Leverage the government's role as a purchaser of and investor in critical goods; . . .
4. Strengthen international trade rules, including trade enforcement mechanisms; . . .
5. Work with allies and partners to decrease vulnerabilities in the global supply chains; . . .
6. Monitor near term supply chain disruptions as the economy reopens from the COVID-19 pandemic.[5]

It is notable that this clear foray into industrial policy is shielded with the technical language of supply chain management, a sign that US governments remain wary of explicit efforts to promote specific industries within the country. This new dedication to upgrading policy, along with the ongoing reluctance to say so explicitly, is also visible in the two enormous industrial policy bills passed by Congress and signed by President Biden in the past few years: the CHIPS Act and the Inflation Reduction Act, which I discuss in the concluding chapter. In the final analysis, whatever names may be used, it is clear that industrial policy is alive and well in the United States, and that its form and function correspond quite well with that of a pluralist, dual fragmented system.

NINE

In Pursuit of Prosperity

Concluding Thoughts and Ways Forward

I began this book with the proposition that state efforts to promote economic upgrading—those actions which come under the rubric of industrial policy—are not doomed to failure. Nor are these efforts guaranteed of success. Indeed, there are no specific policy actions that we can be sure will work every time; the mechanisms needed to move up the value chain are simply too complex and context specific to permit a single rule.

Rather, I have argued, scholars and policymakers should focus on the *coalitions and institutional mechanisms* through which upgrading efforts are developed and implemented. When these are well-structured, ensuring a voice for both state and private actors, effective upgrading policies are more likely to follow. More than that, the relationship between state and private actors—how each is organized and how they interact—can help us understand not only when upgrading policy works, but also the specific form it takes. And this is true not only across national borders, where most political economists have focused their attention, but even across time and economic sectors within the same country.

To briefly recapitulate my argument, I contend that effective policy requires one or more upgrading coalitions as well as one or more upgrading institutions. These can take a wide variety of forms, but, speaking generally, upgrading coalitions are informal groups of influential actors—government officials, business leaders, and others—who stand behind the cooperative upgrading efforts. Institutions, by contrast, are more the formal entities which actually develop and carry out upgrading policies. Upgrading institutions generally follow the structure of upgrading coalitions, whether centralized and cohesive or localized and fragmented, and sometimes members of the informal coalitions are incorporated formally into upgrading institutions as advisory commissions. Upgrading policies, for their part, have the potential to be infinitely diverse, and include everything from research funding to targeted tariff protections to the promotion of networks up and down the value chain.

I argue that when both the state and relevant private interests—including firms, interest groups, and civil society—are cohesively organized, economic policy is characterized by *corporatism*, and when they are both fragmented, it is best described as *pluralist*. A cohesive state facing fragmented private interests leads to a *statist* economic policy, while the reverse leads to *capture* of the state by private interests. Matching levels of cohesion, whether through corporatism or pluralism, are the most likely to produce well considered and appropriate upgrading policies.

Drilling down a bit, I contend that statist forms of upgrading will tend to emphasize visible but largely ineffective government projects and may devolve into clientelism, whereas upgrading policies that are captured by private interests risk acting merely as vehicles for rent-seeking. Upgrading policies developed and implemented in countries, industries, and time-periods where the state and private interests enjoy matched levels of cohesion are likely to be more effective. When both the state and private interests are cohesive, we will observe central planning, along with national upgrading coalitions and institutions. Such systems will be especially effective at managing broad economic transformations. By contrast, when both are fragmented, multiple upgrading coalitions and institutions will form at the industry and the local level. This sort of system will be less effective at national management and transformation, but will excel at detailed, industry-specific innovation.

I test the theory using a classic mixed methods approach, including primary-source based, temporally comparative case studies of France and India, a quantitative examination of OECD countries, and a plausibility probe of the United States. The analyses provide support for the theory and emphasize the critical role played by matching institutional structures in the success of formulating and implementing upgrading policies. They also show how the organizational structures of the state and private interests can vary across time and economic sector within the same country.

To take some specific examples, the analysis of France suggests that upgrading was most effective in industry during the fragmented Fourth Republic and in agriculture during the cohesive Fifth Republic. The dual fragmented nature of industrial upgrading policy in the immediate postwar period was evident in the modernization committees created for each separate industrial sector. While a national plan was crafted, it took a highly decentralized, indicative, and bottom-up form, leading to a highly fragmented, but nevertheless effective, process. By contrast, the matched cohesive approach to upgrading in French agriculture during the Gaullist period, well documented by Keeler (1987), was essentially corporatist. The state cooperated with the powerful FNSEA in order to create a framework to modernize the countryside, one which was later implemented through quasi-public institutions dominated by those interest groups.

To contrast with these successes, French policy was essentially captured by strong agricultural interests during the Fourth Republic. The fragmented state was unable to resist their demands for subsidies and certainly not in a position to force painful modernization on the farming sector. The problems associated with industrial change during the Fifth Republic were the mirror image. Here, a strong Gaullist state dictated terms to fragmented businesses, often creating inefficient national champions which drew significant public attention but frequently fizzled out in the marketplace.

Similar dynamics played out in the Indian case. Civil society and business interests in that country have remained quite fragmented over time, but the structure of state power (though constant in its formal institutions) has evolved considerably. The case study shows that upgrading in India has been most effective during the matched fragmented period of early independence, with Nehru and Shastri in the prime minister's chair, and again in the 1990s and 2000s with coalition governments. Although it is early days, there is reason to believe that with the recentralization of the state under Modi, upgrading policy may return to the ineffective statism of the Indira Gandhi years.

The quantitative analysis, restricted for data reasons to a consideration of OECD countries and to the question of upgrading success (as opposed to form) in industry, provided strong, measurable evidence for the theory. Country-years with matched fragmentation or matched cohesion were significantly more successful in improving their economic indicators than statist or captured economies. And, finally, the plausibility probe of the United States highlighted the important role played by industrial policy even in a country which strongly espouses the free market. The US is an excellent example of a matched-fragmentation approach to upgrading, and its decentralized coalitions and institutions, along with its global dominance in innovation, make the point that this approach is no less effective than systems that rely heavily on central control.

Readers will notice immediately that my theory ascribes a central role in the content and success of upgrading policy to the state. Some may question my argument on its very basic level by pointing to a nation's economic and social fundamentals (education level, capital formation, etc.) as the source of its success or failure. I recognize here the importance of such factors, and I control for them by comparing policies and outcomes within the same countries but across time and sector. Others, more wedded to purely market solutions, will object that state intervention in economic affairs leads inevitably to disaster. I never deny that state intervention *can* lead to disaster, but I follow a large number of political economists in asserting that states can also play a key role in promoting industrial upgrading and modernization. After all, states perform a variety of critical economic functions that are well recognized by neoclassical economics. These include providing a wide variety of public goods, enforcing contracts, protecting property rights, ensuring the provision of market related information, and the like.

My project is self-consciously interdisciplinary. It is rooted primarily in political science, but it draws heavily on insights from economics, history, and sociology. My hope is that it may appeal to scholars in all of those fields, as well as to policymakers interested in the best ways for states to promote economic growth and social stability, a question that has been on the minds of many since the financial crisis and COVID.

Beyond Upgrading?

My purpose in this book has been to understand the politics behind state upgrading policies and their success, but I believe that my theory could potentially be extended to explain a wide variety of economic policies, including trade, welfare, regulation, and incomes. Of course, all of these policies can be components of a broader focus on upgrading, but they have their own drivers as well. Understanding better the interactions between the state and interest groups can shed light on how these, and many other policies, are formulated.

To take an example of how the theory might apply outside upgrading, let us turn to a very brief discussion of another policy area: the welfare state, particularly in France. If we were to apply the theory to this policy area, we might predict that distribution systems would be fragmented in the postwar period, when both state and private institutions were fragmented, but that they might centralize as the state itself became more cohesive in the Fifth Republic. This dynamic is indeed what we observe, but with an interesting caveat.

The size of the French welfare state exploded after the Second World War in response to the increased power of the Left and the near collapse of the traditional, pro-business Right (Nord 2010, Hassenteufel and Palier 2016, Howell 1992, Dutton 2002). In the early years after liberation, the leading figure in this expansion was Pierre Laroque. In common with many French reformers, he was initially inspired by the Beveridge Report, released in Britain during the war years, which called for a coordinated, single-payer welfare system. But the structure of French society was highly fragmented, and the state, fragmented itself, was unable to force a centralized approach (Hassenteufel and Palier 2016).

Rather, the postwar French welfare state came to embody a fragmented structure of state-society relations, with different employer groups, labor unions, and state agencies taking a leading role in creating and managing different components. Farmers had already established a retirement system prior to the war and resisted the idea that their *caisse*, or fund, would be folded into a general system to include the working class. Likewise, many professions balked at the idea of a single system, fearing that their benefits would be controlled and watered down by factory workers and laborers. For their part, pro-natalist and Catholic groups insisted that family policy be separated from income support policy (Nord 2010, Dutton 2002, Palier 2008).

For all of these reasons, the postwar French welfare system saw the development of a separate *caisse* each for workers, farmers, artisans, professionals, and so forth.[1] In general, the funds were administered by elected representatives of employees and employers, generally at a 75% to 25% ratio. As Labor Minister Louis-Paul Aujoulat put it in 1954, the government's intention is "to actively associate participant representatives in the management of the structures of social security."[2]

What is surprising is that the welfare state during the Fifth Republic remained structured in a fragmented fashion, largely as it had been before 1958. This might at first seem to contradict my arguments, but a consideration of the theory of "critical junctures" will show why it does not. While industrial policy was ongoing and always subject to reformulation, especially when the five-year plans came up for renewal, the institutions of the welfare state were more fixed. As a result, the French welfare state is an example of what Thelen (2004) and others have identified as a sticky institution, one whose structure is path dependent and based on the specific configuration of institutions at the time of its development.

That said, while welfare state institutions are sticky, they are by no means fixed. And, indeed, the statist Fifth Republic, facing fragmented interest groups in industry and civil society, has moved to expand the welfare state and to bring it more under state control (Hall 2008, Dutton 2002). In recent decades, the government has taken significantly more control over the various *caisses* that disseminate welfare payments to citizens. As Hall (2008) points out, the old system was difficult to cost control and tended to short-change temporary workers, both of which justified more centralization during the 1980s. I argue here we can also see these shifts as the structure of the welfare state finally catching up to the structure of the underlying state and private institutions underpinning it.

With this in mind, the French welfare state can be characterized as having changed through "layering," where new institutions are layered over the top of existing institutions (Streeck and Thelen 2005). In the French case, the existing mechanisms overseeing the welfare state were not replaced but new regulations and institutions of central control were added to contain their autonomy. In addition, new institutions providing additional welfare services were layered on top of the old welfare system, adding new benefits that had not existed before. These changes reflect, as I argue in Chapter 2, the slow process of institutions coming into alignment with the coalitions that undergird them. As state power became more centralized during the Fifth Republic, the decentralized structure of the French welfare state was increasingly out of sync, and over time a process of centralization took place, though one which did not completely eliminate the original institutional structure.

This slow shift from a fragmented welfare state to a more cohesive one is fully in keeping with the theory, even as it brings to light the importance of understanding mechanisms of institutional change. But what does the theory have to say about the effectiveness of welfare policies based on matching levels of fragmentation? Here, things are not so clear, as what would constitute a successful welfare policy is ambiguous. But the example shows that, for the portion of the argument related to the form of policymaking at least, there is reason to believe that the theory could apply beyond upgrading.

Democracy and State Power

One critical issue that I have spent little time discussing is democracy and its role in upgrading. While I have focused here on the cohesion versus fragmentation of upgrading institutions, as opposed to questions of representation and accountability, I believe that the theory has implications for democracy. Let me take a moment to highlight some of these here.

First, it is notable that the theory points to the downsides of *statist* approaches to upgrading, where cohesive state institutions interact with fragmented private interests. Statism, I argue, tends to incentivize states to focus on large, visible projects and, indeed, on clientelist policies to the exclusion of effective upgrading. When states can safely shut private actors out of the upgrading process, industrial policy is less likely to incorporate the critical, on-the-ground experience that only private actors can provide.

This argument rhymes with the one made by James C. Scott in his well-known book *Seeing Like a State* (1998). Scott's critique of "high modernism" accuses states of implementing strategies of social and economic transformation under the assumption that human societies can be rationalized. My argument also highlights the potential dangers of state efforts at industrial policy that are not constrained or mediated by private interests, and so in that sense reinforces the role of accountability. At the same time, however, the theory sees private sector dominance as equally problematic for upgrading, since it leads to the capture of state institutions.

More broadly, I believe that my theory can help explain the challenges that many authoritarian regimes face in economic development. Because illiberal regimes rarely make room for organized private interests, and because their state structures are generally cohesive, achieving the genuine public-private cooperation necessary for upgrading may be particularly challenging for them. Of course, this fact does not mean that upgrading will be easy or automatic for democratic governments.

With all of this in mind, in addition to democracy's many other salubrious effects, I suspect that it may generally improve the ability of states to engage in the cooperation necessary for upgrading, though it appears unlikely that democracy is a necessary precondition for upgrading. Recent events in China may be an object lesson in what can happen when an unaccountable government, even more centralized under Xi Jinping, oversteps its efforts at economic and social intervention. Despite China's spectacular past success, many of the country's entrepreneurs seem to be seeking an exit, fearful of capricious government action in the wake of the country's zero COVID policy (Yuan 2023).

The Present and Future of Upgrading

Some readers may wonder whether a focus on upgrading policy is passé in a modern global economy more wedded, at least ostensibly, to purely market solutions. I believe it is not. As Haggard (2015) has pointed out, recent events have spurred a comeback for scholars of the developmental state, and the populist wave sweeping much of the world is undermining the faith of many people in pure market solutions. A more active role for the state, in cooperation with the private sector, may be just what capitalism needs to reinvigorate itself.

But is it still possible for countries to engage in robust industrial policy in light of the tremendous constraints imposed by international economic agreements and indeed global markets themselves? This question may seem especially acute for members of the European Union, historically the primary innovators of industrial policy (Gerschenkron 1962). After all, we are no longer operating in a postwar world where national markets are less integrated and countries remain free to use nearly all economic policy instruments. Are the best days of industrial policy behind us?

It is undeniable that international markets and the agreements which regulate and sustain them put certain limitations on the policy options enjoyed by states, or at least by those states—the vast majority—which wish to participate in the world economy. It is no longer possible for most countries to drive up tariffs and quantitative restrictions to insulate their domestic markets, as the purveyors of import substitution did in early decades, at least not without severe backlash. Likewise, governments are restricted, at least somewhat, in their ability to use purchasing, regulation, and subsidies to promote upgrading if these policies discriminate in favor of domestic industries.

But scholars have pointed out that a number of policy instruments are still available for states to encourage upgrading. These include, for example, active labor market policies, the promotion of education, the funding of research, and regulations that promote health and protect the environment (Rodrik 2007, Hall 2008). So, while governments cannot raise tariffs or subsidize domestic industries at will, they can often engage in broader, non-discriminatory horizontal upgrading policies. And indeed, many vertical policies remain open, though in some cases subject to challenge in international forums. Governments can still use finance—subsidies, loans, guarantees, and so forth—to encourage private actors to direct their attention to selected industries or to adopt modern practices. They can still promote linkages between private actors, university researchers, venture capitalists, and the like. And they can use the environment, heath, and defense as justifications for policies that are also concerned with upgrading.

But if industrial policy can survive and indeed flourish in a globalized economy, the recent populist backlash against globalization seen around the world poses a different challenge. Populism, especially of a nationalist variety, might be seen as a natural ally of industrial policy. But a retreat from global economic integration in the name of domestic upgrading would have grave consequences for growth and human development around the world. Economic globalization, whatever its faults, has underpinned decades of unprecedented growth, generating high levels of inequality but also pulling hundreds of millions out of poverty.

The challenge, then, is to make industrial policy and globalization work in tandem for human flourishing. Doing so will require a form of global economic integration that leaves states the necessary room for policy innovation, as well as a form of industrial policy that is not coopted by economic nationalism. I suspect that successful future upgrading initiatives will revolve around sophisticated and careful engagement with globalized value chains.

A brief survey of the world's largest economies shows that industrial and upgrading policy is not only still with us but experiencing something of a comeback. In the United States, as I discussed in the previous chapter, the Biden Administration has developed a comprehensive approach to industrial policy couched as an effort to secure supply chains, promote green technology, and refurbish infrastructure. Indeed, industrial policy in the United States has never gone away, but the dominance of neo-liberal thinking since the 1980s has meant that presidents of both parties have tended to shy away from ramping up upgrading efforts, at least outside of the military. Industrial policy started to get more public support during the Obama Administration's largely successful efforts to confront the 2008 financial crisis, support green initiatives, and save the auto industry, but the failure of one of its grantees, Solyndra, led to a backlash from Republicans (Mazzucato 2015). The Trump Administration, for its part, lacked a cohesive upgrading strategy but certainly did not feel constrained by strict pro-market principles, at least in trade. Perhaps the most significant, and successful, foray into industrial policy in the Trump years was "Operation Warp Speed," which contributed significantly to the early development of a COVID vaccine (Hufbauer and Jung 2021).

These trends have come to a head with Biden, who still avoids the term "industrial policy" but is nevertheless more open about the state's role in promoting upgrading. As discussed in the previous chapter, the administration has embraced an expansive vision of industrial policy, largely under the rubric of supply chain management. And, indeed, two of Biden's most significant legislative successes, the CHIPS Act and the Inflation Reduction Act, both of 2022, are examples of this embrace. According to the White House (2022), the CHIPS Act:

> will strengthen American manufacturing, supply chains, and national security, and invest in research and development, science and technology, and the workforce of the future to keep the United States the leader in the industries of tomorrow, including nanotechnology, clean energy, quantum computing, and artificial intelligence. The CHIPs and Science Act makes the smart investments so that Americans can compete in and win the future.

In keeping with America's pluralist approach to upgrading, the CHIPS Act is focused on catalyzing, rather than replacing, private sector initiative in semiconductors, nanotechnology, and other emerging industries. It also contains a significant regional and local development program. The Inflation Reduction Act of 2022, for its part, is a very eclectic bill, but one that also contains elements of industrial policy, particularly in encouraging demand for clean energy.

The modern enthusiasm for upgrading policy extends well beyond the United States. France under President Emmanuel Macron has also reinvigorated its industrial and upgrading policy, but in a more centralized way in keeping with its institutions. Macron has adopted a number of new initiatives, including financial incentives for upgrading and improved vocational training (Aiginger and Rodrik 2020). Indeed, as the French industry website notes, in March of 2022 Macron went so far as to state:

> I take responsibility for wanting to introduce planning, both in energy production and in the deployment of new industrial sectors, and for implementing these aims subsequently on a regional basis, allowing freedom of adaptation. In this context, the state will have to retake control of several aspects of the energy field [. . .], we will have to take back capital control of several industrial sectors.[3]

The overall French upgrading strategy is to be found in Macron's "France 2030" program, which foresees 100 billion euros of expenditure (French Foreign Ministry 2022). Most recently, in the beginning of 2023, France announced green energy subsidies on the model of the US program, with Finance Minister Bruno Le Maire calling for a "European Inflation Reduction Act" (Caulcutt 2023). Macron's website summarizes his program of industrial policy this way:

> We have too often considered and led our industrial policy in silos, enclosed by ministerial perimeters, as well as following the balance of power between competing institutions. Our environmental, digital, and energy ambitions will not be achieved against, but with, industry, those which must transform themselves radically as well as those which are at the forefront of innovation, taking care for the efficacy and transparency of public action.[4]

More broadly, the European Union has taken upgrading policy on board as a collective tool. Indeed, the foundational Treaty on the Functioning of the European Union identifies the goal of European industrial policy as follows:

> 1) speeding up the adjustment of industry to structural changes; (2) encouraging an environment favourable to initiative and to the development of undertakings throughout the Union, particularly small and medium-sized undertakings; (3) encouraging an environment favourable to cooperation between undertakings; and (4) fostering better exploitation of the industrial potential of policies of innovation, research and technological development.[5]

The Union's recent foray into industrial policy began with the 2010 Lisbon process, which has since been superseded by a series of other initiatives, including Europe 2020 and, most recently, the New Industrial Strategy and, focused on COVID recovery, NextGenerationEU (European Commission 2021). As in the United States, there is a strong focus in these initiatives on green energy, the digital economy, and industrial transitions.

India is another country that is reconsidering the role of upgrading policy. As I discussed in the India case study, the Modi government took the step of eliminating the Planning Commission and replacing it with the more research oriented NITI Aayog. As a result, India's current government is often considered hostile to planning and industrial policy, more so perhaps than any of its predecessors. But as we have seen, hostility toward national planning is not necessarily the same thing as hostility to industrial policy. Prime Minister Modi's signature industrial strategy is termed "Make in India," and focuses on financing and incentivizing industrial development and infrastructure (Prime Minister of India 2022). In December 2022, the government launched an updated variant of this program called "Industrial Policy 2022: Make in India for the World," which Outlook India (2022) characterizes this way:

> The proposed industrial policy focuses on improving competitiveness, achieving international scale, integration with global supply chains, facilitating the movement of the local industry up the value chain, becoming an innovative knowledge economy, improving the ease of doing business, and creating skills and employment. The policy also includes a plan to develop mega clusters that can integrate with global supply chains and serve the needs of key sectors such as heavy engineering, electronics, food processing, drugs, semiconductors, and automobiles.

No survey of the resurgence of upgrading policy would be complete without a brief discussion of China. Despite the country's marketization, Beijing is of course well known for its constant and widespread economic intervention. Not all of this intervention is targeted at upgrading, of course, but much of it is. The central piece of China's upgrading policy is contained in its "Made in China 2025" strategy. This plan was introduced in 2015 and, not surprisingly, is among the largest, most centralized, and most comprehensive industrial policy strategies in the world. Indeed, China has spent, or plans to spend, close to $2 trillion dollars on the program and related initiatives (Lin 2022). China 2025 is truly an upgrading program, as its focus is to move China from a hub of low-skilled manufacturing to a center of global innovation, with a special emphasis on biotechnology, materials, infrastructure, and many other areas (Bloomberg 2022). China industrial policy reflects quite explicitly the Chinese government's fears that the country risks being caught in a middle income trap.

In the final analysis, therefore, while the old mechanisms of industrial policy may be constrained, at least in some cases, the state promotion of upgrading is very much alive. It may just need to take a different form, one that is more subtle and more targeted than the broader state interventions of the past. And indeed, as I argue here, what matters is less the specific policy, which can change according to circumstance, and more the structure of policymaking itself. The most innovative solutions to economic transformation in the future will demand cooperation between business and private interests. To the extent that these solutions, whether centralized or decentralized, are formulated in an accountable and open way, upgrading policy will continue to have a role to play in contributing to a better material future for all citizens.

Notes

Chapter 1

1. https://datahelpdesk.worldbank.org/knowledgebase/articles/906519-world-bank-country-and-lending-groups

2. Governance and Institutions | International Development Association - World Bank

3. Note, however, that the neo-corporatism literature does identify a "state corporatist" model where government takes the leading role. In this formulation, however, interest groups are often creatures of the state and lack genuine independence or connection to the grassroots.

Chapter 2

1. Some readers might wonder if this portion of the theory contradicts the classic veto player argument that the proliferation of actors impedes policy change (see Tsebelis 2002). There is, I believe, no contradiction. My contention here is not that, in fragmented-fragmented systems, more actors are involved in the making of the same decisions. Rather, in these systems I envision micro-coalitions making smaller scale decisions within their own competencies.

2. For simplicity, on the industry side, I consider cases where business and labor are both centralized or both decentralized. I argue, of course, that matching levels of state and business organizational centralization are good for growth. This is also true likely for labor, as the integration of workers aids in keeping inflation down, labor quiescent, and training well organized.

Chapter 3

1. Note that all translations from the French are by the author, unless otherwise noted.

2. See the 1946 Constitution of the French Republic. Available at http://www.conseil-constitutionnel.fr/conseil-constitutionnel/francais/la-constitution/les-constitutions-de-la-france/constitution-de-1946-ive-republique.5109.html

3. See the 1946 Constitution of the French Republic.
4. See the 1946 Constitution of the French Republic.
5. https://www.government.nl/government
6. Bloch-Lainé 1976, 97.
7. See the 1958 Constitution of the French Republic. Constitution of 4 October 1958 | Conseil constitutionnel (conseil-constitutionnel.fr)
8. Constitution of 4 October 1958 | Conseil constitutionnel (conseil-constitutionnel.fr)
9. Constitution of 4 October 1958 | Conseil constitutionnel (conseil-constitutionnel.fr)
10. Constitution of 4 October 1958 | Conseil constitutionnel (conseil-constitutionnel.fr)
11. Vinen 1996 discusses this view.
12. Letter from Ricard to Monnet, dated 5-1-47. Archives nationales du monde du travail, Fond AS/72/109.
13. An example comes from the Archives nationales, Fond 80/AJ/1, which involves an intervention in the planning council by Gingembre, the president of the CGPME, in 1946. Differences between the two groups are also discussed by Ricard, the president of the CNPF, in the Archives nationales du monde du travail, Fond AS/72/109.
14. Quoted in Cleary 1989, 136.

Chapter 4

1. Un Plan Démocratique, by Robert Marjolin. 1/27/47. Archives nationales—Pierrefitte sur Seine. 80/AJ/1.
2. Text of the First Plan (http://www.strategie.gouv.fr/travaux/1946-2016-plan-france-strategie).
3. Déclaration de Le Brun, Secrétaire de la CGT to the Conseil du Plan. 11/26/1946. Archives nationales—Pierrefitte sur Seine. 80/AJ/1.
4. Intervention de Philippe Lamour, S-G of the Confédération générale de l'agriculture. 11/27/1946. Archives nationales—Pierrefitte sur Seine. 80/AJ/1.
5. Intervention de Ricard, President of the CNPF. 11/27/1946. Archives Nationales—Pierrefitte sur Seine. 80/AJ/1.
6. Lettre de Gingembre à Lamour, dated 1/5/52. Archives nationales—Pierrefitte sur Seine. 80/AJ/1.
7. Réponse proposée à Gingembre, 1952. Archives nationales—Pierrefitte sur Seine. 80/AJ/1.
8. Instructions envoyées par M. le président du gouvernement provisoire de la république a M. Le commissaire général du plan, Gouvernement provisoire de la republique, Presidence du Gouvernement. 10.01.1946. Archives nationales—Pierrefitte sur Seine. 80/AJ/1.
9. Instructions envoyées par M. le président du gouvernement provisoire de la république a M. Le commissaire général du plan, Gouvernement provisoire de la republique, Presidence du Gouvernement. 10.01.1946. Archives nationales—Pierrefitte sur Seine. 80/AJ/1.
10. Archives nationales du monde du travail, Fonds 72/AS/1442.
11. Commissariat Général du Plan, 18 Commissions de Modernisation, Archives nationales—Pierrefitte sur Seine. 81AJ/2.

12. Lettre de motivation du Bulletin Mensuel d'information économique (Centre national d'information économique) by Monnet, 10-1-47. Archives nationales du monde du travail, Fonds 72/AS/109.

13. Details on the make-up of the modernization commissions can be found in the Archives nationales du monde du travail, Fonds 72/AS/121, 72/AS/109.

14. Procès-verbal de la première session du conseil du plan, May 16–19, 1946. Archives Nationales de France—Pierrefitte sur Seine. 80/AJ/1.

15. Archives nationales du monde du travail, Fonds 72/AS/121; Text of the Second Plan (http://www.strategie.gouv.fr/travaux/1946-2016-plan-france-strategie)

16. Text of the Third Plan (http://www.strategie.gouv.fr/travaux/1946-2016-plan-france-strategie)

17. Note pour le ministre, dated 3/24/60, by Bertrand Balaresque. Archives nationales—Pierrefitte sur Seine. 540/AP/5.

18. Peyrefitte 2012, location 10315.

19. Text of the Fourth Plan (http://www.strategie.gouv.fr/travaux/1946-2016-plan-france-strategie)

20. Archives nationales du monde du travail, Fonds 81/AJ/1.

21. Archives nationales de France - Pierrefitte sur Seine, Fond 540/AP/5.

22. Note aux ministres, Résumé des étapes de création du plan, Bertrand Balaresque, dated 5/15/62. Archives nationales de France—Pierrefitte sur Seine. 540/AP/5.

23. Fifth Plan of Economic and Social Development (1966), 68. Emphasis in the original. Accessed at: http://www.strategie.gouv.fr/sites/strategie.gouv.fr/files/atoms/files/cinquieme-plan-1966-1970.pdf

24. Though note that the Fourth Plan was the first to be discussed in advance by the National Assembly, as mentioned in a letter from Balaresque, a civil servant in the Ministry of Finance, to Minister Giscard d'Estaing, Archives nationales de France - Pierrefitte sur Seine, Fond 540/AP/5.

25. Document, dated 26-4-67, discussing the participation of the patronat in the Commissions du développement régional (CODER). Archives nationales du monde du travail, Fonds 72/AS/1233.

26. Peyrefitte (2012), location 10435.

27. Synopsis of Non-Tariff Measures for the Protection of Agricultural or in Support of Incomes of Agricultural Producers furnished by the Government of France, General Agreement on Tariffs and Trade, Committee II—Expansion of Trade. European Council Archives, CM2/1959, 649/ab-b. 4 March 1959.

28. Additional Data to the Report Submitted by France on Trade in Agricultural Products, General Agreement on Tariffs and Trade, Committee II—Expansion of Trade. Archives of the Council of the European Union, CM2/1959. 28 October 1959.

29. Debré 1984, 76.

30. Peyrefitte 2012, location 5933.

31. Liste des modifications à apporter au volet agricole du 4e Plan, en date du 4/5/62, Comptes rendu de réunion interministérielle. 09/05/62. Un document destiné au ministre des Finances, daté du 10 mai 1962, résumant les modifications apportées au plan avant le débat parlementaire. Note au minister. 15/01/63. Sur les modifications du plan. Archives nationales de France—Pierrefitte sur Seine. 540/AP/5.

32. Note d'information, Secrétariat Général, Conseil des Communautés Européennes, le 23 Juin 1961. Archives of the Council of the European Union, CM2, 1961, 0115/ac-b/ac-c.

33. Livre blanc des organisations professionnelles agricoles sur le marché commun et l'agriculture. Octobre 1965. Centre des archives contemporaines, Archives nationales de France, 19910148–73.

Chapter 5

1. Portions of the India case study contained in Chapters 5 and 6, which deal with the Nehru and Gandhi periods, are reprinted from two of my previously published articles: Hankla (2006) and Hankla (2008). My thanks go to the publishers of *Business and Politics* (Cambridge) and *Comparative Politics* (City University of New York) for their permission to use this material. The argument presented in this book, as applied to India, depends on establishing the degree to which economic policymaking in the country was decentralized and fragmented or centralized and cohesive, and how this changed over time. The same issues are addressed in these published articles, and so, with thanks to the journals, I am reusing that portion of the articles here. It is important to mention, however, that the bulk of these India chapters are original to the book as they combine the question of varying state organization with varying interest group organization, and apply the two to an understanding of upgrading policy. The chapters also extend the analysis into the 1990s and up to the present. By contrast, the two articles are concerned with the level and distribution of state industrial and trade policies from Indian independence through the 1980s.

2. Ministry of Labour and Employment, Government of India.

3. Congress Election Manifesto—1945 in Zaidi, ed. 1986, 72.

4. Corbridge and Harriss 2000 and Congress Election Manifesto—1945 in Zaidi, ed. 1945.

5. On the formation of the Indian constitution, see Brass 1994, Rudolph and Rudolph 1987, and Corbridge and Harriss 2000.

6. For the classic description of the Congress System, see Kothari 1964. See also Manor 1988, Chhibber and Petrocik 1990, Weiner 1967, Rudolph and Rudolph 1987, and Brass 1994.

7. Detailed descriptions of Congress Party organization are available from Kochanek 1968, Brass 1965, Sirsikar and Fernandes 1984, Weiner 1967, and Kumar 1990.

8. Interviews with a senior Congress Party official and an Indian government official, New Delhi, September and October 2003.

9. Interview with an Indian government official, New Delhi, October 2003.

10. For more on panchayati raj, see Weiner 1967, Brass 1994, and Sirsikar and Fernandes 1984.

11. Brass 1965. He was referring only to the state of Uttar Pradesh, the topic of his study, but the comment can easily be extended nationally.

12. For a description of factions in India, see Brass 1965, Weiner 1967, Kothari 1964, and Brass 1994.

13. For descriptions of the candidate nomination process, see Kochanek 1968, Brass 1965, Rudolph and Rudolph 1987, Sisson 1972, and Sirsikar and Fernandes 1984.

14. Nehru, "Second Five Year Plan," a speech before the Lok Sabha, May 23, 1956, in Government of India, ed. 1958, 98–99.

15. Nehru, "Letter to Chief Ministers," June 3, 1953, in Parthasarathi, ed. 1987, 254.

16. Planning Commission 1958, 45.

17. Planning Commission 1956a, 10.
18. Planning Commission 1958, 66.
19. Hanson 1966, 61.
20. Interviews with a senior Congress Party official and an Indian government official, New Delhi, September and October 2003; Hanson 1966.
21. Hanson 1966. A crore is an Indian measure equivalent to 10 million.
22. Interviews with an Indian government official and a senior Congress Party official, New Delhi, September and October 2003; Corbridge and Harriss 2000.
23. Indian National Congress 1955, 2.
24. Planning Commission 1963, 46–47.
25. Indian National Congress Resolution, Amritsar, 1956, in Zaidi, ed. 1985.
26. Planning Commission 1963, 47.

Chapter 6

1. Interview with an Indian economist, Washington, DC, July 2003; Interview with an Indian trade specialist, New Delhi, October 2003.
2. While most scholars attribute Rajiv Gandhi's inability to implement significant economic reforms to strong interest group opposition, several individuals whom I interviewed dispute this understanding. They argue that a series of scandals, most particularly the Bofors scandal of 1986, put an end to the reforms. In any case, the ability of either scandal or interest group opposition to sidetrack serious economic reform was, I would argue, largely due to the shaky and populist support base of the Congress government.
3. Speeches by Nijalingappa and Indira Gandhi at the 72nd Party Conference, April 37, 1969, in Zaidi, ed. 1984, 239–42.
4. Letter by Indira Gandhi to Congress members, August 18, 1969, in Zaidi, ed. 1984, 267–70.
5. The following account is based on original documents published in Zaidi, ed. 1972. See also Frankel 1978.
6. Presidential Address of Nijalingappa to the Congress (O), December 21, 1969, in Zaidi, ed. 1972, 302–11.
7. Hereafter, I refer to the Congress (R) simply as the Congress, following the convention that accords Mrs. Gandhi's branch of the party the name of the original.
8. Detailed descriptions of Congress Party organization are available from Kochanek 1968, Brass 1965, Sirsikar and Fernandes 1984, Weiner 1967, and Kumar 1990.
9. Sengupta 1995, 239.
10. Interview with an Indian government official, New Delhi, October 2003.
11. Interview with a senior Congress Party official, New Delhi, October 2003. For information on India's trade policy during this period, see also Bhagwati and Srinivasan 1975; Joshi and Little 1994; Agrawal et al. 2000.
12. Interview with an Indian government official, New Delhi, October 2003; Sengupta 1995.
13. Interviews with an Indian government official and a senior Congress Party official, New Delhi, October 2003.
14. For more on the crisis, see Joshi and Little 1994; Srinivasan 1992.
15. Planning Commission 1970, 14–15.

16. Associated Chambers of Commerce and Industry 1969.

17. Sengupta 1995.

18. Monopolies Commission, as quoted in Sudhanshu 1986, 334.

19. Sengupta 1995, 59.

20. Patel 2002, 135.

21. Interview with an Indian government official, New Delhi, October 2003; Bardhan 1984.

Chapter 7

1. This characterization is taken from Gadgil 1993 and Corbridge and Harriss 2000. Mandal refers to the commission report recommending the reservation of a portion of government jobs for backward castes. Mandir refers to the struggle of Hindu nationalists to replace the Babri Mosque in Ayodhya with a Hindu temple.

2. Scheduled castes lie at the bottom of the Indian caste system, and their members are sometimes called Dalits. Above them in the caste hierarchy lie the backward castes and finally the forward castes.

3. Kohli 1990; Interview with an Indian economist, Washington, DC, July 2003.

4. Interview with a prominent Indian scholar, New Delhi, October 2003.

5. Rajiv Gandhi, speech before the Lok Sabha, January 30, 1985, in Shah, ed. 1991.; Kohli 1990.

6. Chakravarty 1991; Interview with an Indian economist, Washington, DC, July 2003.

7. The Janata Dal also led a successful coalition for a time, the United Front.

8. Interview with a US State Department official, Washington, DC, July 2003; Dhar 2003.

9. Congress Election Manifesto—1991 in Zaidi, ed. 1994, 387–88.

10. A large literature exists analyzing the balance of payments crisis and the reforms that followed it. See for example Ahluwalia 1999; Varshney 1999; Jenkins 1999; Sharan and Mukherji 2001; Joshi and Little 1994; Corbridge and Harriss 2000; Dhar 2003; Agrawal et al. 2000; Panagariya 2003; World Bank and ICRIER 2003; and Panagariya 1999.

11. Rao 1993, 14–15.

12. Rao 1993, 20.

13. Interview with senior Indian official, New Delhi, September 2003; Sharan and Mukherji 2001; Brass 1994, and others.

14. "Import-Export Policy to be Amended: Chidambaram," *Economic Times*, July 2, 1991.

15. Interview with prominent Indian economist, Washington, DC, July 2003; Corbridge and Harriss 2000.

16. Interviews with two senior Indian officials, New Delhi, September and October 2003.

17. Interview with senior Congress Party official, New Delhi, October 2003.

18. This argument is based primarily on interviews with a group of eight American and Indian economists and officials. My discussion below is a distillation and extrapolation of the information gained in these interviews.

19. Interview with senior Indian official, New Delhi, October 2003; Jenkins 1999.

Chapter 8

1. These countries are Australia, Austria, Belgium, Canada, Denmark, Finland, France, Germany, Italy, Japan, the Netherlands, Norway, Sweden, Switzerland, the United Kingdom, and the United States.

2. Premus and Bradford 1984, Forward.

3. Department of Energy: https://www.energy.gov/national-laboratories

4. Rodrik and Sabel 2019b, 12.

5. White House 2021b, 12–17.

Chapter 9

1. The structure of the French welfare state is often termed corporatist in the literature because the individual components embody cooperation between business, labor, and the state. By my definition, however, the system is not genuinely corporatist because of its decentralized, fragmented nature. Rather, the French welfare state represents a multitude of specific bargains among different decentralized interests.

2. Speech by Dr. Aujoulat, Archives nationales du monde du travail, Fond 72/AS/475.

3. Emmanuel Macron. As quoted in Industrie Online (2022) Macron II: what industrial policy for the next five years? - Industrie online (industrie-online.com).

4. Emmanuel Macron's Program for Industry. https://www.economie.gouv.fr/france-2030

5. Quoted by the European Parliament (2023). https://www.europarl.europa.eu/factsheets/en/sheet/61/general-principles-of-eu-industrial-policy

Bibliography

Published Secondary Sources

Acemoglu, Daron, and James A. Robinson. 2006. "Economic Backwardness in Political Perspective." *American Political Science Review* 100(1): 115–31.

Acemoglu, Daron, and James A. Robinson. 2012. *Why Nations Fail: The Origins of Power, Prosperity, and Poverty*. New York: Random House, Crown Business.

Adams, William James. 1989. *Restructuring the French Economy: Government and the Rise of Market Competition since World War II*. Washington, DC: The Brookings Institution.

Adams, William James, and Christian Stoffaës, eds. 1986. *French Industrial Policy*. Washington, DC: The Brookings Institution.

Agarwala, Rina. 2019. "The Politics of India's Reformed Labor Model." In *Business and Politics in India*, edited by Christophe Jaffrelot, Atul Kohli, and Kanta Murali. New York: Oxford University Press.

Aghion, Philippe, Jing Cai, Mathias Dewatripont, Luosha Du, Ann Harrison, and Patrick Legros. 2015. "Industrial Policy and Competition." *American Economic Journal: Macroeconomics* 7(4): 1–32.

Agrawal, Pradeep, ed. 2015. *Reviving Growth in India*. New York: Cambridge University Press.

Agrawal, Pradeep, Subir V. Gokarn, Veena Mishra, Kirit S. Parikh, and Kunal Sen. 2000. *Policy Regimes and Industrial Competitiveness*. New York: St. Martin's Press.

Ahluwalia, Isher Judge. 1985. *Industrial Growth in India: Stagnation Since the Mid-Sixties*. New Delhi: Oxford University Press.

Ahluwalia, Montek. 1999. "India's Economic Reforms: An Appraisal." In *India in the Era of Economic Reforms*, edited by Jeffrey D. Sachs, Ashutosh Varshney, and Nirupam Bajpai. New Delhi: Oxford University Press.

Aiginger, Karl, and Dani Rodrik. 2020. "Rebirth of Industrial Policy and an Agenda for the Twenty-First Century." *Journal of Industry, Competition and Trade* 20: 189–207.

Allison, Graham. 1971. *Essence of Decision*. New York: Addison-Wesley.

Amsden, Alice. 1992. *Asia's Next Giant: South Korea and Late Industrialization*. New York: Oxford University Press.

Amsden, Alice. 2001. The Rise of "The Rest": *Challenges to the West From Late-Industrializing Economies*. New York: Oxford University Press.

Andreoni, Antonio. 2017. "Varieties of Industrial Policy: Models, Packages, and Transformation Cycles." In *Efficiency, Finance, and Varieties of Industrial Policy*, edited by Akbar Noman and Joseph Stiglitz. New York: Columbia University Press, 245–305.

Andrews, William G. 1981a. "Introduction: The Impact of France on the Fifth Republic." In *The Fifth Republic at Twenty*, edited by William G. Andrews and Stanley Hoffmann. Albany: State University of New York Press.

Andrews, William G. 1981b. "The Collective Political Executive Under the Gaullists." In *The Fifth Republic at Twenty*, edited by William G. Andrews and Stanley Hoffmann. Albany: State University of New York Press.

Arora, Ashish, and Alfonso Gambardella, eds. 2005. *From Underdogs to Tigers: The Rise and Growth of the Software Industry in Brazil, China, India, Ireland, and Israel*. New York: Oxford University Press.

Arrow, Kenneth J., and Gerard Debreu. 1954. "Existence of an Equilibrium for a Competitive Economy." *Econometrica* 22(3): 265–90.

Athreye, Suma, and Sachin Chaturvedi. 2007. "Industry Associations and Technology-based Growth in India." *European Journal of Development Research* 19(1): 156–73.

Aujac, Henri. 1986. "Introduction to French Industrial Policy." In *French Industrial Policy*, edited by William James Adams and Christain Stoffaës. Washington, DC: The Brookings Institution.

Balakrishnan, Pulapre. 2007. "The Recovery of India: Economic Growth in the Nehru Era." *Economic and Political Weekly* 42(45/46): 52–66.

Balassa, Bela. 1981. "The French Economy under the Fifth Republic, 1958–1978." In *The Fifth Republic at Twenty*, edited by William G. Andrews and Stanley Hoffmann. Albany: State University of New York Press, 204–26.

Balassa, Carol Levy. 1978. *Organized Industry in France and the European Common Market: Interest Group Attitudes and Behavior*. PhD Dissertation, Johns Hopkins University.

Baltagi, Badi H., ed. 2000. *Nonstationary Panels, Panel Cointegration, and Dynamic Panels*. New York: Elsevier Science.

Bardhan, Pranab. 1984. *The Political Economy of Development in India*. New York: Basil Blackwell Publisher.

Bardhan, Pranab. 2016. "State and Development: The Need for a Reappraisal of the Current Literature." *Journal of Economic Literature* 54(3): 862–92.

Bardhan, Pranab. 2019. "Merchants of Hype and Hate: A Political Economic Evaluation of the Modi Regime." In *Majoritarian State: How Hindu Nationalism is Changing India*, edited by Angana P. Chatterji, Thomas Blom Hansen, and Christophe Jaffrelot. London: HarperCollins, 177–92.

Baru, Sanjaya. 2014. The *Accidental Prime Minister: The Making and Unmaking of Manmohan Singh*. New York: Penguin.

Bauchet, Pierre. 1962. *Economic Planning: The French Experience*. Translated by Daphne Woodward. New York: Frederick A. Praeger.

Baum, Warren C. 1958. *The French Economy and the State*. Princeton: Princeton University Press.

Bearce, David H. 2003. "Societal Preferences, Partisan Agents, and Monetary Policy Outcomes." *International Organization* 57(2): 373–410.

Beck, Nathaniel, and Jonathan N. Katz. 1995. "What to do (and not to do) with Time-Series Cross-Section Data." *American Political Science Review* 89(3): 634–47.

Berger, Suzanne. 1972. *Peasants against Politics: Rural Organization in Brittany, 1911–1967*. Cambridge: Harvard University Press.

Berger, Suzanne. 1981a. "Lame Ducks and National Champions: Industrial Policy in the Fifth Republic." In *The Fifth Republic at Twenty*, edited by William G. Andrews and Stanley Hoffmann. Albany: State University of New York Press, 292–310.

Berger, Suzanne. 1981b. "Regime and Interest Representation: The French Traditional Middle Classes." In *Organizing Interests in Western Europe,* edited by Suzanne Berger. New York: Cambridge University Press, 83–102.

Berman, Sheri. 2006. *The Primacy of Politics: Social Democracy and the Making of Europe's Twentieth Century*. New York: Cambridge University Press.

Besley, Timothy, and Torsten Persson. 2011. *Pillars of Prosperity: The Political Economics of Development Clusters*. Princeton: Princeton University Press.

Bhagwati, Jagdish, and Padma Desai. 1970. *India: Planning for Industrialization*. Development Centre of the Organization for Economic Cooperation and Development. London: Oxford University Press.

Bhagwati, Jagdish, and T. N. Srinivasan. 1975. *Foreign Trade Regimes and Economic Development: India*. New York: National Bureau of Economic Research and Columbia University Press.

Bhargava, P. K. 1984. "Transfer of Revenue Resources from the Centre to the States." In *Regional Structure of Development and Growth in India*, edited by G. P. Mishra. Dehli: Ashish.

Bhattacharya, A.K., and Paranjoy GuhaThakurta. 2019. "Contours of Crony Capitalism in the Modi Raj." In *Majoritarian State: How Hindu Nationalism is Changing India*, edited by Angana P. Chatterji, Thomas Blom Hansen, and Christophe Jaffrelot. London: HarperCollins, 193–216.

Bingham, Richard D. 1998. *Industrial Policy American Style*. Armonk, NY: M. E. Sharpe.

Birdsall, Nancy M., Jose Edgardo L. Campos, Chang-Shik Kim, Warner Max Corden, Lawrence MacDonald, Howard Pack, John Page, Richard Sabor, Joseph E. Stiglitz. 1993. *The East Asian Miracle: Economic Growth and Public Policy: Main Report (English)*. World Bank Policy Research Report. Washington, DC: World Bank Group.

Bloomberg. 2022. "China's Vast Blueprint for Tech Supremacy Over U.S.: QuickTake—Bloomberg." January 23, 2022. https://www.bloomberg.com/news/articles/2022-01-23/china-s-vast-blueprint-for-tech-supremacy-over-u-s-quicktake

Brass, Paul R. 1965. *Factional Politics in an Indian State: The Congress Party in Uttar Pradesh*. Berkeley: University of California Press.

Brass, Paul R. 1994. *The Politics of India Since Independence*. New York: Cambridge University Press.

Buigues, Pierre-André, and Khalid Sekkat. 2009. *Industrial Policy in Europe, Japan and the USA: Amounts, Mechanisms and Effectiveness*. New York: Palgrave Macmillan.

Cameron, David R. 1984. "Social Democracy, Corporatism, Labour Quiescence and the Representation of Economic Interests in Advanced Capitalist Society." In *Order and Conflict in Contemporary Capitalism*, edited by John H. Goldthorpe. Oxford: Oxford University Press, 143–78.

Capoccia, Giovanni. 2015. "Critical Junctures and Institutional Change." In *Advances in Comparative-Historical Analysis*, edited by James Mahoney and Kathleen Thelen. New York: Cambridge University Press.

Capoccia, Giovanni, and R. Daniel Kelemen. 2007. "The Study of Critical Junctions: Theory, Narrative, and Counterfactuals in Historical Institutionalism." *World Politics* 59(3): 341–69.

Carey, John M., and Matthew Soberg Shugart. 1995. "Incentives to Cultivate a Personal Vote: A Rank Ordering of Electoral Formulas." *Electoral Studies* 14(4): 417–39.

Caulcutt, Clea. 2023. "France's Le Maire Announces Package to Boost Reshoring of Green Industries." *Politico*, January 4, 2023.

Chagnollaud, Dominique. 1996. "La Haute Administration au Pouvoir? Les 'Grands Commis' de la IVe République." *Pouvoirs* 76: 107–15.

Chakravarty, Nikhil. 1991. "Imperative Before the Lok Sabha." *Economic Times*, June 25, 1991.

Chatterji, Angana P., Thomas Blom Hansen, and Christophe Jaffrelot. 2019. "Introduction." In *Majoritarian State: How Hindu Nationalism is Changing India*, edited by Angana P. Chatterji, Thomas Blom Hansen, and Christophe Jaffrelot. London: HarperCollins, 1–18.

Chaudhuri, Sudip. 2013. "Manufacturing Trade Deficit and Industrial Policy in India." *Economic and Political Weekly* 48(8): 41–50.

Chhibber, Pradeep K. 1999. *Democracy Without Associations: Transformation of the Party System and Social Cleavages in India*. Ann Arbor: University of Michigan Press.

Chhibber, Pradeep K., and John R. Petrocik. 1990. "Social Cleavages, Elections, and the Indian Party System." In *Diversity and Dominance in Indian Politics, Vol. 1*, edited by Richard Sisson and Ramashray Roy. New Dehli: Sage.

Chiang Min-Hua. 2018. *Post-Industrial Development in East Asia: Taiwan and South Korea in Comparison*. New York: Palgrave Macmillan.

Chibber, Vivek. 2003. *Locked in Place: State-Building and Late Industrialization in India*. Princeton: Princeton University Press.

Cimoli, Mario, and Giovanni Dosi. 2017. "Industrial Policies in Learning Economies." In *Efficiency, Finance, and Varieties of Industrial Policy*, edited by Akbar Noman and Joseph Stiglitz. New York: Columbia University Press, 23–64.

Cimoli, Mario, Giovanni Dosi, and Joseph E. Stiglitz, eds. 2009. *Industrial Policy and Development: The Political Economy of Capabilities Accumulation*. New York: Oxford University Press.

Cimoli, Mario, Giovanni Dosi, and Joseph E. Stiglitz. 2009. "The Political Economy of Capabilities Accumulation." In *Industrial Policy and Development: The Political Economy of Capabilities Accumulation*, edited by Mario Cimoli, Giovanni Dosi, and Joseph E. Stiglitz. New York: Oxford University Press.

Cleary, M. C. 1989. *Peasants, Politicians and Producers: The Organisation of Agriculture in France since 1918*. New York: Cambridge University Press.

Clift, Ben. "French Economic Policy: Theory Development and the Three 'I's." In *The Oxford Handbook of French Politics*, edited by Robert Elgie, Emiliano Grossman, and Amy G. Mazur. New York: Oxford University Press, 509–34.

Cohen, Elie, and Michel Bauer. 1985. *Les Grandes Manœuvres Industrielles*. Paris: Belfond.

Cohen, Paul. 2010. "Lessons from the Nationalization Nation: State-Owned Enterprises in France." *Dissent* 57(1): 15–20.

Cole, Alistair. 2008. *Governing and Governance in France*. New York: Cambridge University Press.

Corbridge, Stuart, and John Harriss. 2000. *Reinventing India*. Cambridge: Polity.

Cortell, Andrew P. 2005. *Mediating Globalization: Domestic Institutions and Industrial Policies in the United States and Britain*. Albany: State University of New York Press.

Crozier, Michel. 1970. *La Société bloquée*. Paris: Seuil.

Cruz, Ceci, Philip Keefer, and Carlos Scartascini. 2016. "The Database of Political Institutions Inter-American Development Bank." Updated version of Thorsten Beck, George Clarke, Alberto Groff, Philip Keefer, and Patrick Walsh. 2001. "New Tools in Comparative Political Economy: The Database of Political Institutions." *World Bank Economic Review* 15(1): 165–76.

Culpepper, Pepper D. 2011. *Quiet Politics and Business Power: Corporate Control in Europe and Japan*. New York: Cambridge University Press.

Culpepper, Pepper D., Peter A. Hall, and Bruno Palier, eds. 2008. *Changing France: The Politics that Markets Make*. New York: Palgrave Macmillan.

Culpepper, Pepper D. 2008. "Capitalism, Coordination, and Economic Change: The French Political Economy since 1985." In *Changing France: The Politics that Markets Make*, edited by Pepper D. Culpepper, Peter A. Hall, and Bruno Palier. New York: Palgrave Macmillan.

Dahl, Robert A. 1971. *Polyarchy: Participation and Opposition*. New Haven: Yale University Press.

Dahlman, Carl J. 2009. "Growth and Development in China and India." In *Industrial Policy and Development: The Political Economy of Capabilities Accumulation*, edited by Mario Cimoli, Giovanni Dosi, and Joseph E. Stiglitz. New York: Oxford University Press.

Damodaran, Harish. 2018. *India's New Capitalists: Caste, Business, and Industry in a Modern Nation*. New York: Palgrave McMillan.

Das, Deb Kusum, Abdul Aziz Erumban, and Jagannath Mallick. 2021. "Economic Growth in India During 1950–2015: Nehruvian Socialism to Market Capitalism." *Journal of Economic Surveys* 35(3): 926–51. https://doi.org/10.1111/joes.12350

Dertouzos, Michael L., Richard K. Lester, Robert M. Solow, and the MIT Commission on Industrial Productivity. 1989. *Made in America: Regaining the Productive Edge*. Cambridge, MA: MIT Press.

Devadas, David. 1991. "Dexterous Maneuvering by Narasimha Rao." *Economic Times*, June 25, 1991.

Dhar, P. N. 2003. The *Evolution of Indian Economic Policy, Selected Essays*. New Dehli: Oxford University Press.

Doner, Richard F. 2009. *The Politics of Uneven Development: Thailand's Economic Growth in Comparative Perspective*. New York: Cambridge University Press.

Doner, Richard F., and Ben Ross Schneider. 2016. "The Middle-Income Trap: More Politics than Economics." *World Politics* 68(4): 608–44.

Doner, Richard F., Gregory W. Noble, and John Ravenhill. 2021. *The Political Economy of Automotive Industrialization in East Asia*. New York: Oxford University Press.

Dutton, Paul V. 2002. *Origins of the French Welfare State*. New York: Cambridge University Press.

Duverger, Maurice. 1964. *Political Parties: Their Organization and Activity in the Modern State*. London: Methuen.

Easterly, William. 2002. *The Elusive Quest for Growth*. Cambridge: MIT Press.

Easton, David. 1993. "Political Science in the United States: Past and Present." In *Discipline and History: Political Science in the United States*, edited by James Farr and Raymond Seidelman. Ann Arbor: University of Michigan Press, 291–310.

Eckstein, Harry. 1972. "Case Study and Theory in Political Science." In *Handbook of Political Science*, vol. 7, edited by Fred I. Greenstein and Nelson W. Polsby. Reading, MA: Addison-Wesley, 79–137.

Ehrlich, Sean. 2011. *Access Points: An Institutional Theory of Policy Bias and Policy Complexity*. New York: Oxford University Press.

Ehrmann, Henry W. 1957. *Organized Business in France*. Princeton: Princeton University Press.

Eichengreen, Barry. 2007. *The European Economy since 1945*. Princeton: Princeton University Press.

Esping-Andersen, Gøsta. 1990. *The Three Worlds of Welfare Capitalism*. Princeton: Princeton University Press.

Estrin, Saul, and Peter Holmes. 1983. *French Planning in Theory and Practice*. London: George Allen & Unwin.

Evans, Peter. 1995. *Embedded Autonomy: States and Industrial Transformation*. Princeton: Princeton University Press.

Evans, Peter B., Dietrich Rueschemeyer, and Theda Skocpol. 1985. *Bringing the State Back In*. New York: Cambridge University Press.

Falleti, Tulia G., and James Mahoney. 2015. "The Comparative Sequential Method." In *Advances in Comparative-Historical Analysis*, edited by James Mahoney and Kathleen Thelen. New York: Cambridge University Press.

Farhang, Sean, and Miranda Yaver. 2016. "Divided Government and the Fragmentation of American Law." *American Journal of Political Science* 60(2): 401–17.

Fasteau, Mark, and Ian Fletcher. 2024. *Industrial Policy for the United States*. New York: Cambridge University Press.

Felipe, Jesus. 2015. "Modern Industrial Policy." In *Development and Modern Industrial Policy in Practice: Issues and Country Experiences*, edited by Jesus Felipe. Cheltenham: Edward Elgar and Asian Development Bank.

Felipe, Jesus, Utsav Kumar, and Arnelyn Abdon. 2013. "Exports, Capabilities, and Industrial Policy in India." *Journal of Comparative Economics* 41(3): 939–56.

Ferraz, João, David Kupfer, and Felipe Silveira Marques. 2014. "Industrial Policy as an Effective Development Tool: Lessons from Brazil." In *Transforming Economies: Making Industrial Policy Work for Growth, Jobs and Development*, edited by José M. Salazar-Xirinachs, Irmgard Nübler, and Richard Kozul-Wright. Geneva: International Labour Organization.

Flechtner, Svenja, and Stephan Panther. 2016. "Economic Inequality, Political Power, and Political Decision-Making: The Case of the 'Middle-Income Trap.'" In *Varieties of Economic Inequality*, edited by Sebastiano Fadda and Pasquale Tridico. London: Routledge.

Frankel, Francine. 1978. *India's Political Economy, 1947–1977*. Princeton: Princeton University Press.

Frears, J. R. 1981. "Parliament in the Fifth Republic." In *The Fifth Republic at Twenty*, edited by William G. Andrews and Stanley Hoffmann. Albany: State University of New York Press.

Freeman, John R. 1989. *Democracy and Markets: The Politics of Mixed Economies*. Ithaca: Cornell University Press.

Frieden, Jeffry. 1991. *Debt, Development, and Democracy: Modern Political Economy and Latin America, 1965–1985*. Princeton: Princeton University Press.

Frieden, Jeffry. 2020. *Global Capitalism: Its Fall and Rise in the Twentieth Century*. New York: W. W. Norton.

Gadgil, V. N. 1993. "Party Organization." In *Challenges Before the Nation*, edited by Pranab Mukherjee. New Dehli: Vikas and the Indian National Congress.

Garrett, Geoffrey. 1998. *Partisan Politics in the Global Economy*. New York: Cambridge University Press.

Gehlbach, Scott, and Edmund J. Malesky. 2010. "The Contribution of Veto Players to Economic Reform." *Journal of Politics* 72(4): 957–75.

Gereffi, Gary. 2018. *Global Value Chains and Development: Redefining the Contours of 21st Century Capitalism*. New York: Cambridge University Press.

Gerschenkron, Alexander. 1962. *Economic Backwardness in Historical Perspective: A Book of Essays*. New York: Harvard University and Belknap Presses.

Gilpin, Robert. 2001. *Global Political Economy: Understanding the International Economic Order*. Princeton: Princeton University Press.

Gingrich, Jane. 2015. "Coalitions, Policies, and Distribution: Esping-Andersen's *Three Worlds of Welfare Capitalism*." In *Advances in Comparative-Historical Analysis*, edited by James Mahoney and Kathleen Thelen. New York: Cambridge University Press.

Goyer, Michel. 2008. "The Transformation of Corporate Governance in France." In *Changing France: The Politics that Markets Make*, edited by Pepper D. Culpepper, Peter A. Hall, and Bruno Palier. New York: Palgrave Macmillan.

Gueldry, Michel R. 2001. *France and European Integration: Toward a Transnational Polity?* Westport, CT: Praeger.

Guha, Ramachandra. 2019. *India After Gandhi: The History of the World's Largest Democracy*. New York: HarperCollins.

Hacker, Jacob S., Paul Pierson, and Kathleen Thelen. 2015. "Drift and Conversion: Hidden Faces of Institutional Change." In *Advances in Comparative-Historical Analysis*, edited by James Mahoney and Kathleen Thelen. New York: Cambridge University Press.

Hackett, John, and Anne-Marie Hackett. 1965. *Economic Planning in France*. New York: Harvard University Press.

Haggard, Stephan. 1990. *Pathways from the Periphery: The Politics of Growth in the Newly Industrializing Countries*. Ithaca: Cornell University Press.

Haggard, Stephan. 2015. "The Developmental State is Dead: Long Live the Developmental State!" In *Advances in Comparative-Historical Analysis*, edited by James Mahoney and Kathleen Thelen. New York: Cambridge University Press.

Haggard, Stephan. 2018. *Developmental States*. New York: Cambridge University Press.

Hall, Peter A. 1986. *Governing the Economy: The Politics of State Intervention in Britain and France*. Oxford: Oxford University Press.

Hall, Peter A. 2008. "Introduction: The Politics of Social Change in France." In *Changing France: The Politics that Markets Make*, edited by Pepper D. Culpepper, Peter A. Hall, and Bruno Palier. New York: Palgrave Macmillan, 1–25.

Hall, Peter A., and David Soskice. 2001. *Varieties of Capitalism: The Institutional Foundations of Comparative Advantage*. New York: Oxford University Press.

Hancké, Robert. 2002. *Large Firms and Institutional Change: Industrial Renewal and Economic Restructuring in France*. New York: Oxford University Press.

Hankla, Charles R. 2006. "Party Linkages and Economic Policy: An Examination of Indira Gandhi's India." *Business and Politics* 8(3), Article 4: 1–29.

Hankla, Charles R. 2008. "Parties and Patronage: An Analysis of Trade and Industrial Policy in India." *Comparative Politics* 41(1): 41–60.

Hankla, Charles, and Daniel Kuthy. 2012. "Economic Liberalism in Illiberal Regimes: Authoritarian Variation and the Political Economy of Trade." *International Studies Quarterly* 57(3): 492–504.

Hanson, A. H. 1966. *The Process of Planning: A Study of India's Five-Year Plans, 1950–1964*. London: Royal Institute of International Affairs and Oxford University Press.

Hansen, Wendy, and Kee Ok Park. 1995. "Nation-State and Pluralistic Decision-Making in Trade Policy." *International Studies Quarterly* 39(2): 181–211.

Harrison, Ann, and Andrés Rodríguez-Clare. 2010. "Trade, Foreign Investment, and Industrial Policy for Developing Countries." In *Handbook of Development Economics, Vol. 5*, edited by Dani Rodrik and Mark Rosenzweig. Boston: Elsevier, North-Holland, 4039–214.

Hassenteufel, Patrick, and Bruno Palier. 2016. "The French Welfare System." In *The Oxford Handbook of French Politics*, edited by Robert Elgie, Emiliano Grossman, and Amy G. Mazur. New York: Oxford University Press, 60–80.

Hausmann, Ricardo, and Dani Rodrik. 2003. "Economic Development as Self Discovery." *Journal of Development Economics* 72(2): 603–33.

Hayek, Friedrich von. 2005 [1945]. *The Road to Serfdom: Condensed Version*. London: Institute of Economic Affairs.

Hayward, J. E. S. 1966. *Private Interests and Public Policy: The Experience of the French Economic and Social Council*. New York: Barnes and Noble.

Hayward, Jack. 1986. *The State and the Market Economy: Industrial Patriotism and Economic Intervention in France*. New York: New York University Press.

Hayward, Jack. 2016. "The State Imperative." In *The Oxford Handbook of French Politics*, edited by Robert Elgie, Emiliano Grossman, and Amy G. Mazur. New York: Oxford University Press, 44–59.

Heckscher, Eli, and Bertil Ohlin. 1933. *International and Inter-Regional Trade*. Cambridge: Harvard University Press.

Heda, H. C. 1958. *On the High Seas: Reflections on Congress*. New Delhi: Institute of National Affairs.

Henisz, Witold J. 2000. "The Institutional Environment for Economic Growth." *Economics and Politics* 12(1): 1–31.

Herring, Ronald J. 1999. "Embedded Particularism: India's Failed Developmental State." In *The Developmental State*, edited by Meredith Woo-Cumings. Ithaca: Cornell University Press.

Hitchcock, William I. 1998. *France Restored: Cold War Diplomacy and the Quest for Leadership in Europe, 1944–1954*. Chapel Hill: University of North Carolina Press.

Hoffmann, Stanley. 1974. *Decline or Renewal? France since the 1930s*. New York: Viking Press.

Hollingsworth, Joseph, Philippe Schmitter, and Wolfgang Streeck. 1994. *Governing Capitalist Economies: Performance and Control of Economic Sectors*. New York: Oxford University Press.

Howell, Chris. 1992. *Regulating Labor: The State and Industrial Relations Reform in Postwar France*. Princeton: Princeton University Press.

Hsueh, Roselyn. 2023. *Micro-Institutional Foundations of Capitalism: Sectoral Pathways to Globalization in China, India, and Russia*. New York: Cambridge University Press.

Huber, John D. 1996. "The Vote of Confidence in Parliamentary Democracies." *American Political Science Review* 90(2): 269–82.

Hufbauer, Gary Clyde, and Euijin Jung. 2021. *Scoring 50 Year of US Industrial Policy, 1970–2020*. Peterson Institute for International Economics. PIIE Briefings 21–5.

Huntington, Samuel P. 1968. *Political Order in Changing Societies*. New Haven: Yale University Press.

Immergut, Ellen M. 1990. "Institutions, Veto Points, and Policy Results: A Comparative Analysis of Health Care." *Journal of Public Policy* 10(4): 391–416.

Iversen, Torben, and David Soskice. 2019. *Democracy and Prosperity: Reinventing Capitalism through a Turbulent Century*. Princeton: Princeton University Press.

Jaffrelot, Christophe, Atul Kohli, and Kanta Murali. 2019. "Introduction." In *Business and Politics in India*, edited by Christophe Jaffrelot, Atul Kohli, and Kanta Murali. New York: Oxford University Press.

Jenkins, Rob. 1999. *Democratic Politics and Economic Reform in India*. Cambridge: Cambridge University Press.

Johnson, Chalmers. 1982. *MITI and the Japanese Miracle*. Stanford: Stanford University Press.

Joshi, Vijay, and I. M. D. Little. 1994. *India: Macroeconomics and Political Economy, 1964–1991*. Washington, DC: The World Bank.

Judt, Tony. 2006. *Postwar: A History of Europe since 1945*. New York: Penguin.

Judt, Tony. 2011. *Marxism and the French Left: Studies on Labour and Politics in France, 1830–1981*. New York: New York University Press.

Kabra, Kamal Nayan. 1998. *Development Planning in India*. New York: Sage.

Kahler, Miles, and David A. Lake, eds. 2013. *Politics in the New Hard Times: The Great Recession in Comparative Perspective*. Ithaca: Cornell University Press.

Kaplinsky, Raphael, and Mike Morris. 2001. *A Handbook for Value Chain Research*. Paper prepared for the International Development Research Centre.

Kathuria, Vinish, S. N. Rajesh Raj, and Kunal Sen. 2012. "State–business relations and productivity in Indian industry." In *State-Business Relations and Economic Development in Africa and India, edited by Kunal Sen*. Abington: Taylor & Francis Group.

Katzenstein, Peter. 1985. *Small States in World Markets: Industrial Policy in Europe*. Ithaca: Cornell University Press.

Kedward, Rod. 2005. *France and the French: A Modern History*. Woodstock: Overlook Press.

Keeler, John T. S. 1981a. "The Corporatist Dynamic of Agricultural Modernization in the Fifth Republic." In *The Fifth Republic at Twenty*, edited by William G. Andrews and Stanley Hoffmann. Albany: State University of New York Press, 271–91.

Keeler, John T. S. 1981b. "Corporatism and Official Union Hegemony: The Case of French Agricultural Syndicalism." In *Organizing Interests in Western Europe*, edited by Suzanne Berger. New York: Cambridge University Press, 185–208.

Keeler, John T. S. 1987. *The Politics of Neocorporatism in France: Farmers, the State, and Agricultural Policy-making in the Fifth Republic*. New York: Oxford University Press.

Keeler, J. T. S. 2000. "A Response to Andrew Moravcsik." *Journal of Cold War Studies* 2(3): 74–76.

Keller, Matthew R., and Fred Block. 2015. "Do as I Say or as I Do? US Innovation and Industrial Policy since the 1980s." In *Development and Modern Industrial Policy in Practice: Issues and Country Experiences*, edited by Jesus Felipe. Cheltenham: Edward Elgar and Asian Development Bank.

Kenworthy, Lane. 2003. "Quantitative Indicators of Corporatism." *International Journal of Sociology* 33(3): 10–44.

Ketels, Christian H. M. 2007. "Industrial Policy in the United States." *Journal of Industry, Competition Trade* 7: 147–67.

Kindleberger, Charles. 1963. "The Postwar Resurgence of the French Economy." In *In Search of France*, edited by Stanley Hoffmann. New York: Harvard University Press.

Knudsen, Ann-Christina L. 2009. *Farmers on Welfare: The Making of Europe's Common Agricultural Policy*. Ithaca: Cornell University Press.

Kochanek, Stanley A. 1968. *The Congress Party of India: The Dynamics of One-Party Democracy*. Princeton: Princeton University Press.

Kochanek, Stanley A. 1974. *Business and Politics in India*. Berkeley: University of California Press.

Kochanek, Stanley A. 1976. "Mrs. Gandhi's Pyramid: The New Congress." In *Indira Gandhi's India: A Political System Reappraised*, edited by Henry C. Hart. Boulder: Westview Press.

Kochanek, Stanley. 1995. "The Transformation of Interest Politics in India." *Pacific Affairs* 68(4): 529–50.

Kohli, Atul. 1990. *Democracy and Discontent: India's Growing Crisis of Governability*. New York: Cambridge University Press.

Kohli, Atul. 2000. "Centralization and Powerlessness: India's Democracy in a Comparative Perspective." In *Politics and the State in India*, edited by Zoya Hasan. New Delhi: Sage Publications.

Kohli, Atul. 2004. *State-Directed Development: Political Power and Industrialization in the Global Periphery*. New York: Cambridge University Press.

Kothari, Rajni. 1964. "The Congress 'System' in India." *Asian Survey* 4(12): 1161–73.

Kothari, Rajni. 1975. "Continuity and Change in the Party System." In *Citizens and Parties: Aspects of Competitive Politics in India*, edited by D. L. Sheth. New Dehli: Allied Publishers.

Krueger, Anne O. 1990. "Government Failures in Development." *Journal of Economic Perspectives* 4(3): 9–23.

Krugman, Paul. 1986. *Strategic Trade Policy and the New International Economics*. Boston: MIT Press.

Krugman, Paul. 2021. "Wonking Out: Economic Nationalism, Biden-Style." *New York Times*, June 11, 2021.

Kuisel, Richard F. 1981. *Capitalism and the State in Modern France*. New York: Cambridge University Press.

Kumar, K. N. 1990. *Political Parties in India: Their Ideology and Organization*. New Dehli: Mittal Publications.

Kuttner, Robert. 2021. "Bringing the Supply Chain Back Home." *The New York Review of Books*. Nov. 21, 2021.

Lal, Deepak. 2000. *The Poverty of "Development Economics."* Cambridge, MA: MIT Press.

Lallement, Michel. 2008. "New Patterns of Industrial Relations and Political Action since the 1980s." In *Changing France: The Politics that Markets Make*, edited by Pepper D. Culpepper, Peter A. Hall, and Bruno Palier. New York: Palgrave Macmillan.

Lauber, Volkmar. 1981. "The Gaullist Model of Economic Modernization." In *The Fifth*

Republic at Twenty, edited by William G. Andrews and Stanley Hoffmann. Albany: State University of New York Press, 227–39.

Lehne, Richard. 2013. *Government and Business: American Political Economy in Comparative Perspective*. New York: CQ and Sage.

Levy, Jonah D. 1999. *Tocqueville's Revenge: State, Society, and Economy in Contemporary France*. Cambridge: Harvard University Press.

Lévy, Raymond. 1986. "Industrial Policy and the Automobile Industry." In *French Industrial Policy*, edited by William James Adams and Christian Stoffaës. Washington, DC: The Brookings Institution.

Lewis, John P. 1997. *India's Political Economy: Governance and Reform*. New Delhi: Oxford University Press.

Lewis, William Arthur. 1950. *Industrial Development in the Caribbean*. Berkeley: University of California Press.

Lieberman, Evan S. 2015. "Nested Analysis: Toward the Integration of Comparative-Historical Analysis with Other Social Science Methods." In *Advances in Comparative-Historical Analysis*, edited by James Mahoney and Kathleen Thelen. New York: Cambridge University Press.

Lieshout, Robert H., Mathieu L. L. Segers, and Anna M. van der Vleuten. 2004. "De Gaulle, Moravcsik, and The Choice for Europe." *Journal of Cold War Studies* 6(4): 89–139.

Lijphart, Arend, and Markus M. L. Crepaz. 1991. "Corporatism and Consensus Democracy in Eighteen Countries: Conceptual and Empirical Linkages." *British Journal of Political Science* 21(2): 235–46.

Lijphart, Arend. 1999. *Patterns of Democracy: Government Forms and Performance in Thirty-Six Countries*. New Haven: Yale University Press.

Lin, Justin Yifu. 2017. "Industrial Policy Revisited: A New Structural Economics Perspective." In *Efficiency, Finance, and Varieties of Industrial Policy*, edited by Akbar Noman and Joseph Stiglitz. New York: Columbia University Press, 225–44.

Lin, Liza. 2020. "China's Trillion-Dollar Campaign Fuels a Tech Race With the U.S." *Wall Street Journal*. June 11, 2020. https://www.wsj.com/articles/chinas-trillion-dollar-campaign-fuels-a-tech-race-with-the-u-s-11591892854

Lincicome, Scott. 2021. *Industrial Policy: A Bad Idea is Back*. CATO Institute Policy Report.

Loriaux, Michael. 1999. "The French Developmental State as Myth and Moral Ambition." In *The Developmental State*, edited by Meredith Woo-Cumings. Ithaca: Cornell University Press.

MacRae, Duncan, Jr. 1967. *Parliament, Parties, and Society in France, 1946–1958*. New York: St. Martin's Press.

Mahoney, James. 2003. "Strategies of Causal Assessment in Comparative Historical Analysis." In *Comparative Historical Analysis in the Social Sciences*, edited by James Mahoney and Dietrich Rueschemeyer. New York: Cambridge University Press.

Mahoney, James, and Kathleen Thelen. 2010. *Explaining Institutional Change: Ambiguity, Agency, and Power*. New York: Cambridge University Press.

Mahoney, James, and Kathleen Thelen. 2015. "Comparative-Historical Analysis in Contemporary Political Science." In *Advances in Comparative-Historical Analysis*, edited by James Mahoney and Kathleen Thelen. New York: Cambridge University Press.

Mahtab, Harekrushna. 1950. *The Road Ahead.* Delhi: Atma Ram and Sons.

Maier, Charles S., and Dan S. White, eds. 1968. *The Thirteenth of May: The Advent of de Gaulle's Republic*. New York: Oxford University Press.

Majumdar, Sumit K. 2012. *India's Late Late Industrialization: Democratizing Entrepreneurship*. New York: Cambridge University Press.

Manor, James. 1988. "Parties and the Party System." In *India's Democracy: An Analysis of Changing State-Society Relations*, edited by Atul Kohli. Princeton: Princeton University Press.

Manor, James. 1992. "The State of Governance." In *Foundations of India's Political Economy*, edited by Subroto Roy and William E. James. New Delhi: Sage.

Manor, James. 2019. "Can Modi and the BJP Achieve and Sustain Hegemony?" In *Majoritarian State: How Hindu Nationalism is Changing India*, edited by Angana P. Chatterji, Thomas Blom Hansen, and Christophe Jaffrelot. London: HarperCollins, 117–32.

Mazzucato, Mariana. 2015. *The Entrepreneurial State: Debunking Public vs. Private Sector Myths*. New York: PublicAffairs.

McCauley, Darren. "Interest Groups: Moving Beyond State-Centric Models." In *The Oxford Handbook of French Politics*, edited by Robert Elgie, Emiliano Grossman, and Amy G. Mazur. New York: Oxford University Press, 417–38.

McGillivray, Fiona. 1997. "Party Discipline as a Determinant of the Endogenous Formation of Tariffs." *American Journal of Political Science* 41(2): 584–607.

McGillivray, Fiona. 2004. *Privileging Industry: The Comparative Politics of Trade and Industrial Policy*. Princeton: Princeton University Press.

Meckstroth, Theodore W. 1975. "'Most Different Systems' and 'Most Similar Systems': A Study in the Logic of Comparative Inquiry." *Comparative Political Studies* 8(2): 132–57.

Milberg, William, Xiao Jiang, and Gary Gereffi. 2014. "Industrial Policy in the Era of Vertically Specialized Industrialization." In *Transforming Economies: Making Industrial Policy Work for Growth, Jobs and Development*, edited by José M. Salazar-Xirinachs, Irmgard Nübler, Richard Kozul-Wright. International Labour Organization.

Mioche, Philippe. 1987. *Le Plan Monnet: Genèse et Élaboration, 1941–1947*. Paris: Publications de la Sorbonne.

Mitchell, Jonathan, Christopher Coles, and Jodie Keane. 2009. "Upgrading Along Value Chains: Strategies for Poverty Reduction in Latin America." Overseas Development Institute (ODI) Policy / Briefing Paper.

Mitra, Subrata K. 1994. "Party Organization and Policy Making in a Changing Environment: The Indian National Congress." In *How Political Parties Work*, edited by Kay Lawson. New Delhi: Bloomsbury.

Mitra, Subrata K., and V. B. Singh. 1999. *Democracy and Social Change in India*. New Delhi: Sage.

Moravcsik, Andrew. 1998. *The Choice for Europe: Social Purpose and State Power from Messina to Maastricht*. New York: Cornell University Press.

Moravcsik, Andrew. 2000. "De Gaulle Between Grain and Grandeur: The Political Economy of French EC Policy, 1958–1970." *Journal of Cold War Studies* 2(3 & 4): 3–43, 4–68.

Mukherjee, Andy. 2022. "Oops, Wrong Hyundai. India's Industrial Policy Misfires—Again." *Bloomberg*. September 27, 2022. https://www.bloomberg.com/opinion/articles/2022-09-27/india-s-industrial-policy-misfires-again-with-hyundai-gaffe?leadSource=uverify%20wall

Murali, Kanta. 2019. "Economic Liberalization and the Structural Power of Business in India." In *Business and Politics in India*, edited by Christophe Jaffrelot, Atul Kohli, and Kanta Murali. New York: Oxford University Press.

Neustadt, Richard E. 2021 [1960]. *Presidential Power: The Politics of Leadership*. New York: Hassell Street.

Noman, Akbar, and Joseph Stiglitz. 2017. Learning, Industrial, and Technology Policies: An Overview. In *Efficiency, Finance, and Varieties of Industrial Policy,* edited by Akbar Noman and Joseph E. Stiglitz. New York: Columbia University Press, 1–20.

Nooruddin, Irfan. 2011. *Coalition Politics and Economic Development: Credibility and the Strength of Weak Governments*. New York: Cambridge University Press.

Nord, Philip. 2010. *France's New Deal: From the Thirties to the Postwar Era*. Princeton: Princeton University Press.

North, Douglass C. 1990. *Institutions, Institutional Change and Economic Performance*. Cambridge: Cambridge University Press.

North, Douglass C., and Barry R. Weingast. 2000. "Institutional Analysis and Economic History." *Journal of Economic History* 60(2): 414–17.

Ocampo, José Antonio. 2017. "Dynamic Efficiency: Structural Dynamics and Economic Growth in Developing Countries." In *Efficiency, Finance, and Varieties of Industrial Policy*, edited by Akbar Noman and Joseph Stiglitz. New York: Columbia University Press, 65–102.

Olson, Mancur. 1971. *The Logic of Collective Action: Public Goods and the Theory of Groups*. Cambridge, MA: Harvard University Press.

Ornston, Darius. 2012. *When Small States Make Big Leaps: Institutional Innovation and High-Tech Competition in Western Europe*. Ithaca: Cornell University Press.

Osafo-Kwaako, Philip, and James A. Robinson. 2013. "Political Centralization in Pre-Colonial Africa." *Journal of Comparative Economics* 41(1): 6–21.

Outlook India. 2022. "Here Are Key Things To Know About Industrial Policy 2022: Make In India For The World (outlookindia.com)." December 22, 2022. https://www.outlookindia.com/business/here-are-key-things-to-know-about-industrial-policy-2022-make-in-india-for-the-world--news-244881

Pack, Howard, and Kamal Saggi. 2006. "Is There a Case for Industrial Policy? A Critical Survey." *The World Bank Research Observer* 21(2): 267–97.

Palier, Bruno. 2008. "The Long Goodbye to Bismarck? Changes in the French Welfare State." In *Changing France: The Politics that Markets Make*, edited by Pepper D. Culpepper, Peter A. Hall, and Bruno Palier. New York: Palgrave Macmillan.

Palshikar, Suhas. 2019. "Toward Hegemony: The BJP Beyond Electoral Dominance." In *Majoritarian State: How Hindu Nationalism is Changing India*, edited by Angana P. Chatterji, Thomas Blom Hansen, and Christophe Jaffrelot. London: HarperCollins, 101–16.

Panagariya, Arvind. 1999. "Trade Policy in South Asia: Recent Liberalisation and Future Agenda." *World Economy* 22(3), 353–78.

Panagariya, Arvind. 2010. *India: The Emerging Giant*. New York: Oxford University Press.

Panagariya, Arvind. 2003. "India: Internal Sector Reforms in the 1990s and Their Impact." Paper Presented at the Workshop on Trade Policies of South Asian Countries, October 16–17, 2003, New Dehli. Sponsored by the Indian Council for Research on International Economic Relations and the World Bank.

Parthasarathi, G., ed. 1987. *Jawaharlal Nehru Letters to Chief Ministers, 1947–1964, Volume 3*. New Dehli: Government of India and Oxford University Press.

Patel, I. G. 2002. *Glimpses of Indian Economic Policy: An Insider's View*. New Delhi: Oxford University Press.

Patnaik, Prabhat. 2000. *The State in India's Economic Development*. In *Politics and the State in India*, edited by Zoya Hasan. New Delhi: Sage Publications.

Paus, Eva. 2014. "Latin America and the Middle-Income Trap." ECLAC, Financing for Development Series, no. 250. Santiago, Chile: CEPAL.

Pierson, Paul. 2015. Power and Path Dependence. In *Advances in Comparative-Historical Analysis*. Edited by James Mahoney and Kathleen Thelen. New York: Cambridge University Press.

Pieter van Dijk, Meine, and Jacques Trienekens. 2012. *Global Value Chains: Linking Local Producers from Developing Countries to International Markets*. Amsterdam: Amsterdam University Press.

Pinglé, Vibha. 1999. *Rethinking the Developmental State: India's Industry in Comparative Perspective*. New York: Saint Martin's Press.

Polanyi, Karl. 2001 [1944]. *The Great Transformation: The Political and Economic Origins of Our Time*. Boston: Beacon Press.

Porter, Michael. (2011 [1990]). *The Competitive Advantage of Nations*. New York: The Free Press.

Prebisch, Raúl. 1959. "Commercial Policy in the Underdeveloped Countries." *American Economic Review* 49(2): 251–73.

Rai, Haridwar and Pandey, Jawahar Lal. 1971. *Intra-Party Democracy: The Experience of the Indian National Congress. In Indian Political Parties: Programmes, Promises, and Performance*. Edited by L. M. Singhvi, Subhash Kashyap, and J. P. Sharma. Dehli: The Institute of Constitutional and Parliamentary Studies, and Research Publications in the Social Sciences.

Rangnekar, D. K. 2012. *Politics of Poverty: Planning India's Development*. Los Angeles: Sage.

Ricardo, David. 2004 [1817]. *The Principles of Political Economy and Taxation*. New York: Dover.

Rioux, Jean-Pierre. 1987. *The Fourth Republic, 1944–1958*. Translated by Godfrey Rogers. New York: Cambridge University Press.

Rodrik, Dani. 2007. *One Economics, Many Recipes: Globalization, Institutions, and Economic Growth*. Princeton: Princeton University Press.

Rodrik, Dani. 2008. "Normalizing Industrial Policy." Commission on growth and development working paper; no. 3 Washington, D.C.: World Bank Group. http://documents.worldbank.org/curated/en/524281468326684286/Normalizing-industrial-policy

Rodrik, Dani, and Charles Sabel. 2019a. "An Industrial Policy for Good Jobs." Project Syndicate, May 8, 2019. https://www.project-syndicate.org/commentary/industrial-policy-for-good-jobs-by-dani-rodrik-and-charles-sabel-2019-05

Rodrik, Dani, and Charles Sabel. 2019b. "Building a Good Jobs Economy." Working Paper.

Rodrik, Dani. 2021. "The Metamorphosis of Growth Policy." Project Syndicate, Oct. 11, 2021. https://www.project-syndicate.org/commentary/new-growth-policies-for-developing-countries-by-dani-rodrik-2021-10?barrier=accesspaylog

Rogowski, Ronald. 1987. "Trade and the Variety of Democratic Institutions." *International Organization* 41(2): 203–23.

Romer, Paul M. 1986. "Increasing Returns and Long-Run Growth." *Journal of Political Economy* 94(5): 1002–37.

Root, Hilton. 1996. *Small Countries, Big Lessons: Governance and the Rise of East Asia*. Hong Kong: Oxford University Press and the Asian Development Bank.

Rosenstein-Rodan, P. N. 1943. "Problems of Industrialisation of Eastern and South-Eastern Europe." *Economic Journal* 53.

Rosenthal, Stuart S., and William C. Strange. 2004. "Evidence on the Nature and Sources of Agglomeration Economies." In *Handbook of Regional and Urban Economics* 4, edited by J. Vernon Henderson and Jacques-François Thisse, 2119–71.

Ross, George. 1981. "Gaullism and Organized Labor: Two Decades of Failure?" In *The Fifth Republic at Twenty*, edited by William G. Andrews and Stanley Hoffmann. Albany: State University of New York Press, 330–47.

Rudolph, Lloyd I., and Susanne Hoeber Rudolph. 1987. *In Pursuit of Lakshmi: The Political Economy of the Indian State*. Chicago: University of Chicago Press.

Salazar-Xirinachs, José M., Irmgard Nübler, and Richard Kozul-Wright. 2014. *Transforming Economies: Making Industrial Policy Work for Growth, Jobs and Development*. Geneva: International Labour Organization.

Salvati, Michele. "May 1968 and the Hot Autumn of 1969: The Responses of Two Ruling Classes." In *Organizing Interests in Western Europe*, edited by Suzanne Berger. New York: Cambridge University Press, 331–66.

Schattschneider, E. E. 1935. *Politics, Pressures and the Tariff*. New York: Prentice-Hall.

Schmall, Emily, Karan Deep Singh, and Sameer Yasir. 2021. "In Rare Show of Weakness, Modi Bows to India's Farmers." *New York Times*, Nov. 21, 2021. https://www.nytimes.com/2021/11/18/world/asia/india-farmers-modi.html

Schmidt, Vivien A. 1996. *From State to Market? The Transformation of French Business and Government*. New York: Cambridge University Press.

Schmidt, Vivien A. 2009. "Putting the Political Back into Political Economy by Bringing the State Back in Yet Again." *World Politics* 61(3): 516–48.

Schmidt, Vivien A. 2016. "Varieties of Capitalism: A Distinctly French Model?" In *The Oxford Handbook of French Politics*, edited by Robert Elgie, Emiliano Grossman, and Amy G. Mazur. New York: Oxford University Press, 606–35.

Schmitter, Philippe C. 1974. "Still the Century of Corporatism?" *The Review of Politics* 36(1): 85–131.

Schrank, Andrew, and Josh Whitford. 2009. "Industrial Policy in the United States: A Neo-Polanyian Interpretation." *Politics & Society* 37(4).

Schultze, Charles L. 1983. "Industrial Policy: A Dissent." *The Brookings Review*.

Scott, James C. 1999. *Seeing Like a State*. New Haven: Yale University Press.

Shah, M. C., ed. 1991. *Rajiv Gandhi in Parliament*. Delhi: Shipra Publications.

Sharan, Vyuptakesh, and Indra Nath Mukherji. 2001. *India's External Sector Reforms*. New Dehli: Oxford University Press.

Sharma, Mihir. 2022. "Make in India? It will take more than Subsidies." *Bloomberg*, November 13, 2022. https://www.bloomberg.com/opinion/articles/2022-11-10/modi-s-make-in-india-push-needs-more-than-subsidies

Sheahan, John. 1963. *Promotion and Control of Industry in Postwar France*. Cambridge, MA: Harvard University Press.

Shiller, Robert J. 2006. *Irrational Exuberance*. New York: Crown Business.

Shonfield, Andrew. 1965. *Modern Capitalism: The Changing Balance of Public and Private Power*. New York: Oxford University Press.

Shugart, Matthew Soberg, and John M. Carey. 1992. *Presidents and Assemblies: Constitutional Design and Electoral Dynamics*. Cambridge: Cambridge University Press.

Singh, Ajit. 2009. "The Past, Present, and Future of Industrial Policy in India." In *Industrial Policy and Development: The Political Economy of Capabilities Accumulation*, edited by Mario Cimoli, Giovanni Dosi, and Joseph E. Stiglitz. New York: Oxford University Press.

Singh, Mahendra Prasad. 1981. *Split in a Predominant Party*. New Dehli: Shakti Malik.

Singh, Tavleen. 1991. "A Forced Consensus." *Economic Times*, June 25, 1991.

Sinha, Aseema. 2005. "Understanding the Rise and Transformation of Business Collective Action in India." *Business and Politics* 7(2).

Sinha, Aseema. 2019. "India's New Porous State." In *Business and Politics in India*, edited by Christophe Jaffrelot, Atul Kohli, and Kanta Murali. New York: Oxford University Press.

Siripurapu, Anshu, and Noah Berman. 2022. "Is Industrial Policy Making a Comeback?" *Council on Foreign Relations Backgrounder*.

Sirsikar, V. M., and L. Fernandes. 1984. *Indian Political Parties*. New Delhi: Meenakshi Prakashan.

Sisson, Richard. 1972. *The Congress Party in Rajasthan*. Berkeley: University of California Press.

Smith, Adam. 2013 [1776]. *The Wealth of Nations*. Project Gutenberg. http://www.gutenberg.org/files/3300/3300-h/3300-h.htm

Solow, Robert M. 1970. *Growth Theory: An Exposition*. New York: Oxford University Press.

Srinivasan, T. N. 1992. "Planning and Foreign Trade Reconsidered." In *Foundations of India's Political Economy*, edited by Subroto Roy and William E. James. New Delhi: Sage.

Steinberg, David. 2015. *Demanding Devaluation: Exchange Rate Politics in the Developing World*. Ithaca: Cornell University Press.

Steinmo, Sven. 2010. *The Evolution of Modern States: Sweden, Japan, and the United States*. New York: Cambridge University Press.

Stiglitz, Joseph E., and Bruce C. Greenwald. 2015. *Creating a Learning Society*. New York: Columbia University Press.

Stoffaës, Christian. 1986. Industrial policy and the steel industry. In *French Industrial Policy*, edited by William James Adams and Christian Stoffaës. Washington, DC: The Brookings Institution.

Stone, Brewer Stevenson. 1994. "Governmental Corruption in China and India." Unpublished Dissertation, Harvard University.

Streeck, Wolfgang, and Kathleen Thelen. 2005. *Beyond Continuity: Institutional Change in Advanced Political Economies*. New York: Oxford University Press.

Sudhanshu, S. N. T. 1986. *Industrial Licensing Policy and Growth of Industries in India*. New Delhi: Deep and Deep.

Suleiman, Ezra N. 1974. *Politics, Power, and Bureaucracy in France: The Administrative Elite*. Princeton: Princeton University Press.

Taylor, Mark Zachary. 2016. *The Politics of Innovation: Why Some Countries are Better than Others at Science and Technology*. New York: Oxford University Press.

Thelen, Kathleen. 2004. *How Institutions Evolve: The Political Economy of Skills in Germany, Britain, the United States, and Japan*. Cambridge: Cambridge University Press.

Thelen, Kathleen. 2014. *Varieties of Liberalization and the New Politics of Social Solidarity*. New York: Cambridge University Press.

Thimmaiah, G. 1985. "Inter-State Disparities in Financial Allocations." In *Regional Structure of Development and Growth in India*, edited by G. P. Mishra. Delhi: Ashish.

Tsebelis, George. 2002. *Veto Players: How Institutions Work*. New York: Princeton University Press.

Varshney, Ashutosh. 1998. *Democracy, Development, and the Countryside: Urban-Rural Struggles in India*. New York: Cambridge University Press.

Varshney, Ashutosh. 1999. "Mass Politics or Elite Politics? India's Economic Reforms in Comparative Perspective." In *India in the Era of Economic Reforms*, edited by

Jeffrey D. Sachs, Ashutosh Varshney, and Nirupam Bajpai. New Delhi: Oxford University Press.

Vijayabaskar, Manimegalai, and Suresh Babu. 2014. *Building Capabilities in the Software Service Industry in India: Skill Formation and Learning of Domestic Enterprises in Value Chains*. Geneva: International Labour Office.

Vinen, Richard. 1995. *Bourgeois Politics in France, 1945–1951*. New York: Cambridge University Press.

Vinen, Richard. 1996. *France, 1934–1970*. New York: St. Martin's Press.

Wade, Robert. 1990. *Governing the Market: Economic Theory and the Role of Government in East Asian Industrialization*. Princeton: Princeton University Press.

Wade, Robert H. 2012. "Return of Industrial Policy?" *International Review of Applied Economics* 26(2).

Wade, Robert H. 2015. "The Role of Industrial Policy in Developing Countries." *Rethinking Development Strategies after the Financial Crisis—Volume I: Making the Case for Policy Space*. Paris: OECD, 67–79.

Waldner, David. 1999. *State Building and Late Development*. Ithaca: Cornell University Press.

Wanjari, Dhananjay Soindaji. 2022. *Inheritance, Hierarchy and Caste: Origins of Political Decay in India*. Washington, DC: Sage.

Warwick, Ken. 2013. "Beyond Industrial Policy: Emerging Issues and New Trends." OECD Science, Technology and Industry Policy Papers, No. 2. Paris: OECD Publishing. http://dx.doi.org/10.1787/5k4869clw0xp-en

Wehner, Joachim. 2010. *Legislatures and the Budget Process: The Myth of Fiscal Control*. New York: Palgrave Macmillan.

Weiner, Myron. 1989. "The 1971 Elections: India's Changing Party System." In *The Indian Paradox: Essays in Indian Politics*, edited by Ashutosh Varshney. New Delhi: Sage.

Weiner, Myron. 1967. *Party Building in a New Nation: The Indian National Congress*. Chicago: University of Chicago Press.

Weiss, Linda. 2014. *America Inc.? Innovation and Enterprise in the National Security State*. Ithaca: Cornell University Press.

Wilson, Frank L. 1987. *Interest-Group Politics in France*. New York: Cambridge University Press.

Woo-Cumings, Meredith, ed. 1999. *The Developmental State*. Ithaca: Cornell University Press.

World Bank Commission on Growth and Development. 2008. *The Growth Report: Strategies for Sustained Growth and Inclusive Development*. Washington, DC: The World Bank.

World Bank. 2003. Volume I: An Overview. Paper Presented at the Workshop on Trade Policies of South Asian Countries, October 16-17, 2003, New Dehli. Sponsored by the Indian Council for Research on International Economic Relations (ICRIER) and the World Bank.

World Bank. 2021. *World Development Indicators*. Washington, DC.

Wright, Gordon. 1964. *Rural Revolution in France: The Peasantry in the Twentieth Century*. Stanford: Stanford University Press.

Yoffie, David B., and Joseph L. Badaracco. 1983. "'Industrial Policy': It Can't Happen Here." *Harvard Business Review*, November 1983.

Yuan, Li. 2023. "Entrepreneurs Flee China's Heavy Hand." *New York Times*, January 19, 2023.

Zalk, Nimrod. 2014. "Industrial Policy in a Harsh Climate: The Case of South Africa." In *Transforming Economies: Making Industrial Policy Work for Growth, Jobs and Development*, edited by José M. Salazar-Xirinachs, Irmgard Nübler, and Richard Kozul-Wright. Geneva: International Labour Organization.

Ziegfeld, Adam. 2012. "Coalition Government and Party System Change: Explaining the Rise of Regional Political Parties in India." *Comparative Politics* 45(1): 69–87.

Ziegler, J. Nicholas. 1997. *Governing Ideas: Strategies for Innovation in Germany and France*. Ithaca: Cornell University Press.

Zysman, John. 1977. *Political Strategies for Industrial Order: State, Market and Industry in France*. Berkeley: University of California Press.

Zysman, John. 1981. "The Interventionist Temptation: Financial Structure and Political Purpose." In *The Fifth Republic at Twenty*, edited by William G. Andrews and Stanley Hoffmann. Albany: State University of New York Press, 252–70.

Published Primary Sources

Associated Chambers of Commerce and Industry of India (ASSOCHAM). December 18, 1967. "India: The Way Ahead," Speech by C. A. Pitts, President of ASSOCHAM, Calcutta.

Associated Chambers of Commerce and Industry of India (ASSOCHAM). 1969. "Fiftieth Annual Report."

Bharatiya Janata Party. 2000. *BJP Resolutions: Economic, 1980–1999*. New Delhi: Bharatiya Janata Party.

Bidault, Georges. 1967. *Resistance: The Political Biography of Georges Bidault*. New York: F. A. Praeger.

Bloch-Lainé, François. 1976. *Profession: Fonctionnaire, Entretiens avec Françoise Carrière*. Paris: Editions du Seuil.

Blum, Léon. 1958a. *L'Oeuvre de Léon Blum, 1945–47*. Paris: Éditions Alban Michel.

Blum, Léon. 1958b. *L'Oeuvre de Léon Blum, 1947–50*. Paris: Éditions Alban Michel.

Centre for the Study of Developing Societies. 1967. National Election Survey, Delhi.

Centre for the Study of Developing Societies. 1971. All India Survey, Delhi.

Centre for the Study of Developing Societies. 1996. Post-Election Poll, Delhi.

Commisariat Général du Plan. Texts of the first through fifth plans. (http://www.strategie.gouv.fr/travaux/1946-2016-plan-france-strategie)

Congressional Research Service. 2019. "The Made in China 2025 Initiative: Economic Implications for the United States." Updated April 12, 2019.

Debré, Michel. 1981. "The Constitution of 1958: Its Raison d'etre and How It Evolved." In *The Fifth Republic at Twenty*, edited by William G. Andrews and Stanley Hoffmann. Albany: State University of New York Press.

Debré, Michel. 1984. *Trois républiques pour une France: Mémoires*. Paris: Editions Albin Michel.

de Gaulle, Charles. 1971. *Memoirs of Hope: Renewal and Endeavor*. Translated by Terence Kilmartin. New York: Simon and Schuster.

European Commission. 2021. "Updating the 2020 New Industrial Strategy: Building a Stronger Single Market for Europe's Recovery." EUR-Lex - 52021DC0350 - EN - EUR-Lex (europa.eu).

European Parliament. 2022. "General principles of EU industrial policy | Fact Sheets on the European Union | European Parliament (europa.eu)." https://www.europarl.europa.eu/factsheets/en/sheet/61/general-principles-of-eu-industrial-policy

Federation of Indian Chambers of Commerce and Industry (FICCI). March 22–24, 1957. The Proceedings of the 13th Annual Meeting, New Delhi.

French Embassy to the United States. *Major Addresses, Statements, and Press Conferences of General Charles de Gaulle, May 19, 1958–January 31, 1964*. New York: French Embassy Press and Information Division.

French Foreign Ministry. 2022. "France Relance recovery plan: building the France of 2030—Ministry for Europe and Foreign Affairs (diplomatie.gouv.fr)." https://www.diplomatie.gouv.fr/en/french-foreign-policy/economic-diplomacy-foreign-trade/promoting-france-s-attractiveness/france-relance-recovery-plan-building-the-france-of-2030/

Government of India, ed. 1958. *Jawaharlal Nehru's Speeches, Volume 3*. Delhi: Government of India.

Groupe de Travail du Comité Interministériel des Entreprise Publiques. 1967. Rapport sur Les Entreprises Publiques (Rapport Nora).

Hawley, Josh. 2021. "The Only Way to Solve Our Supply Chain Crisis, Rethink Trade." *New York Times, October 29, 2021*.

Indian National Congress. 1950. *Our Immediate Programme*. New Delhi: All Indian Congress Committee.

Indian National Congress. 1950. *President's Letter About the Second Five Plan to the All Indian Congress Committee*. New Delhi: All Indian Congress Committee.

Indian National Congress. 1955. *President's Letter About the Second Five Plan to the All Indian Congress Committee*.

Indian National Congress. 1957. *Congress and the General Elections*. New Delhi: Indian National Congress.

Indian National Congress. 1985. *100 Years—The Milestones*. New Delhi: All India Congress Committee and New Public Press.

Indian National Trade Union Conference (INTUC). May 1956. "A Brief Review of the Eighth Annual Session," Surat.

Indian National Trade Union Conference (INTUC). April 24, 1960. "Address by Shri G. Ramanujam." 11th Session, New Delhi.

Indian National Trade Union Conference (INTUC). May 12, 1968. "Presidential Address by V. V. Dravid." 17th Session, Ahmedabad.

Indian National Trade Union Conference (INTUC). May 12–13, 1968. "Brief Review of the 17th Session, Ahmedabad."

Industrie Online (2022) "Macron II: what industrial policy for the next five years?"– Industrie online (industrie-online.com). https://www.industrie-online.com/en/p/actualite-2/actualites/macron-ii-quelle-politique-industrielle-pour-les-5-prochaines-annees

Maier, Charles S., and Dan S. White, eds. 1968. *The Thirteenth of May: The Advent of de Gaulle's Republic*. New York: Oxford University Press.

Mendès-France, Pierre. 1963. *A Modern French Republic*. Translated by Anne Carter. New York: Hill and Wang.

Monnet, Jean. 1978. *Memoirs*. Translated by Richard Mayne. Garden City: Doubleday and Company.

Newfarmer, Richard, ed. 1984. "Policies for Industrial Growth in a Competitive World: A Volume of Essays Prepared for the Use of the Subcommittee on Economic Goals and Intergovernmental Policy, Joint Economic Committee, Congress of the United States." Washington, DC: US Government Printing Office.

Peyrefitte, Alain. 2012. *Charles De Gaulle: Biographie, Tome 1*. Paris: Fayard.

Pinay, Antoine. 1984. *Un Français comme les autres*. Paris: Belfond / Jean-Cyrille Godefroy.

Pisani, Edgard. 1974. *Le général indivis*. Paris: Albin Michel.

Planning Commission, Government of India. 1956a. "Second Five Year Plan: Summary."

Planning Commission, Government of India. 1956b. "Second Five Year Plan."

Planning Commission, Government of India. 1958. *The New India: Progress Through Democracy*. New York: Macmillan Company.

Planning Commission, Government of India. 1963. *The Planning Process*. New Delhi: Government of India.

Planning Commission, Government of India. 1970. "Fourth Five Year Plan, 1969–74."

Planning Commission, Government of India. 1985. "Seventh Five Year Plan, 1985–90, Volume 1."

Planning Commission, Government of India. 1980. "Sixth Five Year Plan, 1980–85."

Planning Commission, Government of India. 1992. "Eighth Five Year Plan, 1992–97, Volume 1."

Premus, Robert, and Charles H. Bradford. 1984. "Industrial Policy Movement in the United States: Is it the Answer?: A Staff Report for the Joint Economic Committee of the Congress of the United States." Washington, DC: US Government Printing Office.

Prime Minister of India. 2022. "Make In India | Prime Minister of India (pmindia.gov.in)." https://www.pmindia.gov.in/en/major_initiatives/make-in-india/

Rao, P. V. Narasimha. 1993. "The Tasks Ahead," Presidential Address at the Congress Session, Tirupati, April 1992. In *Challenges Before the Nation*. Edited by Pranab Mukherjee. New Dehli: Vikas and the Indian National Congress.

République Française. Texts of the Constitutions of the Fourth and Fifth Republics. https://www.elysee.fr/en/french-presidency/founding-texts ; http://www.conseil-constitutionnel.fr/conseil-constitutionnel/francais/la-constitution/les-constitutions-de-la-france/constitution-de-1946-ive-republique.5109.html

Sengupta, Nitish K. 1995. *Inside the Steel Frame: Reminiscences and Reflections of a Former Civil Servant.* New Delhi: Vikas Publishing House.

White House. 2021a. "FACT SHEET: Biden-Harris Administration Announces Supply Chain Disruptions Task Force to Address Short-Term Supply Chain Discontinuities | The White House."

White House. 2021b. "Building Resilient Supply Chains, Revitalizing American Manufacturing, and Fostering Broad-Based Growth." White House Supply Chain Program: https://www.whitehouse.gov/wp-content/uploads/2021/06/100-day-supply-chain-review-report.pdf

White House. 2022. "FACT SHEET: CHIPS and Science Act Will Lower Costs, Create Jobs, Strengthen Supply Chains, and Counter China | The White House." https://www.whitehouse.gov/briefing-room/statements-releases/2022/08/09/fact-sheet-chips-and-science-act-will-lower-costs-create-jobs-strengthen-supply-chains-and-counter-china/

Zaidi, A. M., ed. 1972. *The Great Upheaval: '69–'72.* New Delhi: Orientalia.

Zaidi, A. M., ed. 1984. *Aloud and Straight: Frank Talks at Party Meetings.* New Delhi: Indian Institute of Applied Political Research.

Zaidi, A. M., ed. 1985. *A Tryst with Destiny: A Study of Congress Economic Policy Resolutions of INC Passed During the Last 100 Years.* New Delhi: Indian Institute of Applied Political Research.

Zaidi, A. M., ed. 1986. *The Annual Register of Indian Political Parties, 1984.* New Delhi: Indian Institute of Applied Political Research.

Zaidi, A. M., ed. 1986. *Promises to Keep: A Study of the Election Manifestoes of the Indian National Congress, 1937–1985.* New Delhi: Indian Institute of Applied Political Research.

Zaidi, A. M., ed. 1994. *The Annual Register of Indian Political Parties, 1991 Part 2.* New Delhi: Indian Institute of Applied Political Research.

Archival Sources

Le Centre d'acceuil et de recherche des Archives nationales (CARAN), Archives nationales de France, Paris

F/60/3102
F/10/5638
F/12/11419
C/15748
4/AG/13
4/AG/15
4/AG/54

Le Centre d'archives contemporaines, Archives nationales de France, Fontainebleu

19910148–73
19771525–49
19850271–2

Central Archives of the Council of the European Union

CM1/1963
CM2/1958
CM2/1959
CM2/1962
CM2/1963

Archives nationales du monde du travail

72 AS 101
72 AS 109
72 AS 112
72 AS 114
72 AS 121
72 AS 122
72 AS 126
72 AS 136
72 AS 1233
72 AS 1381
72 AS 1382
72 AS 1442
72 AS 1505
72 AS 1385
72 AS 473
72 AS 474
72 AS 593
72 AS 475
72 AS 529

Archives nationales de France—Pierrefitte sur Seine

80/AJ/1
81 AJ 2
81 AJ 4
F 60 610
F 60 423
F 60 914
540 AP 5
540 AP 6
81 AJ 1
F 60 3024
540 AP 7

Multiple Elite Interviews in New Delhi and Washington DC, 2003

Index